TEXAS CEMETERIES

Clifton and Shirley Caldwell
Texas Heritage Series
Number Five

TEXAS CEMETERIES

*The Resting Places of Famous, Infamous,
and Just Plain Interesting Texans*

BILL HARVEY

University of Texas Press, Austin

Fourth paperback printing, 2007

Requests for permission to reproduce material from this work should be sent to:
Permissions
University of Texas Press
P.O. Box 7819
Austin, TX 78713-7819
www.utexas.edu/utpress/about/bpermission.html

♾ The paper used in this book meets the minimum requirements of ANSI/NISO Z39.48-1992 (R1997) (Permanence of Paper).

Library of Congress Cataloging-in-Publication Data

Harvey, Bill, 1950–
    Texas cemeteries / by Bill Harvey. — 1st ed.
        p.   cm. — (Clifton and Shirley Caldwell Texas heritage series ; no. 5)
    Includes bibliographical references and index.
    ISBN 978-0-292-73465-4 (alk. paper)   ISBN 978-0-292-73466-1 (pbk. : alk. paper)
    1. Cemeteries—Texas—Directories.   2. Cemeteries—Texas—History.   3. Texas—
History, local.   4. Texas—Biography.   5. Texas—Genealogy—Handbooks, manuals, etc.
6. Photography—Texas—Amateurs' manuals.   I. Title.   II. Series.
F387.H355   2003
929'.5'025764—dc21   2002013123

*For Sabrina, Dad, and all those Texans
who answered the call.*

CONTENTS

ぅ

ACKNOWLEDGMENTS

T his book was a wonderful project of almost six years' length. It began as a hobby of sorts, until I showed some of the photographs and notes I had taken to a friend, Paul Montgomery. Paul introduced me to Shannon Davies, who looked over the initial scribblings and helped launch the project. Shannon was a great source of encouragement, and I am quite indebted to both Shannon and Paul. Bill Bishel, of the University of Texas Press, patiently waited for the volume and provided ideas critical to its content.

Many people around the state provided information and help in finding gravesites, including Chanté Bryant, Llano Cemetery, Amarillo; Byron Kreuger, Austin Memorial Park, Austin; Kay Ann Yaklin, City of Austin; Greg Kreuger, Oakwood Cemetery, Austin; Alexandra Smith, Forest Lawn Cemetery, Beaumont; Edwina Thomas, Brenham; Monroe Shaw, Greenleaf Cemetery, Brownwood; Paul Dickey, Dreamland Cemetery, Canyon; Raymond Bouska, Greenwood Cemetery, Dallas; Pat Patterson, Laurel Land Cemetery, Dallas; Barbara Gross, Sparkman-Hillcrest Memorial Park, Dallas; Kathy Johnson and Gail Heedley, Mount Olivet Cemetery, Fort Worth; Linda McBee, Galveston; Bonnie Ambrus, Glenwood Cemetery, Houston; Sammy Smith, City of Lubbock Cemetery, Lubbock; Eunice Anderson, Uvalde; James E. Evans, Oakwood Cemetery, Waco; and Joe Bob Wells, Richland Springs.

Myretta Bell made a first review of the book, and her suggestions and ability to find errors were invaluable. Sherri Moore also reviewed the manuscript and provided many helpful comments. My love to my sister, Marilyn, for taking long trips to distant cemeteries and for reminding me with regularity, "I can't wait until that book is finished!"

Finally—for my friend John Graves—thanks for your inspiration and the wonderful hours spent talking on your back porch.

INTRODUCTION

⨍

In the summer of 1967 I landed my first full-time job. The opportunity arose when a classmate resigned his job at Mount Olivet Cemetery, located just down the street from my northeast Fort Worth high school. He had been responsible for watering the acres of grass at the cemetery, and the tools of his trade—sprinkler heads, pipe wrenches, and joint sealant—now lay in want of new hands. He drove his own tractor and was his own supervisor, left alone to water the grass after class each day until the summer sun disappeared behind the headstones. It was a job highly coveted by the entire gang of boys who played football in the vacant lot across the road from Mount Olivet. All of us applied. Proving that in the corporate world it is not what you know but whom you know, the grounds superintendent recognized me as one of an endless stream of past neighborhood newspaper carriers. He gave me the job. It was to begin for me a lifelong interest in cemeteries.

As water streams arched over headstones and shrubs, I often walked among the names and dates, trying to imagine how they might have looked and how they had lived. Friends were at rest in Mount Olivet. Occasionally, when the grass around the gravesite of a baseball teammate browned, I lingered over his flat, brass marker, daydreaming of once again lolling in left field while Terry patrolled center. The cemetery was replete with the people and history of Fort Worth, for each stone marked a life lived and memories created, some seemingly eternal, some painfully ephemeral.

Working in the cemetery was a perfect union of my love of the outdoors and my love for history. The Fort Worth Independent School District was serious about the subject of Texas history as an element of public education. Maybe the state school board thought we might forget the Alamo, I do not know, but the people and stories of Texas never left me.

So why stop and walk through a cemetery in which none of your relatives are buried or where you know of no prominent person resting there? I suggest that the reason is that each cemetery is the same and each is different. A casual walk through a cemetery, any cemetery, provides a subtle sense of place and time, of what a town was in the past in contrast to what it is now. Cemeteries provide direct and often poignant links to our story, and no other section of a town more accurately records the legacy of its citizenry. For example, one need only stroll through the Old City Cemetery in Gonzales and feel the German presence recorded there to understand that Gonzales' legacy is one of European immigrants in search of a better life in a distant and frequently dangerous land. The cemeteries of old Indianola, each with markers recording the seemingly instantaneous passing of entire families, document a populace that flirted with the catastrophic hurricanes, floods, and disease that swept the Texas coast in the late 1800s. And the huge granite mausoleums that line the streets of Oakwood Cemetery in Fort Worth stand in silent testimony to the rich trail-driving and ranching heritage that sprung from the Texas plains like prairie grasses.

In a broader sense, Texas' cemeteries reflect the entire American experience and the immense contribution that Texans made in the invention and reinvention of our nation. Texas has always been a place where big dreams and big landscapes collided to produce big legends. Texans are a pioneering people, independent, industrious, curious, bawdy, brave, proud, and occasionally outrageous. Texas is the final resting place of suffragists, industrialists, teachers, heroines, villains, and an American president. It is the home of innumerable veterans whose solitary white gravestones, scattered to every corner of the state, provide a sobering reminder of the staggering human currency paid to protect our homes and loved ones.

Researching Texas history and traveling to hundreds of cemeteries tucked away in every corner of Texas were a revelation to me—an introduction to people and places that I scarcely knew existed. Terry Jordan's book *Texas Graveyards* was an important source of information about cemeteries, but unlike that book, the present volume is not about the cultural significance of cemeteries, the occult mysticism that surrounds them, or a guide to deciphering the symbolism and traditions of burial. Jordan's book and similar texts were written by people who understand that side of the gravestone much better than I. Rather, this book is about the richness of humanity.

Every cemetery has a story. In some cases, the story is the cemetery itself (Cowboy Cemetery near Mercury is a great example), sometimes it is both the cemetery and those buried there (Texas State Cemetery, Austin), and sometimes it springs from remarkable people in an otherwise unremarkable cemetery.

In each cemetery listed, I searched for its story. As a result, some listings have extensive descriptions of the cemetery itself and minimal reference to the people who are at rest there. For other cemeteries, there is no description of the site itself but rather only references to those buried. Therein lies some level of what appears at first blush to be inconsistency among entries, but in fact, one finds remarkable uniformity in and among cemeteries, because each does have its own story.

Traveling across Texas and slowly walking through hundreds of cemeteries was a wonderful experience. I came away from that journey with insights previously unheld. First, the contribution made by Texas' women to the state's history, culture, and quality of life is enormous and (in my view) largely underappreciated. Texas women have been great athletes, philanthropists, civic leaders, and pioneers. Of all the lessons learned in this exercise, that was perhaps the most personally important and gratifying.

Second, the human capital cost of warfare is enormous. The rows of silent gravestones in our national cemeteries are a testament to young lives lost in defense of ideals that may be well worth that cost, but they also speak to our responsibility to ensure that warfare is an instrument of absolute last resort. Yet these gravestones also underscore the courage and commitment to comrades-in-arms that Texans have carried with them to all corners of the earth as they were called to service of this state and this nation. To those who read this book, it may seem I have a bias to military figures, particularly those Texans who have been awarded the Congressional Medal of Honor. Perhaps that is the case, but to include one recipient in these pages requires inclusion of all; no one sacrifice is any greater than another, and so all of those medal recipients who could be located have been included.

The choice of the biographical sketches was made using three criteria. First, the deceased is buried in Texas in a public cemetery. Many noteworthy Texans lie at rest in family cemeteries on private property, and their gravesites are not readily accessible. Further, many other notable Texans are buried in cemeteries outside the state, and those people were excluded. The second criterion was that of verifying the actual burial site. The gravesites of many Texans whose contribution should be acknowledged herein simply could not be found. Third, the person was a significant figure in Texas history or made a substantial contribution to its broadly defined culture. Texas history, folklore, and culture directly reflect the people who settled this state, fought for its independence, settled its frontiers, trailed its cattle, educated its young, and participated in its eternally wacky politics. Yet, if it appears as though a favorite cemetery, someone you know, or a prominent Texan is missing from this book and should be found among its pages, you are probably right: No single volume can encompass this state.

My hope is that this book helps you find, visit, and enjoy just a few of the many stories to be discovered in Texas' estimated thirty-five thousand graveyards. In a very real sense, producing *Texas Cemeteries* was a means to understanding the people who lived and died in a state that I have passionately loved my entire life. The responsibility inherent with being a native son, for me at least, required an interweaving of geography, history, and legend so that I could fully understand who I am. Somehow those of us lucky enough to have been born in Texas believe that we are different from those born somewhere else—not better, necessarily, but surely different. I always wondered why we believed that. Now I know.

LOCATING THE CEMETERY
AND GRAVESITE YOU
ARE SEEKING

TIPS ON FINDING THE CEMETERY

Estimates have placed the number of cemeteries in Texas as high as thirty-five thousand. Cemeteries are scattered throughout the state, and many have the same name. For example, there are at least thirty-five cemeteries named Evergreen in Texas and two cemeteries with that name in each of Bee, Harris, McLennan, and Runnels counties. But finding a cemetery or an individual gravesite is not impossible; in most cases it is only a matter of locating the right maps or library resources. Here are some good starting places.

County Road Maps from the Texas Department of Transportation

Of the map resources available for finding a Texas cemetery, I have found the county road maps from the Texas Department of Transportation (TXDOT) to be very useful. TXDOT produces detailed road maps of each Texas county, and the locations and names of cemeteries within a county usually can be found on its TXDOT map. These maps are especially useful for finding locations of cemeteries within urban areas, and they negate the need for purchasing individual maps of cities.

TXDOT county road maps are available in two forms, as singular sheets or in a bound volume of all Texas counties. These maps can be purchased from TXDOT, but most libraries maintain copies, and individual maps are often available at TXDOT district offices around the state. Information about purchasing maps, locations of district offices, and other useful information is available on the TXDOT website at <www.dot.state.tx.us>.

County Genealogical Societies

Almost every Texas county has a genealogical society, and its members are accurate and generous repositories of local history. In many counties, members of these societies have surveyed every identified cemetery in a county and have catalogued each of the gravesites in those cemeteries (up to the publication date of the catalogue, of course).

Finding a member of a county genealogical society is usually as easy as contacting the county clerk's office, the public library in the county seat, or a local funeral home. For example, the Rosenberg Library in Galveston has an extensive section on local history, including records of the local cemeteries. After inquiring at the library about the location of the gravesite of Angelina Dickinson, I was directed to a Galveston resident who helped in the search. A local funeral home provided maps of the Galveston cemeteries for me at no charge and then faxed them to me so I would have them when I visited two days later.

The Lorenzo de Zavala State Archives and Library

The Lorenzo de Zavala State Archives and Library Building, 1201 Brazos Street, Austin (directly east of the Texas State Capitol in the downtown area), is a terrific resource. Housed on the first floor of the building is a large, well-staffed Genealogy Collection with records of every sort imaginable, including complete cemetery records for many Texas counties. In many cases, not only are all the cemeteries in individual counties enumerated, but all the gravesites in those cemeteries are inventoried as well. If you know the county in which a person is buried, there is an excellent possibility the gravesite is recorded in one of these volumes.

The Genealogy Collection includes an extensive microfiche collection and a useful array of other historical resources. The staff of the Genealogy Collection is helpful and available Tuesday–Saturday from 8:00 A.M. until 5:00 P.M.

U.S. Geological Survey Resources

The U.S. Geological Survey (USGS) has mapped the entirety of the United States, and these maps (called "quadrangles" or "quads") show the location of the surveyed cemeteries within the confines of that quadrangle. Each quadrangle map has a unique name and number. USGS quadrangles are produced at different scales, and the most useful scale for locating cemeteries is 1/24,000 (also referenced as 7.5-minute series maps). Many libraries maintain a complete set of these maps, and the maps can be purchased from the USGS.

The USGS maintains a website <http://mapping.usgs.gov> that allows easy access to a searchable database of all the surveyed cemeteries within a county, the location of the cemetery expressed as latitude and longitude, and the name of the 7.5-minute quadrangle map upon which the cemetery appears. However, my experience is that some cemeteries in a county do not appear in this database. Still, having access to the latitude and longitude of a cemetery can be very useful in finding the location of a cemetery using Global Positioning System (GPS) technology.

Using GPS

The Global Positioning System (GPS) is a worldwide radio-navigation system formed from a constellation of twenty-four satellites and associated ground stations. The technology works by triangulation, with position on the surface of the earth calculated from signals transmitted from these satellites and received by a GPS unit. Upon receipt of these signals, geographic position (latitude and longitude) of the receiver is displayed.

GPS is a powerful navigation technology that is readily available, inexpensive, and easy to use. In fact, many automobile manufacturers include GPS units as an option to help motorists locate destinations, speed of travel, estimated time of arrival, and current position. An internal function—often referred to as a "Go To" function—is used to navigate to that known location stored in memory. For example, if you enter the GPS coordinates for the Greenwood Cemetery in Weatherford and turn your GPS unit on as you travel, the unit's "Go To" function will direct you to the cemetery. Further, many websites now have GPS coordinates for specific gravesites that can be downloaded.

Entering these coordinates into the GPS unit will allow you to locate the gravesite almost immediately. As you thumb through this book, you will find GPS locations of all the cemeteries referenced in this volume. These are included to aid you in finding cemeteries throughout the state. But GPS locations for individual gravesites are not included—that would eliminate most of the fun of discovery!

SKIPPING STONES — TIPS FOR FINDING A GRAVESITE

Searching for a particular gravesite in a cemetery can be either great fun or a great source of frustration, depending on the size of the cemetery, the condition of the marker, and the depth of your patience. But here are some techniques that greatly enhance your skill in locating the site you wish to find.

Contact the Cemetery's Administrator

If the gravesite you seek is in an expansive cemetery like Sparkman-Hillcrest in Dallas or Glenwood Cemetery in Houston, do not waste your time trying to locate the site on your own. These cemeteries are much too large for you to experience much success by walking or driving through the cemetery. Some cemeteries have twenty thousand or more gravesites, and finding a site without knowing its location in advance is akin to looking for a particular rock in a quarry. If you are searching for a series of sites, you may find some of them, but you will not find them quickly and it is highly unlikely that you will find them all. For example, I invested more than a hundred hours walking through Oakwood Cemetery in Austin, searching for about fifty individual gravesites, and there were several I could not find. A call to the administration office yielded quick results. The bottom line is that if time is at all a consideration, begin your search in the cemetery office.

The administrators at urban cemeteries are extraordinarily helpful in locating gravesites. In many cases, they will provide not only the location of the site but a map of the cemetery as well. On several occasions a cemetery manager actually accompanied me through the cemetery to help in my search and provided interesting information in addition to that which I was seeking. The administrator of the Greenwood Cemetery in Dallas spent a very cold, wet morning showing me the interesting sites there and explained in detail the many types of stone used in grave markers, how they were carved, and the source of the stone. The staff at Mount Olivet Cemetery in Fort Worth quickly aided in my search and provided stacks of information about other cemeteries in Tarrant County as well. If your travels do not allow you to visit the cemetery during regular business hours, consider writing to the cemetery administrator prior to visiting and asking for a map of the cemetery with the gravesites indicated. It works.

Check for Local Cemetery Associations

In many cemeteries, administration is provided by local volunteers, usually in the form of a cemetery association. Quite often the phone number or address of an association representative is provided on the cemetery premises, either near one or more of the entrances, on the cemetery maintenance building, or on the door of the cemetery administration building. Also, check the local phone book; in some instances the phone numbers of local associations are listed there. On a venture to the Prairie Lea Cemetery in Brenham, after having looked two hours for a headstone, I found a phone number for the local cemetery association and called. Within a matter of seconds I was told exactly where to look, and the location was right on target.

Search East to West

In most cemeteries, the people interred there are laid to rest facing eastward. Markers are not called *head*stones without reason; the markers stand at the head of the deceased's burial plot, and the inscriptions on the headstones appear on the east face of the stone. So, if you start from the east and go west in most cemeteries, the inscriptions on the stones will be easily readable as you walk or drive. That is not always the case, however; many of the stones in the International Order of Odd Fellows Cemetery in Georgetown face west, and the stones in the Panteon-Hidalgo Cemetery in New Braunfels face to every point of the compass. But the majority of cemeteries are laid out so that an east-to-west line of travel will save a lot of time in finding gravesites.

Find the Large Upright Monuments and Mausoleums

If you are searching for the gravesite of a prominent person, particularly one buried before World War II, look for an upright marker bearing the family name of the deceased. Many notable people buried in the late 1800s and early 1900s have large markers, obelisks, statues, or granite slabs as headstones. The oldest parts of the cemetery will almost invariably have the largest concentration of upright markers. This is an excellent means for immediately finding the historic section of the cemetery.

If the deceased was wealthy, do not neglect the mausoleums. The cluster of private mausoleums in Fort Worth's Oakwood Cemetery looks like a housing development where each successive builder tried to outdo his neighbor. Two of Texas' most wealthy and successful cattlemen, Samuel Burk Burnett and John B. Slaughter, each rest in huge private mausoleums across a paved road from one another in this cemetery.

Know the Deceased's Date of Death

Quite often burials are clustered by date of death. In some ethnic-German cemeteries, for example, burials take place in near chronological order, so that knowledge of the deceased's date of death will lead you to the gravesite rather easily. In other cemeteries, the oldest parts of the graveyard are also clustered and tend to have the vast majority of upright monuments. For example, walking into the Salado Cemetery, one notices that most of the upright and ornate monuments are located in a fairly small area in the center of the cemetery. If the date of death of the person you are seeking is not within a decade of the dates on the stones most proximate to where you are looking, there is a strong likelihood that the person whose gravesite you are seeking is buried somewhere else in the cemetery. This location method does not always work, but it is a great way to find a site in the majority of cemeteries I visited.

Look for Texas Historical Markers

If you are searching for the gravesite of a prominent local person or historical figure, keep an eye out for historical markers placed by the Texas Historical Commission. The historical marker may not mark the site you are looking for, but it is likely to be in a part of the cemetery where other interesting gravesites are located. Two of the most historically significant gravesites in all of Texas are in the Greenwood Cemetery at Weatherford. The graves of cattle trail legends Bose Ikard and Oliver Loving are in that cemetery, and both headstones are small, rather inconspicuous stones that lie flat on the ground. However, both men's graves are also marked by Texas historical markers, easily seen from almost any vantage point in the cemetery. This strategy, as simple as it seems, works superbly. It is also an effective way to find information about local citizens or notable Texans who might be buried there. While visiting the Greenleaf Cemetery in Brownwood, I spotted a historical marker for writer Robert Howard (creator of Conan the Barbarian), for whom I had no burial site location information prior to my visit. I would have missed his grave without the guidance of the marker.

Use the Burial Lists at National Cemeteries

Finding a gravesite in one of the national cemeteries is easy because complete lists of all burials in these cemeteries are maintained on the premises of each. For example, the Fort Sam Houston National Cemetery has gravesite listings and maps available in several kiosks throughout the cemetery. Each tombstone in these cemeteries has a grave number on the back of the stone, so locating a gravesite is a simple matter.

SHOOTING STONES— TAKING GREAT PHOTOS IN A CEMETERY

ॐ

S hooting good photographs in a cemetery is no more difficult than in any other type of outdoor location, and any camera will take excellent photos of headstones or cemetery statuary under favorable light conditions. Like landscape photography, almost everything of interest in a cemetery is stationary, which multiplies the options for use of slower film speeds (sharper images), narrow lens apertures (greater depth of field), and long exposure times (low-light conditions). Unlike most landscape photography, there is little color and contrast variation in headstones. Still, there can be some situations unique to cemeteries that require a little work and planning if you want to capture a good image.

EQUIPMENT

In addition to a camera and a tripod, a few other items might come in handy when shooting photos in a cemetery:

- A gallon-size water container (for wetting and cleaning headstones)
- A white umbrella (for shade and rain protection)
- A ladder or step stool (for unusual points of view)
- White poster board (for shade and bounced flash)
- Grass clippers (for removing stray blades)
- A blanket (a lifesaver if you are wearing shorts and want to kneel)
- A broom or brush (for cleaning markers)
- A small rake (for removing debris and reptiles)

A word of caution is appropriate. Cemeteries, particularly those that are not regularly maintained and have high grass or accumulated debris, are havens for wildlife of every sort—including snakes and insects capable of quickly disturbing your visit. Stone markers can be especially attractive to snakes seeking a place to bask in the sun and warm their bodies. The cracks and crevices in and around headstones make excellent hiding places for spiders and my personal nemesis, scorpions. Before setting up to photograph objects in any cemetery, take a minute or two to closely examine the immediate area around and on the marker or statue. The largest snake I have ever seen crawled leisurely from under a flat marker in a McCulloch County cemetery and into my camera viewfinder.

COMPOSITION TIPS

Like flash photography, composition is an art in itself. But following some easy composition tips will result in much better photos.

Clean Up the Area

First, make sure your subject and its surrounding areas are reasonably clear of litter. A modicum of leaves and sticks can actually add to the character and mood of an image, but too much organic litter is distracting. Raking away grass clippings and leaves that have accumulated around the base of a stone provides a much cleaner image, and I have often used a pair of grass clippers to trim upright blades of tall grass standing in front of a marker.

Headstones, much like statues, are also a favorite perching place for birds, and a little housecleaning goes a long way. Dousing the headstone with plain water and brushing it with a broom quickly remove bird droppings, loose dirt, and other debris, as well as providing better contrast between the inscriptions and the marker itself. Although many cemeteries have a readily available source of water, carrying a gallon or two along with you is a good idea.

After selecting your subject and before you snap the picture, take a few seconds to examine the edges of the viewfinder closely for distractions. A camera does not "see" the same way our eye gathers information. When we look at a subject, we tend to focus on what is important to us as we see it in the viewfinder. Somehow, our mind seems to filter out the distractions that our eyes see but do not register. We may see a perfectly carved granite headstone and not notice the weeds, wilted flowers, dead sticks, and loose papers around its base—

unless we take time to really look for them. However, the camera sees everything, and the beauty of an immaculately carved headstone or statue may be lost in the chaos of distractions captured in the exposure. I once spent several hours in a cemetery waiting for that single moment when the setting sun set the stone of an angel perfectly aglow. Later, upon viewing the image, I was thrilled with the light that bathed her face. However, also captured in the photo was a water sprinkler. Below eye level and unnoticed, it appearing to be growing out of her foot.

Consider the Point of View

Point of view, the camera position relative to the subject, is a critical element in taking good photos in general and cemetery photos in particular. Burial grounds are full of upright headstones, markers, statues, fences, and shrubs—all in proximity to one another. Such visual background noise can be distracting in the final image. Consider the relative position of the camera to the subject, and then select the light and background that best remove any distractions that compete with the viewer's attention to the main subject. Take a few seconds to look at the background and edges of the viewfinder before you shoot; sometimes just moving a few inches can make a big difference in the impact of the printed image.

Because headstones and markers come in so many shapes and sizes, managing the angle of view (the position of the camera relative to eye level) takes on a new significance. The most pedestrian photos in the world are photos of headstones shot "head-on" at eye level, while different perspectives captured by an unusual angle of view can be very interesting. For example, statues shot from a bird's-eye view or obelisks photographed from directly below the spire can produce intriguing and powerful images.

Finding interesting angles of view is a snap when photos are shot from elevated positions or from ground-level positions. Not only is a short stepladder necessary to get directly above upright markers and flat markers, but the elevated angle of view also creates unique perspectives. Similarly, a blanket provides a nice means of kneeling or lying on the ground to explore unusual angles of view below those of eye level.

Clearly, there is no "best" point of view or angle of view. But often there are better ones than the first one you see. Composition is all about exploring alternatives to standing in front of the subject and firing the shutter. When you are photographing headstones and markers, you are not working with the most inherently colorful or dynamic subjects. Taking a little time to find an unusual point of view can make a big difference.

Choosing the Right Film for Your Camera

Any film will suffice when taking cemetery photos, but the choice of film speed can have a noticeable effect on the quality of the final image. Clarity of image is paramount in shooting headstones or statuary because much of the beauty and information conveyed is in the detail of the object. Film is a light-sensitive medium, and images are captured on the film by controlling its exposure to light. The film speed is a measure of the film's sensitivity to light and is indicated by its ISO rating. The higher the ISO number, the more sensitive the film is to light, and the less light is required to capture the image. Although faster film—say, ISO 400—can certainly be used to shoot headstones or other images in a cemetery, the trade-off comes in image quality. In general, the "faster" the film (the higher the ISO number), the "grainier" the final image. I have had excellent results using "daylight" film with a film speed of ISO 200 or less. The quality of the image is sharp, and the colors are usually as vibrant as can be expected under the circumstances. After all, as often as not you are photographing a rock!

Artificial lighting, low light, and the highly polished surface of crypts in a mausoleum cause some unique problems. Ordinary tungsten-filament light bulbs tend to give most "daylight" films a warmer tone than that observed by our eye. Special indoor films, or "tungsten" films, compensate for the color shift and are readily available. However, unless you are planning to shoot a whole roll of film in a mausoleum, you might consider using daylight film and a flash unit.

Using a Tripod

In low-light situations, particularly when using slower ISO films (especially slower than ISO 100), a tripod or its equivalent is a necessity for sharp image production. Lengthened exposure times (slow shutter speeds) go hand in hand with dim light. If the camera's exposure time setting is 1/30th second or longer, it is virtually impossible to operate a handheld camera without generating movement sufficient to produce a blurred final image.

A tripod will save film costs and perhaps prevent return trips to rephotograph markers. Tripods can be exorbitantly expensive, but I have used a small, lightweight "backpack" tripod (purchased for $15) that worked quite well. If your camera cannot be mounted on a tripod, a beanbag placed on the ground, a nearby marker, a ladder rung, or a box will produce a stable photography platform.

Although flash photography is an alternative to slow shutter speeds and a tripod, polished stone and metal markers tend to reflect the light back into the camera lens, much like the flash reflection created by eyeglasses worn by a portrait subject. For most of us, slowing the shutter speed is certainly easier and usually more reliable than flash photography.

LIGHTING

For consistently good-quality photographs, consider shooting headstones, markers, and statuary on cloudy or rainy days. The diffuse light tends to soften images, provides a subtle mood, and relieves problems like reflectance and uneven lighting produced by direct sunlight. The contrast is often not as good on cloudy days, but in general, there is not much contrast inherent in the subject or its environment. Plus, you can correct some of the difficulty with contrast by using one of a series of color-correcting lens filters. If you must photograph on sunlit days, early morning and late afternoon provide the best lighting for upright markers; midday sunlight provides good lighting for flat headstones.

SHOOTING FLAT HEADSTONES

Midday sunlight tends to be harsh, particularly in a cemetery with few or no trees, and the direct overhead rays striking markers that are set flat with the ground can be blinding. In addition, sunlight filtering through tree leaves usually provides a dappling effect on the surface of a stone or marker, making correct film exposure more difficult. But solutions to the problems of midday sun are easily found in a gallon of water and a white golf umbrella.

Stones and metal markers can get very hot when exposed to direct sunlight, even in winter months (remember the snakes and insects). Water slowly poured onto the surface of the stone cools the surface and reduces its reflectance. The water also collects in the carvings of the stone, making the letters and numerals much easier to visualize by improving the contrast between the inscription and its surroundings.

On very hot days, wet the stone thoroughly, let it dry, and then wet it again. The water evaporates more slowly after the second wetting, allowing time to focus the camera, secure a good exposure, and snap the shutter.

A white golf umbrella provides an excellent means of shading flat markers and provides uniform lighting across the face of the stone. Golf umbrellas are inexpensive and large, perfect for providing maximum shade with frugality. Although any color of umbrella will suffice, white umbrellas allow more light penetration through the fabric onto the marker, again facilitating longer exposure times. Colored umbrellas will work, but my red one, for example, tends to produce an unnatural color and allows less illumination of the subject.

Since flat markers are just that, flat with the ground, they are considerably more challenging to photograph than are upright markers. Interesting points of view are harder to find when shooting flat markers, largely because the markers tend to be two-dimensional. But a stepladder provides some alternatives because it allows the photographer to position the camera above and away from the marker. The quality and choices in composition of flat marker photos are much better when the camera is elevated. For example, before I used a stepladder, most of my photos of flat markers were accentuated by the presence in the image of one or both of my feet.

SHOOTING UPRIGHT HEADSTONES

Early morning or late afternoon sunlight is much less direct, creating warmer tones and eliminating the glare or reflectance that is characteristic of almost all polished stone markers. Unfortunately, photographing upright markers and statues depends upon the east-west orientation of the structure and its engraving. Markers usually receive morning sunlight because most people are buried facing east, but that is not always the case. For example, many of the numerous upright markers in the Texas State Cemetery are engraved or carved on both sides of the stones. Letters and numerals on upright markers can be hard to visualize clearly through the camera lens at midday, when the sun is directly overhead, because there is little contrast between the carvings and the surface. Moreover, upright markers with raised letters and numerals can produce long and rather ugly shadows on the marker face during midday. Still, as with flat headstones, the contrast of carvings and inscriptions on upright markers can be enhanced by pouring water on the stone's surface.

If your desire is to photograph upright stones in a cemetery, plan on being in the cemetery at sunrise and sunset to take advantage of sun angles and the direction of light. For example, shooting an east-facing marker at sunset results in the full sun directly behind the marker and shining straight into the camera lens. Unless you choose to fill the frame with the headstone or statue so that the backlighting is completely blocked, the resulting image will often be poorly exposed. In addition, an east-facing monument itself shades the markings on it as the sun sets in the west, making the inscription difficult to read. The bottom line is that east-facing stones are best photographed in the morning, and west-facing stones are best photographed in the afternoon.

Using a Flash

In some lighting situations, a flash unit can vastly improve the quality of the photos you take. However, if there is insufficient ambient light to illuminate a marker fully, then using a flash unit will illuminate the stone, but the background of the photo will be almost totally black. Flash units therefore should be used only to supplement natural light and not to replace it. Flash photography is an art in itself, and its nuances are beyond the scope of this volume. Still, here are some ideas that will help you use a flash to photograph cemetery objects.

Again, highly polished headstones and metal markers tend to reflect the flash strobe back into the lens, particularly if you photograph the marker head-on. Head-on pictures are usually not very interesting even in the best of light, and when flash is used, the results are often terrible: a huge light burst in the middle of the image. You can generally get better results by taking an angled, indirect shot of the headstone, usually from the left or right side of the marker. A little water on the stone sometimes, but not always, helps reduce reflectance.

When headstones are in bright overhead light, the shadows from surrounding vegetation and the shadows cast by the stone itself often obscure inscriptions and other details. These can be revealed, and shadows lightened, by using your flash; this technique, called fill flash, illuminates those areas that ambient light does not reach. Keep in mind that reflectance off the face of the stone may still be a problem if the shot is taken head-on.

Fill flash also works well to illuminate an upright marker when the sun is shining on the side of the stone opposite the engraved side. For example, using a fill flash on an east-facing marker at sunset, when the west face is being illuminated, can produce a well-exposed image. The fill flash brightens the shaded side of the stone, and the attendant backlighting provided by the sun can be quite beautiful. This technique, in my opinion, works nicely when photographing statuary. The fill-flash exposure of a statue against a clear blue sky can be striking and "opens" the statue's numerous shadows and its subtlety.

If your flash-head angle is adjustable, try bouncing the flash off a sheet of white poster board and onto the subject. Position the white poster board over or near the marker or crypt face, making sure that the poster board does not appear in your viewfinder. Aim the flash unit at the white poster board surface, and bounce the flash off the poster board onto the subject. Be sure to use only white poster board; otherwise the subject may pick up the color cast by the board.

A bounce flash technique can be useful if you are photographing in a mausoleum. The flash tends to overcome the tint of tungsten lights in a mausoleum and also compensates for low light levels. I have generally found that daylight film used in conjunction with a bounced flash yields quite satisfactory results in these situations.

Using Lens Filters

Lens filters come in a variety of sizes and colors and can produce dramatic special effects. Three types of filters can be handy in photographing cemetery stones: a polarizing filter, a warming filter, and a UV/haze filter.

Polarizing filters work in the same manner as polarizing sunglasses and are effective in removing reflecting light from surfaces like polished stone, glass, or water. Polarizing filters are most useful for increasing general outdoor color saturation and contrast. Polarization is angle-dependent, and as you aim your camera either more into or away from the sun, the effect will gradually diminish. There is no polarizing effect if your lens is pointed directly toward or away from the sun.

Warming filters do a great job of improving image quality on rainy and overcast days, although these filters are more useful for capturing landscape images than for creating images of headstones. On overcast days or in shadows on sunny days, the light is a bit cool and bluish. The yellow-amber 81 series of filters remove the blue tone, resulting in a warmer tone to the photo.

Film often exhibits sensitivity to invisible, ultraviolet (UV) light.

Ultraviolet filters absorb UV light, usually without affecting visible light. These filters are used most often outdoors, especially at high altitudes, where the UV-absorbing atmosphere is thinner, and over long distances, such as marine scenes. Ultraviolet light can show up as a bluish color cast with color film, or it can cause a low-contrast haze that diminishes details, especially when viewing distant objects.

UV/haze filters absorb the ultraviolet rays that can make outdoor photographs hazy and indistinct. These filters also serve as a lens protector and can be kept mounted to the camera lens at all times.

AROUND THE STATE

✤

Abilene

Elmwood Memorial Park
Highway 277 at Twilight Trail
N 32 24.862, W 099 48.021

JESSIE KENAN WILDER JONES

Jessie Jones (1882–1969) dedicated much of her public life to civic service. On a trip to Colorado with her children in the 1930s she found that there was no shady spot along the road where she could stop with her children and rest or eat lunch. Apparently, as she ate under the shade of a railroad trestle, an idea took root. At a highway beautification meeting, she proposed a project to construct roadside parks. The concept gained momentum after finding a champion in Governor Miriam Ferguson. The multitude of roadside parks that now dot the Texas landscape are the direct result of her interests. Her service to the people of Abilene continued throughout her life, and her gifts touched the lives of every citizen of that city.

Acton

Acton Cemetery
FM 4, near intersection with FM 1192
N 32 26.412, W 097 41.062

Acton Cemetery has within its confines the smallest state park in all of Texas. Located in the center of this beautiful country cemetery is the gravesite of Elizabeth Crockett (1788–1860), the second wife of Alamo hero Davy Crockett. In the family plot next to her are two of

WESTWARD-FACING STATUE
OF ELIZABETH CROCKETT,
ACTON CEMETERY, ACTON.

her children, Matilda Porter Crockett (1823–1864) and Robert Patton Crockett (1816–1889). Mrs. Crockett received a grant of 320 acres in Hood County (although it was still part of Johnson County at the time) from the state of Texas for her husband's sacrifice at the Alamo. Their 0.006-acre gravesite is maintained by the Texas Parks and Wildlife Department as a state historic site and is marked by an immense granite stone (erected in 1911) and the westward-facing statue of Elizabeth Crockett.

The cemetery also has several excellent examples of limestone false crypts, most of which are near the Crockett gravesite. The excellent stonework of these crypts, particularly the monolithic limestone tables that cover them, is among the finest to be found in Texas. A series of impressive oak trees surrounds these crypts, and these trees were alive with both raucous chickadees and barking squirrels on the November day that took me there.

Along the back border of the Acton Cemetery is a rock fence meticulously constructed of unmortared limestone. In several places, trees have grown through and toppled a bit of the fence, but it remains in remarkably good condition and is a monument to patient hands.

If you visit the Acton Cemetery, try to go after the first freeze of the fall. This cemetery is replete with native Texas pecan trees that produce an abundance of nuts. Walking among the markers in the cemetery, I gathered a small sack of the richest pecans imaginable.

Alleyton

Alleyton Cemetery
FM 102, south of Interstate 10
N 29 42.495, W 096 28.865

DALLAS STOUDENMIRE

Dallas Stoudenmire (1845–1882) is said to have looked the part of a lawman. At six feet four inches, he had dark brown hair, green eyes, and the long moustache characteristic of the day. His reputation as a gunfighter grew from his participation in several shoot-outs near Columbus, Texas. When he later traveled west to El Paso, Stoudenmire was hired as city marshal on April 11, 1881. His career as marshal was short, about a year, but eventful.

His reputation and ability to outshoot and outdraw anyone looking for trouble had an immediate calming influence on the town.

GRAVESITE OF DALLAS STOUDENMIRE, ALLEYTON CEMETERY, ALLEYTON.

Four days after assuming office, Stoudenmire was involved in the legendary "Four Dead in Five Seconds" shoot-out. The gunplay took the lives of an innocent bystander (accidentally shot by Stoudenmire), former city marshal George Campbell (probably shot by Stoudenmire), local ruffian John Hale (definitely shot by Stoudenmire), and Constable Gus Krempku (shot by John Hale shortly before his own demise).

But as is often the case, those who "live by the gun" eventually "die by the gun," and Stoudenmire proved no exception. During his tenure a feud developed between Stoudenmire and three brothers, George (Doc), Frank, and James Manning. On the afternoon of September 18, 1882, Stoudenmire agreed to meet in the Manning Saloon, have a drink with the brothers, and sign a peace treaty. But the situation rapidly deteriorated when Doc Manning and Stoudenmire reached for their guns. In the ensuing gunfight Stoudenmire was wounded and fell into a wrestling match in the street with Manning. During the life-or-death struggle, Jim Manning shot and killed Stoudenmire. Both James and Doc Manning went on trial for murder, and each was acquitted in separate trials.

The body of Dallas Stoudenmire was returned to Alleyton and was buried in a simple grave surrounded by an ironwork fence. The grave is just inside the gate to the cemetery along its only dirt road. A new Confederate marker, signifying his service during the Civil War, marks his gravesite.

Amarillo

Llano Cemetery
2900 S. Hayes St.
N 35 11.097, W 101 49.913

LEE AND MARY ELIZABETH GILBERT BIVINS

Lee Bivins (1862–1929) was born in Farmington, Grayson County. By the age of twenty he had accumulated his own herd and established

BIVINS FAMILY PLOT, LLANO CEMETERY, AMARILLO.

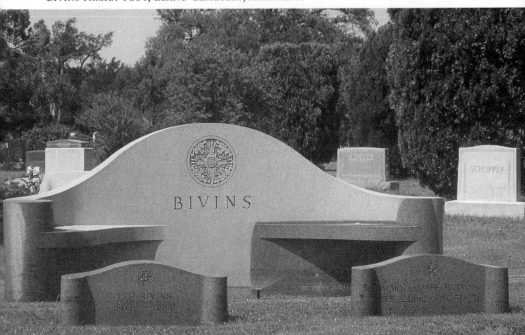

two general stores in Sherman. On August 18, 1882, he married his childhood sweetheart, Mary Gilbert (1862–1951). Bivins moved the family to the Panhandle in 1890 and there acquired his first ranch, the Mulberry Pasture, south of Claude.

In the 1920s Bivins was said to be the largest individual cattle owner in the world and the largest landowner west of the Mississippi. At one time he leased or owned more than a million acres of land, and Texas legend has it that he once rode a horse ninety miles from Dalhart to Amarillo without leaving his property.

Mrs. Bivins put the family money to many philanthropic uses (including the donation of the family home as a library), public charities, and support for needy families in the area. She actively supported the Amarillo Tuberculosis Association, the School Children's Relief Fund, and the American Red Cross.

JOHNSON BLAIR CHERRY

Johnson Blair Cherry (1901–1966) began his football-coaching career in Ranger after graduating from Texas Christian University in 1924. In 1930 Cherry took the job as head coach at Amarillo High School, where his teams won four state championships in seven years. Cherry was hired at the University of Texas in 1937 and served as first assistant on the Longhorn staff for ten years. When Dana X. Bible retired after the 1946 season, Cherry was named head coach. In Cherry's four years at Texas, he had one Southwest Conference championship and an overall record of 32-10-1. Cherry was voted into the Texas Sports Hall of Fame in 1966.

THOMAS E. CREEK

Lance Corporal Thomas E. Creek (1950–1969) was a member of Company I, Third Battalion, Ninth Marines, Third Marine Division. Near Cam Lo, Vietnam, on February 13, 1969, his rifle squad was providing security for a convoy when a mine detonated, destroying one of the vehicles and halting the others. When a grenade landed between Creek and several companions, he fell on it and saved the lives of his fellow Marines. For his gallant sacrifice, Thomas Creek was awarded the Congressional Medal of Honor.

CAL FARLEY

Cal Farley (1895–1967) settled in Amarillo in 1923 after service in World War I. A gifted athlete and a savvy businessman, Farley began his business career upon acquiring a rundown tire shop that he built into a lucrative business. In January 1934 he helped found the Maverick Club, an organized sports program with a goal of providing boys a place for exercise and learning. In 1939 he founded Cal Farley's Boys Ranch and soon devoted his full attention to helping homeless and delinquent boys.

Farley was a district governor of Rotary International and is in the Panhandle Sports Hall of Fame. He was named Outstanding Citizen of Texas and given the Veterans of Foreign Wars Silver Citizenship Medal, the Bronze Keystone Award of the Boys Clubs of America, and an honorary doctor of humanities degree from Texas Technological College (now Texas Tech University) in 1963.

DUTCH MANTELL

Dutch Mantell (1881–1941) was born Alfred Albert Joe de Re la Gardiur, in Diekirch, Luxembourg. Although he began his sports career as a prizefighter, he took up wrestling and became a champion in the sport. He became an American citizen in 1906 and for the next six years toured the nation as a wrestler.

From 1913 to 1915 he was a cast member of Hollywood's Keystone Cops. In 1925 Mantell made Amarillo his permanent home, and there he helped promote the Wun-Stop-Duzzit tire business, which belonged to his close friend Cal Farley. Mantell was the inspiration for Farley's Flying Dutchman trademark. Although he was a tough—often mean—competitor in the ring, outside the ropes Dutch Mantell was generous and kind to a fault. Much of his fortune was handed over to those in need. After his death, his estate was split between two organizations he had helped build—the Maverick Club in Amarillo and Cal Farley's Boys Ranch.

AUSTIN A. MEREDITH

Austin A. Meredith (1891–1963) was one of Texas' most influential water conservationists. As early as 1926, Meredith recognized the need for a water storage reservoir on the Canadian River as a reliable water source for the Panhandle and South Plains areas. Largely as a result of his work, in 1953 the Texas Legislature created the Canadian River Municipal Water Authority. On July 1, 1962, Meredith joined U.S. Secretary of the Interior Stewart Udall in officially beginning construction of the Sanford Dam on the Canadian River. After his death, Congress named the reservoir formed by the dam "Lake Meredith."

Bascom Nolley Timmons

Bascom Timmons (1890–1987) was born in Collin County, Texas. He developed an interest in politics and national affairs at an early age and was writing newspaper articles by age 18. At the 1912 Democratic National Convention he represented the *Washington Post* and was the youngest reporter in attendance. Timmons established his own Washington news bureau in the mid-1920s and soon had nationwide distribution of his news reports. Timmons wrote three biographies: *Garner of Texas* (1948), *Portrait of an American: Charles Gates Dawes* (1953), and *Jesse H. Jones: The Man and the Statesman* (1956). Timmons was a lifelong animal lover and had 125 of his cats buried in a cat cemetery in Washington, D.C.

Anderson

Odd Fellows Cemetery
FM 149, west of Anderson
N 30 29.210, W 095 59.840

Benjamin Briggs Goodrich

Benjamin Briggs Goodrich (1799–1860) studied medicine in Baltimore and practiced throughout the South prior to his 1834 arrival in Texas. He settled in Washington, Texas, and as one of the four delegates from Washington to the Convention of 1836, Goodrich signed the Texas Declaration of Independence.

Athens

Athens City Cemetery
Prairieville St. at Mack St.
N 32 11.985, W 095 51.321

Clinton W. Murchison, Sr.

Clinton Murchison, Sr. (1895–1969), was born in Tyler and, after service in World War I, partnered with his lifelong friend Sid W. Richardson in the oil business. Murchison's exploration and development business was very successful, and in 1925 he sold his holdings for $5 million. In 1929 Murchison formed the Southern Union Gas Company and in 1945 formed Delhi Oil Corporation. An astute businessman, Murchison expanded his business interests into a wide assortment of enterprises, including insurance, building materials, banking, cattle, and transportation.

Austin

Austin Memorial Park

2800 Hancock Dr.
N 30 19.705, W 097 45.030

Austin Memorial Park was begun about 1941 after all the available lots in the principal city cemetery, Oakwood Cemetery, had been sold. The cemetery is rather unique in that it overlays a dense limestone formation, such that about 75 percent of the gravesites are actually excavated from underlying rock. As a result, it requires about five times as many man-hours to dig a grave in this cemetery as it does in a dirt cemetery.

DANA X. BIBLE

Dana X. Bible (1891–1980) came to Texas in 1916 to coach the freshman football team at Texas A&M. In 1917 he was promoted to head coach and won the first of five Southwest Conference championships he would win at the school.

In the 1922 Dixie Classic, Bible inadvertently created the famous Texas A&M "Twelfth Man" tradition. Playing heavily favored Centre College, A&M had only eighteen roster players at kickoff. Early in the contest, three Aggies were lost to injury, and the team faced possible forfeiture of the game because of a lack of players. Bible called upon a reserve halfback, E. King Gill (who was in the press box, keeping statistics for the team), to suit up and be ready to play if needed. The Aggies defeated Centre College, and although Gill never took the field, his determination to play if called upon became a legend. In the tradition of the twelfth man, A&M students stand throughout football games to show their willingness to play if needed.

Bible left A&M for a stint at the University of Nebraska but soon returned to Texas and assumed the head coaching position at the University of Texas. Bible won Southwest Conference titles in 1943 and 1945, retired from coaching in 1946, and was UT athletic director from 1947 to 1956. Bible was a charter member of the National Football Hall of Fame and was inducted into the Texas Sports Hall of Fame in 1959.

BIBB FALK

Bibb Falk (1899–1989) coached and was the last surviving member of the 1920 White Sox, a team rebuilt after the World Series "Black Sox" gambling scandal destroyed the 1919 team. Falk has the distinction of having been the player who replaced Shoeless Joe Jackson in left field after Jackson was banned from the sport. Falk played for the Chicago White Sox, 1920–1928, and the Cleveland Indians, 1929–1932. He had a .314 batting average in 1,354 games.

In April 1940, Falk assumed the coaching duties of the University of Texas baseball team, leading the Longhorns to the conference championships in 1940 and 1941. At the outbreak of World War II, Falk enlisted in the Army Air Corps and served until his return to the university in 1946. Under his leadership, Texas became the first college team to win back-to-back national championships, in 1949 and 1950.

Falk remained at Texas until 1967, compiling a 478–176 record (278–84 in the Southwest Conference), and recorded fifteen outright Southwest Conference championships. He was elected to the Texas Baseball Hall of Fame in 1988.

FRANCIS AUGUSTUS HAMER

Francis A. (Frank) Hamer (1884–1955) was the embodiment of the twentieth-century Texas Ranger. Flinty, tough as nails, and an expert shot, Hamer served two years with the Rangers (1906–1908) and resigned to become marshal of Navasota, a position he held until moving to Harris County in 1911. Frank Hamer rejoined the Texas Rangers in 1915 and became a legend as he took on the bandits who

TEXAS RANGER FRANK HAMER AND HIS SON BILLY (KILLED ON IWO JIMA) AT REST NEXT TO EACH OTHER IN AUSTIN MEMORIAL PARK, AUSTIN.

NOVELIST JAMES MICHENER CHOSE AUSTIN AS HIS RESIDENCE AFTER COMPLETING HIS NOVEL *TEXAS*. AUSTIN MEMORIAL PARK, AUSTIN.

ruled the Texas border. In 1921 he moved to Austin and rose to the rank of captain.

Although Frank Hamer's contributions to law enforcement in the years after he left the Texas-Mexico border were impressive, he is perhaps best known for his role in tracking down the legendary outlaws Clyde Barrow and Bonnie Parker. On February 1, 1934, Hamer was assigned a position as special investigator for the Texas prison system, with the expressed assignment of putting an end to the crime spree of "Bonnie and Clyde." Relentlessly tracking the pair for months, he set a trap for them near Gibsland, Louisiana, and on May 23, 1934 (with the aid of several other officers), sprung an ambush that ended the crime spree.

Hamer's gravesite is marked by a simple stone in Austin Memorial Park, and he is at rest next to his son Billy Hamer, who as a member of the Third Marine Division was killed in action on the island of Iwo Jima.

JAMES A. MICHENER

James Michener (1907–1997) was one of America's most prolific and beloved writers. His success began with *Tales of the South Pacific*, which won the 1948 Pulitzer Prize. Michener's royalties from the play allowed him to concentrate on writing novels, and his forty-plus books have sold an estimated seventy-five million copies worldwide.

HARVEY PENICK

Harvey Penick (1904–1995) was one of golf's finest and, in his later years, most acclaimed teachers. Penick coached the University of Texas golf team to twenty-two Southwest Conference titles during his tenure (1931–1963). His list of students reads like a who's who of the golf world, including Tom Kite, Ben Crenshaw, and six members of the Ladies Professional Golf Association Hall of Fame.

His first golf instruction book, *Harvey Penick's Little Red Book* (cowritten with Bud Shrake in 1992) became the all-time best-selling sports book, and it remained on the *New York Times* best-seller list for fifty-four weeks. Penick was inducted into both the Texas Golf Hall of Fame (1979) and the Texas Sports Hall of Fame (1984).

ZACHARY THOMSON SCOTT, JR.

Zachary Thomson Scott, Jr. (1914–1965), was born in Austin, and his acting career began at Austin High School. After graduation from the University of Texas in 1939, he undertook his acting career in earnest and was soon on Broadway. His first starring role in the movies was in 1944, and he would appear in more than thirty motion pictures during his career. He received an Academy Award nomination for his acting in *The Southerner.*

Hornsby Cemetery
FM 969, approximately 1 mile west of FM 973
N 30 15.372, W 097 37.289

REUBEN HORNSBY

Hornsby Bend, also known as Hornsby or Hornsby's, was named for Reuben Hornsby (1793–1879), who settled there in 1832 and served as postmaster during the Republic of Texas era. The Hornsby Community may be the oldest settlement in Travis County. The Hornsby Cemetery is located near the site of the original home of the Hornsby family and is likely the oldest cemetery in Travis County. It is partially surrounded by a sturdy stone fence, and a Texas historical marker in the cemetery speaks to the fate of Texas Rangers killed by local Indians.

Hornsby landed in Texas at Velasco in 1830 and received a grant from Stephen Austin in the new Austin Colony near the present site of Austin. A surveyor by trade, Hornsby selected and surveyed his one-labor headright at Hornsby Bend, east of the Colorado River and

BASEBALL HALL OF FAME LEGEND ROGERS HORNSBY IS AT REST IN THE RUSTIC HORNSBY CEMETERY, NEAR AUSTIN.

thirty miles north of Bastrop. He occupied this headright in July 1832 and received title on March 4, 1841. At that date, the Hornsby home was the northernmost on the Colorado and was often the target of Indian raids. In June 1836, Indians killed one of Reuben's sons, Daniel, and a companion while the boys were fishing in the Colorado River.

ROGERS HORNSBY

Rogers Hornsby (1896–1963) is generally considered the finest right-handed hitter in the history of professional baseball. Called the "Rajah of Swat," Hornsby began his career in 1915 with the St. Louis Cardinals. He led the National League in batting seven times and batted over .400 in three seasons. In the years 1921–1925 his batting averages were .397, .401, .384, .424 (a modern record), and .403; a record considered by some as the most extraordinary period of batting greatness in baseball history. Hornsby's lifetime batting average was .358, the highest in National League history and second only to the .367 of Ty Cobb. Hornsby was named most valuable player of the National League in 1925 and 1929. He managed the St. Louis Cardinals to their first world championship in 1926. In 1942 he was elected to the Baseball Hall of Fame.

Oakwood Cemetery

1601 Navasota St.
N 30 16.586, W 097 43.719

In 1839, as Austin gained favor as the location for the capital of the Republic of Texas, a cemetery was established in what is now the southwest part of the current Oakwood Cemetery. It was not until September 1856 that the cemetery became city property, when the Texas Legislature transferred the tract to the city of Austin. Although the cemetery had a succession of names, it was christened as Oakwood Cemetery in 1912.

Temple Beth Israel has provided care of the two Hebrew sections of Oakwood Cemetery since 1876. One is located in the southwest corner of Oakwood; the other (also enclosed) is located on the north side of the tract. Oakwood is acceptably maintained, and the oak, mature cedar, and pecan trees provide lovely shade in the hot Texas summers. The cemetery office is housed in a cut-limestone building located near the cemetery's center.

Oakwood is a large cemetery with interesting gravesites spread throughout. Information concerning gravesite locations can be obtained at the office between about 8:00 A.M. and 4:00 P.M. Monday through Friday. However, if you plan to get information concerning Oakwood Cemetery prior to visiting, you should call the Austin Parks and Recreation Department for contact information. Another great source of information on gravesite locations in Oakwood is contained on microfiche in the Genealogy Collection at the Lorenzo de Zavala State Archives and Library Building, 1201 Brazos Street.

Oakwood Cemetery exemplifies the history of Texas perhaps more than any other cemetery in the state, largely as a result of Austin's role in its exploration and governance. Oakwood also is a testament to the remarkable contribution that Texas' women have made to the state's history and heritage. Some of Texas' most prominent women are at peace in Oakwood, including Annie Webb Blanton, Ima Hogg, and Anna Pennybacker.

A random walk through Oakwood in 1995 and the chance discovery of the gravesite of one of Texas' most famous women provided inspiration for this volume. A small state historical marker located in the south central area of the cemetery indicates the grave of Susanna Dickinson (1814–1883). As I stood facing her gravestone, I wondered how many living Texans knew where this Alamo survivor had finally

GRAVESITE OF SUSANNA DICKINSON HANNIG, SURVIVOR OF THE ALAMO.
OAKWOOD CEMETERY, AUSTIN.

been laid to rest. She had witnessed and survived one of the defining moments in Texas history.

Following her husband, Almaron, to the Alamo mission, she and her baby daughter had survived the battle. It was Susanna Dickinson who would deliver the message of defeat to Gen. Sam Houston. She had been swept into history in the blink of an eye, only to settle into Austin and the quiet life of a cabinetmaker's wife. Although John Wayne immortalized her in a film version of the story of the Alamo, I suspect that the location of her gravesite remains a mystery to most— as it is with many of the old ones.

WILMER ALLISON

Wilmer Allison (1904–1977) began his successful career as a tennis player when he enrolled in the University of Texas in 1925. Allison won the Wimbledon doubles title in 1929 and 1930 (with partner John Van Ryn) and won the U.S. Open Championship in 1935. Allison was elected to the Texas Sports Hall of Fame in 1957.

LAURINE C. ANDERSON

Laurine (L. C.) Anderson (1853–1938) received his B.A. from Fisk University and came to Texas in 1879 to assist his brother, E. H. Anderson, at Prairie View Normal Institute (now Prairie View A&M University). L. C. Anderson was the first president of the Colored Teachers State Association. He served as president of the college from 1885 to 1889 and embarked on a personal crusade to improve educational conditions for African-American Texans. Anderson left Prairie View after seventeen years and moved to Austin to serve for thirty-two years as principal of the school for African Americans that later was named Anderson High School in his honor.

JOHN BARCLAY ARMSTRONG

John Barclay Armstrong (1850–1913) was known as "McNelly's Bulldog." He arrived in Texas in 1871, and in 1875 he enlisted in the Texas Ranger company led by Capt. Leander McNelly. That same year, he accompanied McNelly to the Rio Grande, quickly rising to the rank of sergeant. When McNelly retired from Ranger service, Armstrong was named second lieutenant of the Special Force of Texas Rangers under 1st Lt. Jesse L. Hall (1877).

John B. Armstrong's most daring act was the capture of gunman John Wesley Hardin. Hardin was wanted for the murder of a Brown County lawman and had fled Texas before he could be arrested. Armstrong tracked Hardin to Alabama and then to Florida, where he confronted the outlaw and four of his gang on a train in Pensacola. With lightning-fast reaction, Armstrong shot and killed one of Hardin's men, struck Hardin unconscious with his pistol, and took the remaining gang members into custody.

Armstrong returned Hardin to Texas, where Hardin stood trial and was sentenced to twenty-five years in prison. In 1882 Armstrong established the fifty-thousand-acre Armstrong Ranch in Willacy County. Armstrong is a member of the Texas Ranger Hall of Fame.

Eugene C. Barker

Eugene C. Barker (1874–1956) was born in Walker County, Texas. After his father's death in 1888, he moved to Palestine, where he worked as a blacksmith during the day and attended school at night. Barker enrolled in the University of Texas in September 1895 and really never left. He received a B.A. degree (1899) and an M.A. (1900) and then served the history department as tutor (1899–1901), instructor (1901–1908), adjunct professor (1908–1911), associate professor (1911–1913), professor (1913–1951), and professor emeritus (1951–1956). In 1910 Barker assumed the chair of the University of Texas history department, a position he held until 1925. When the title of distinguished professor was inaugurated in 1937, Barker was among the first three professors to be so honored.

Barker's contributions to the understanding and documentation of Texas history were immense. He wrote several volumes on Texas history and served as managing editor of the *Southwestern Historical Quarterly* and director of the Texas State Historical Association (1910–1937). He was a revered teacher and one of the recognized leaders of the faculty. In 1950 the University of Texas named the Barker Texas History Center in his honor, the first time that such an honor had been bestowed upon a living faculty member.

Annie Webb Blanton

A lifelong educator, Annie Webb Blanton (1870–1945) came to Austin in 1888 to teach elementary and secondary school. She attended the University of Texas, supporting herself by teaching, and graduated in 1899. From 1901 to 1908 Blanton taught English at North Texas State Normal College (now the University of North Texas) in Denton, where she became active in the Texas State Teachers Association. In 1916 she was elected as the first female president of the association.

In 1918 women obtained the right to vote in Texas primaries, and they immediately began to flex their democratic muscles. The suffragists backed Annie Blanton in a run for state superintendent of public instruction, and in the July 1918 primary, when Texas women exercised their voting rights for the first time, Blanton defeated the incumbent. Her victory in the November general election made her the first woman in Texas elected to statewide office. She served two terms as superintendent and then ran unsuccessfully for Congress. She earned her master's degree in 1923, taught in the UT education department until 1926, and then took a leave of absence to pursue a Ph.D. from Cornell University. After returning to the University of Texas in 1927, she remained a professor of education there until her death. Annie Blanton published several books during her career and founded the Delta Kappa Gamma Society (an honorary society for women teachers).

ALBERT SIDNEY BURLESON

Albert Sidney Burleson (1863–1937) represented Texas in the Fifty-sixth through the Sixty-third U.S. Congresses (1899–1913). Woodrow Wilson appointed him postmaster general in 1913, and he served in that capacity until 1921. During his tenure the post office developed the parcel post and airmail service. Burleson was chairman of the U.S. Telegraph and Telephone Administration in 1918 and chairman of the U.S. Commission to the International Wire Communication Conference in 1920.

OSCAR B. COLQUITT

Oscar Branch Colquitt (1861–1940) served as Texas state senator (1895–1899) and succeeded John H. Reagan as state railroad commissioner (1903–1911). He made an unsuccessful run for governor in 1906 but was elected to the office in 1910. After being reelected in 1912, he held the office until 1915.

ABNER COOK

Abner Cook (1814–1884) came to Texas in 1839, just as the republic was beginning construction of its new capital, Austin. In 1847 Cook built a residence for Thomas Ward (commissioner of the General Land Office), the first of many homes and commercial buildings he would design in Austin. Among his many works is the Texas Governor's Mansion.

JOHN C. DUVAL

John C. (Texas John) Duval (1816–1897) came to Texas in 1835, where he joined a company organized by his brother Capt. Burr H. Duval to fight in the Texas Revolution. Both John and Burr Duval were with James W. Fannin when he surrendered to Mexican forces. In the Goliad Massacre, Burr Duval was killed, but John escaped. He went on to serve with William A. A. (Bigfoot) Wallace as a member of John C. (Jack) Hays' company of Texas Rangers (1845) and later served in the Confederate army.

In his later years, Duval took up writing and has been called the first Texas "man of letters." His account of his escape from the Goliad Massacre is a Texas classic. Duval also wrote *The Adventures of Bigfoot Wallace, the Texas Ranger and Hunter* (1870), and at the time of his death, he was the last surviving member of Fannin's ill-fated force.

REBECCA JANE GILLELAND FISHER

Rebecca Jane Gilleland Fisher (1831–1926) settled with her family in Refugio County in 1837. In 1840, Comanche Indians attacked the Gilleland home, killed Rebecca's parents, and took her and her brother, William, as captives. Texas soldiers under the command of Albert Sidney Johnston later rescued the children.

Rebecca Gilleland attended Rutersville College from about 1845 to 1848 and married Orceneth Fisher, a Methodist minister. Rebecca Fisher became one of Texas' most important historian-preservationists. She was a charter member of the Daughters of the Republic of Texas and served as its state president for eighteen years. Her portrait was the first of a woman to be hung in the Senate Chamber at the Texas Capitol.

GEORGE WASHINGTON GLASSCOCK

George Washington Glasscock (1810–1868) was born in Hardin County, Kentucky. In 1830 he went to St. Louis, Missouri, and for a period in 1832 partnered with Abraham Lincoln in a flatboating business. In 1835 he moved to Texas and participated in the Siege of Bexar. He represented Travis and Williamson counties in the Tenth and Eleventh state legislatures. Glasscock County was named in his honor.

THOMAS GREEN

Thomas Green (1814–1864) left the study of law to come to Texas and fight in the Texas Revolution. He served in Isaac N. Moreland's company, which operated the Twin Sisters cannons in the Battle of San Jacinto. Green settled in Texas and began a long career in public and military service. He fought in the U.S.-Mexican War in 1846, and after secession in 1861, he was elected colonel in the Fifth Texas Volunteer Cavalry, part of Gen. H. H. Sibley's brigade. In the spring of 1863 Green commanded the First Cavalry Brigade in Louisiana and was promoted to the rank of brigadier general.

In April 1864 he led a division in successful attacks on federal forces at the Battle of Mansfield and then at the Battle of Pleasant Hill. A few days later, on April 12, 1864, he was killed while leading an attack on federal gunboats patrolling the Red River at Blair's Landing. Tom Green County was named in his honor.

ANDREW JACKSON HAMILTON

Andrew Jackson Hamilton (1815–1875) was educated and admitted to the practice of law in Alabama. In 1846 he came to Texas with his brother Morgan. After practicing law in La Grange and Austin, he was appointed acting attorney general in 1849. Hamilton actively opposed secession, was elected to the U.S. Congress in 1859, and participated on the House committee formed in 1860–1861 to search for a solution to the growing North–South crisis. He returned to Texas in 1861 but left for Mexico in the face of rumored assassination plots. President Abraham Lincoln appointed him military governor of Texas in 1862, and he served as provisional governor for approximately one year (1865–1866). He ran for governor on the Republican ticket in 1869 but lost to Edmund J. Davis.

JAMES M. HILL

James Hill (1818–1904) came to Texas with his father, Texas patriot Asa Hill, in 1835. After the fall of the Alamo, Hill and his father joined Sam Houston's army. At San Jacinto, James M. Hill served in Company H of Col. Edward Burleson's First Regiment, Texas Volunteers. James Hill was one of the those few who witnessed the first postbattle meeting between Houston and Gen. Santa Anna. Hill also appears in William Henry Huddle's painting *The Surrender of Santa Anna*, now hanging in the Texas Capitol.

Hill joined his two brothers and father in the Somervell Expedition, continuing on to Mexico with the men of Mier Expedition. All of the family members were captured. His personal reminiscences of the Battle of San Jacinto have become an important part of the historical documentation of the conflict.

IMA HOGG

Ima Hogg (1882–1975) was the daughter of Governor James Stephen Hogg and was born in Mineola, Texas. As a young woman, she studied music, and although she became an accomplished pianist, Ima Hogg's contributions to Texas came through her generosity and philanthropy.

Her family fortune had gushed from the earth in the form of oil discovered on the Hogg property in Brazoria County. By the 1920s she had begun what would be lifelong devotion to public giving. She founded the Houston Child Guidance Center (1929) and the Hogg Foundation for Mental Hygiene (which later became the Hogg Foundation for Mental Health) at the University of Texas. She was elected to the Houston School Board (1943) and the presidency of the Houston Symphony Society (1946) and in 1948 became the first female president of the Philosophical Society of Texas.

In the 1950s Ima Hogg restored the Hogg family home at Varner Plantation near West Columbia, and in 1958 she donated her home to the state of Texas as Varner-Hogg Plantation State Historical Park. She served in a multitude of organizations throughout the rest of her life. In 1969, along with Oveta Culp Hobby and Lady Bird Johnson, she was honored as one of the first three women to be members of the Academy of Texas, which honors persons who "enrich, enlarge, or enlighten" knowledge in any field.

JAMES STEPHEN HOGG

James S. Hogg (1851–1906) was the first governor of Texas born on Texas soil. After studying law, he was elected county attorney of Wood County in 1878 and served as district attorney for the Seventh District (1880–1884). In 1886 he was elected attorney general and became a nineteenth-century consumer advocate. He succeeded in a series of initiatives that returned land holdings to the state, set aside money for schools and institutions, and broke up the Texas Traffic Association (a freighting cartel operating in violation of state law).

Hogg recognized the need for a new means of regulating the powerful railroad interests and was a leading proponent of the establishment of the Texas Railroad Commission. Running on that platform, he was elected governor in 1891. His tenure in office was marked by his attempts to level the business playing field and to provide secure funding for higher education. After his public service, Hogg returned to private life, where he continued a lucrative law practice and championed progressive reforms. Jim Hogg County was named in his honor.

THE HOLLAND FAMILY

Bird Holland (?–1864) came to Texas around 1837 and by 1840 had settled in Travis County. During the U.S.-Mexican War, he was elected captain of a company of volunteers but became seriously ill in Matamoros and resigned his command. After the war, he served as chief clerk and assistant secretary in the State Department. He was appointed secretary of state on March 16, 1861.

In all likelihood, Bird Holland was the father of three sons— James, Milton, and William—born as a result of his relationship with a slave named Matilda. William H. Holland (1841–1907) was born into slavery in Marshall in 1841, and his brother Milton (1844–1910, also born into slavery) was born either in Carthage or Austin. At some point in the 1850s Bird Holland apparently purchased the three brothers' freedom and sent them to Ohio. There both William and Milton attended the Albany Enterprise Academy, a school owned and operated by African Americans.

As the Civil War erupted, Bird Holland volunteered for duty in the Confederate army and served as adjutant of Col. Richard B. Hubbard's Twenty-second Texas Infantry. Two of his sons volunteered for service in the Union army. Milton joined the Fifth United States Colored Troops in Athens, Ohio, in 1863 and fought in the Petersburg campaign in Virginia during 1864 and at Fort Fisher, North Carolina, in January 1865. He rose to the rank of regimental sergeant major. William enlisted in the Union army's Sixteenth United States Colored Troops.

On April 8, 1864, Bird Holland was killed while leading his Confederate regiment at the Battle of Mansfield, Louisiana. Five months later, his son Milton would charge into the history of the Union army. During the night of September 28–29, Maj. Gen. Benjamin Butler's Army of the James crossed the James River to assault the Richmond defenses north of the river. The columns attacked at dawn. After initial Union successes at New Market Heights and Fort Harrison, the Confederates rallied and stalled the federal onslaught. When all of the white commanding officers either died or became disabled during

AFRICAN AMERICAN LEADER WILLIAM HOLLAND LIES AT REST IN OAKWOOD CEMETERY, AUSTIN. HIS FATHER, BIRD HOLLAND, IS BURIED NEARBY.

engagements at Chaffin's Farm and New Market Heights, Virginia (September 28 and 30, 1864), Milton Holland assumed command and led the troops in battle. Holland's troops suffered heavy casualties but won the battle. Although wounded, he led a charge on Fort Harrison later the same day. Milton Holland was cited for his bravery and valor on the battlefields of Virginia and was the first African American born in Texas to win the Congressional Medal of Honor (it is likely that Milton Holland was the first person born on Texas soil to win the Congressional Medal of Honor). After the Civil War, Milton led a prosperous life in Washington, D.C.

Milton's brother William entered Oberlin College in Ohio in 1867 and returned to Texas after two years to teach school in Austin. He later moved to Waller County and in 1876 won election to the Fifteenth Legislature in 1876 as a representative from that county. In the legislature he sponsored the bill providing for Prairie View Normal College (now Prairie View A&M University). William Holland was instrumental in establishing the Deaf, Dumb, and Blind Institute for Colored Youth in 1887, and Governor Lawrence S. Ross appointed him to serve as the institute's first superintendent.

The legacy of the Holland family is one of kindness and service to country and to fellowman. Had Bird Holland not purchased the freedom of his sons, it is unlikely that Milton and William would have enjoyed the opportunities they had as they grew into manhood. The clear irony of the death of Bird Holland in defense of the Confederacy—with its attendant stance on slavery—and the triumph of Milton Holland as he fought to maintain the Union and to deliver all Americans from slavery is one of the most compelling in Texas history. William went on to serve Texas in a series of important roles, and every graduating class at Prairie View A&M speaks to his dedication to the education of African American Texans. Bird Holland was laid to rest next to his wife, Matilda Rust, in Oakwood Cemetery in 1865, and his son William was buried there (next to his mother—also named Matilda) in another section of Oakwood. Milton Holland was honored by burial at Arlington National Cemetery, Virginia.

JOHN B. JONES

Major John B. Jones (1834–1881) was commander of the famous Frontier Battalion of the Texas Rangers. Established by the Fourteenth Legislature, the Frontier Battalion was ordered to end the long history of Indian raids on the frontier and to provide a much needed law enforcement presence in the state. Perhaps Jones' most famous law enforcement episode involved a gunfight in Round Rock that resulted in the death of train robber Sam Bass on July 19, 1878.

GEORGE WASHINGTON LITTLEFIELD

George Washington Littlefield (1842–1920) came to Texas in 1850 and grew up on the family plantation in Gonzales County. Littlefield enlisted in the Confederate army and served with Company I, Eighth Texas Cavalry (Terry's Texas Rangers), which fought in the Army of Tennessee. After the war, he returned to Texas and began a series of business ventures, including his entry into the cattle business. By 1881 Littlefield had become a wealthy man.

When George Littlefield moved to Austin in 1883, he was one of the largest landowners in Texas and, upon moving to the capital, he expanded his activities into the banking business. In 1911 Governor Oscar B. Colquitt appointed Littlefield to the Board of Regents of the University of Texas. Over the next decade Littlefield donated generously to the university, providing more money than any other single donor in the first fifty years of the institution.

JANE MCCALLUM

Jane McCallum (1877–1957) was born in La Vernia, Texas, and in 1896 married Arthur Newell McCallum, Sr. She settled with her husband in Austin, where he was school superintendent from 1903 to 1942. Jane McCallum jumped into politics as a supporter of prohibition and as a suffragist. In 1915 she was elected president of the Austin Women's Suffrage Association and soon was a recognized leader in the statewide campaign to secure the vote for Texas' women.

In 1926 she actively campaigned for Daniel J. Moody's run for the office of governor, and after his election she was appointed secretary of state, a position she held until 1933. After leaving office, she remained active in Austin civic affairs.

ELISHA MARSHALL PEASE

Elisha Marshall Pease (1812–1883) arrived in Texas in 1835 and immediately became involved in the smoldering Texas Revolution. At Washington-on-the-Brazos in March 1836 he authored part of the Constitution of the Republic of Texas. Pease served in a variety of positions in the republic and was the state's first comptroller of public accounts.

After annexation, Pease represented Brazoria County in the first three legislatures and was elected governor in (1853–1857). While in office, Pease's administration established the permanent school fund and supervised the building campaign that led to the completion of the Governor's Mansion, the General Land Office building, and a new Capitol.

ORAN MILO ROBERTS

Oran M. Roberts (1815–1898) came to Texas in 1841, where he settled in San Augustine and began a successful law practice. He served as district attorney (1844–1846) and was appointed district judge. After service in the Confederacy, he was appointed chief justice of the Texas Supreme Court in 1864 and served until he was removed along with other state incumbents in 1865. In 1874 he once again began service on the Texas Supreme Court and was chief justice for four years. In 1878 he was elected governor and served two terms. Upon his retirement Roberts was immediately appointed professor of law at the University of Texas, a position he held for the next ten years. Roberts County is named in his honor.

JOHN H. ROGERS

John H. Rogers (1863–1930) joined the Texas Rangers in 1882, rising to the rank of captain in 1892. During his service he was twice wounded, and as a result of one of the wounds his arm was shortened, after which he carried a specially constructed Winchester rifle. In 1913 President Woodrow Wilson appointed Rogers as U.S. marshal for the Western District of Texas, and he served in that position for eight years. Rogers later served during the tenure of Governor Dan Moody as a Ranger captain (1927–1930). John Rogers is a member of the Texas Ranger Hall of Fame.

JAMES GIBSON SWISHER

James Gibson Swisher (1794–1862) served in the War of 1812 and participated in the Battle of New Orleans. In 1833 he arrived in Texas and settled in Washington County. Swisher was elected captain of a military company organized in Washington Municipality at the beginning of the Texas Revolution. He participated in the Siege of Bexar in December 1835 and was one of the three commissioners to negotiate the surrender of the city on December 11, 1835. Swisher remained with the army until he was elected one of four delegates from Washington Municipality to the Convention of 1836. James Swisher signed the Texas Declaration of Independence and the Constitution of the Republic of Texas.

BEN THOMPSON WAS BURIED IN OAKWOOD CEMETERY, AUSTIN, AFTER DYING IN A SAN ANTONIO GUNFIGHT.

BEN THOMPSON

Ben Thompson (1842–1884) was born in England and brought to Austin as a child. He became one of Texas' most notorious gunmen. Thompson served for a period as city marshal of Austin, but his gunplay and love for drink and gambling led to his eventual demise. He was killed along with flamboyant outlaw-turned-lawman John King Fisher in a San Antonio vaudeville theater on March 11, 1884.

ELIZABETH ELLEN JOHNSON WILLIAMS

Lizzie E. Johnson Williams (1840–1924) came to Texas around 1844. She earned a degree in 1859 from the Chappell Hill Female College in

Washington County and began a career as a schoolteacher. In 1873 she began teaching from her home and keeping books for prominent cattlemen of the area. An astute businesswoman, she quickly realized the profits to be made in the cattle business. She achieved legendary status as an early Texas "cattle queen" and is thought to be the first woman in Texas to ride the Chisholm Trail with a herd of cattle that she had acquired under her own brand.

Texas State Cemetery
909 Navasota St.
N 30 16.016, W 097 43.604

The Texas State Cemetery is located approximately one mile east of the State Capitol between Navasota and Comal streets. General Edward Burleson was the first person buried at the Texas State Cemetery. After his death in 1851, a committee of the Texas House of Representatives convened to plan a funeral, and Andrew Jackson Hamilton provided a parcel of his personal property in east Austin as a state burial ground. The state of Texas assumed ownership of the site in 1854, and from 1856 to 1866, burials of Texas leaders, Civil War generals, and those who had fought for Texas Independence were common.

As the 1800s drew to a close, the state of Texas assumed management of the Confederate Men's and Women's Home. As the survivors of the Civil War began to pass slowly into history, many of them were buried at the state cemetery. The early part of the twentieth century saw a substantial change in the cemetery. Civil War hero Albert Sidney Johnson was memorialized with a beautiful monument upon which Elizabet Ney carved his likeness. Several of Texas' most famous and prominent citizens were reinterred at the cemetery, including Stephen F. Austin, Joanna Troutman, and Gen. John Wharton. Between 1929 and 1936 more than seventy Texas notables were brought to the Texas State Cemetery. Many of Texas' earliest patriots are buried there. Several of those who signed the Texas Declaration of Independence are buried in the state cemetery, including John W. Bunton (1807–1879), William C. Crawford (1804–1895), Richard Ellis (1781–1846), Thomas Jefferson Gazley (1798–1853), Jesse Grimes (1788–1866), Bailey Hardeman (1795–1836), William Menefee (1796–1875), Martin Parmer (1778–1850), Robert Potter (1799–1842), William B. Scates (1802–1882), and Edwin Waller (1800–1881).

In 1994 Lieutenant Governor Bob Bullock organized a full-scale

THE GRAVESITE OF THE "FATHER OF TEXAS," STEVEN F. AUSTIN, IS MARKED BY A
STATUE CREATED BY SCULPTOR POMPEO COPPINI. TEXAS STATE CEMETERY,
AUSTIN.

renovation of the cemetery, and the results are impressive. It has a lovely visitor's center, a gallery, a pond, a columbarium wall, and a memorial plaza. All Confederate headstones were taken down and cleaned and were replaced if damaged. Trees, shrubbery, flowers, and grass were planted for the beautification phase of the project. In March 1997, Governor George W. Bush and Lieutenant Governor Bullock rededicated the site.

The gallery and visitors center are open Monday–Friday, 8:00 A.M.–5 P.M., and the cemetery grounds are open seven days a week, 8:00 A.M.–5 P.M. Guided tours may be booked by calling the administration office at 512-463-0605.

STEPHEN FULLER AUSTIN

Stephen Fuller Austin (1793–1836) is generally considered the "Father of Anglo-American Texas." Austin was successful in bringing the first colonists (the Old Three Hundred) to Texas in 1825, and he obtained contracts for six hundred more colonists (1827–1828). Austin was the dominant figure in the colonization and early administration of Texas. A statue of Austin, created by Pompeo Coppini, marks his gravesite, and both the city of Austin and Austin County were named in his honor.

ROY BEDICHEK

Roy Bedichek (1878–1959) was a beloved Texas writer and folklorist. Bedichek was close friends with both J. Frank Dobie and Walter Prescott Webb, and at their urging he began to write a series of books, including his classic *Adventures with a Texas Naturalist* (1947). *Karánkaway Country* (1950) won the Carr P. Collins Award for the best Texas book of the year, as did *Educational Competition: The Story of the University Interscholastic League of Texas* (1956).

PETER HANSBOROUGH BELL

Peter H. Bell (1812–1898) came to Texas to fight in the Texas Revolution and was a participant in the Battle of San Jacinto. He joined the Texas Rangers under John C. (Jack) Hays in 1840, participated in the Somervell Expedition (1842), and fought with distinction under Gen. Zachary Taylor in the U.S.-Mexican War. Bell was twice elected governor of Texas (1849, 1851) and served in the U.S. Congress (1853–1857). Bell County was named in his honor.

Bob Bullock

Bob Bullock (1929–1999) grew up in Hillsboro and was first elected to public office as a state representative in 1956. That set in motion a dedication to public service that lasted until he stepped down as lieutenant governor in 1999. His career marked him as one of the finest and most innovative public servants in the history of the state of Texas. He was appointed Texas secretary of state and was an advocate for voting rights for eighteen-year-old Texans. Bullock was elected state comptroller after leaving the secretary of state's office and was Texas' chief financial officer and tax collector for sixteen years. While in office as lieutenant governor, he was instrumental in the renovation of the Texas State Cemetery. Bullock's service to Texas is summed up in his trademark saying, "God bless Texas."

John Wheeler Bunton

John W. Bunton (1807–1879) represented Mina at the Convention of 1836 at Washington-on-the-Brazos, signed the Texas Declaration of Independence, and helped in drafting the constitution of the new republic. Bunton participated in the Siege of Bexar on December 5–10, 1835, and at the Battle of San Jacinto he served on the staff of Gen. Sam Houston. After the Texas Revolution, he represented Bastrop County in the House of Representatives in the First Congress of the Republic of Texas. He later resided in Austin County and was elected to the House of Representatives in the Third Congress, where he is credited for the bill that established the Texas Rangers, the bill providing postal service, and the bill outlining the judiciary system.

Edward Burleson

Edward Burleson (1798–1851) had a long and distinguished military service to Texas that began soon after he arrived in 1830. In October 1835 (in Gonzales) he was elected lieutenant colonel of the infantry in Gen. Stephen F. Austin's army and on November 24, 1835, Burleson became general of the volunteer army and replaced Austin. He participated in the Siege of Bexar, and on December 6 he entered Bexar with Benjamin R. Milam. His volunteer army disbanded on December 20, 1835, and Burleson left San Antonio prior to the battle that would take the lives of the Alamo garrison. At the Battle of San Jacinto he commanded the First Regiment. After the Texas Revolution, Burleson served as colonel of the Frontier Rangers and participated in several engagements with native Indians, defeating the Cherokees under

Chief Bowl (1839) and the Comanches at the Battle of Plum Creek (1840). Burleson died in 1851, and his burial was the first in what would eventually become the Texas State Cemetery. He is the namesake of Burleson County.

JOHN BOWDEN CONNALLY, JR.

John Connally, Jr. (1917–1993), was born near Floresville, Texas, and educated at the University of Texas and the UT Law School (1941). He began his career in politics at the foot of Congressman Lyndon B. Johnson. Connally was commissioned in the U.S. Naval Reserve in 1941 and served with distinction in the Pacific theater of war.

After returning home, he managed five of LBJ's major political campaigns, including Johnson's reelection to the U.S. House of Representatives in 1946, the 1941 and 1948 races for the U.S. Senate, and the election to the presidency in 1964. In 1962 Connally won a runoff by twenty-six thousand votes and was elected governor of Texas. The next year, he survived serious gunshot wounds from an assassin's bullets while riding in the front seat of the automobile carrying John F. Kennedy. Connally was reelected governor in both 1964 and 1966. In 1971 he became Nixon's secretary of the treasury.

WILLIAM GORDON COOKE

William Gordon Cooke (1808–1847) volunteered for service in the New Orleans Greys and arrived with the second company at Velasco, Texas, on October 25, 1835, to fight in the Texas Revolution. Cooke participated in the storming of Bexar, led the party that finally forced the Mexican capitulation, and received the flag of surrender. At the Battle of San Jacinto he served on Gen. Sam Houston's staff and was in charge of the guard on the prisoners when Gen. Antonio López de Santa Anna was captured. Cooke is credited with saving Santa Anna's life by preventing the general's execution so that he could be brought before General Houston.

After the Texas Revolution, Cooke explored and mapped much of north central Texas. He established Fort Johnson and Fort Preston on the Red River and Cedar Springs Post on the Trinity River, the first permanent structures at the future site of Dallas. Cooke County was named in his honor.

EDMUND J. DAVIS

Edmund J. Davis (1827–1883) came to Texas in 1848 and studied law. He was admitted to the bar in 1849, and in 1853 he became district attorney of the Twelfth Judicial District at Brownsville. In 1856 Governor Elisha M. Pease named him judge of the same district, a position he held until 1861.

As the Civil War approached, Davis joined Sam Houston in opposition to secession and was forced to flee Texas in 1862. After a meeting with President Lincoln, Davis received a colonel's commission and authorization to recruit the cavalry regiment that became the First Texas Cavalry (U.S.). Davis and the First Texas were engaged throughout much of the remainder of the war, and in 1864 Davis was promoted to brigadier general. For the rest of the war he commanded Gen. Joseph J. Reynolds' cavalry in the Division of Western Mississippi. In the election of 1869 Davis defeated Andrew J. Hamilton in the governor's race. The Davis administration was rocky as it struggled with Reconstruction politics in Texas. Davis ran for reelection in December 1873 and was defeated by Richard Coke.

JAMES FRANK DOBIE

J. Frank Dobie (1888–1964) was one of Texas' most prolific and loved folklorists. His first book, *Vaquero of the Brush Country* (1929), established his place in southwestern literary culture. Two years later Dobie published *Coronado's Children* (1931), which won the Literary Guild Award and vaulted him into national prominence. Over the course of his career Dobie wrote many of Texas' most beloved volumes and inspired generations of future Texas authors.

JAMES EDWARD AND MIRIAM AMANDA WALLACE FERGUSON

James Edward (Pa) Ferguson (1871–1944) was elected Texas governor in 1914. During his first term, the Texas Legislature passed important education bills and a substantial increase in the holdings of the state prison system. Ferguson's reelection in 1916 was largely without incident, but during his second term he engaged the University of Texas in a bitter dispute. The controversy arose when Ferguson objected to certain faculty members and requested that they be fired. The Board of Regents refused, and the governor responded by vetoing the university budget. But this was only the first of Ferguson's troubles.

Accused of questionable ethics in office, Ferguson was indicted by the Travis County grand jury in July 1917. The Speaker of the Texas House called a special session to consider impeachment of Ferguson, and the Senate convicted Ferguson on five articles. The Court of Impeachment ordered his removal from office, and he eventually resigned. Ferguson sought the Democratic nomination again in 1918 but was defeated by William Hobby. But Ferguson was not through with Texas politics, not by a long shot.

Miriam Amanda (Ma) Ferguson (1875–1961) was born in Salado and married Jim Ferguson in 1899. After his resignation from office, Jim Ferguson could not legally have his name on the ballot in 1924. So he encouraged his wife to run for governor, and she entered the race. Miriam Ferguson quickly assured Texans that, if elected, she would follow the advice of her husband and that Texas thus would gain "two governors for the price of one." In November 1924 she handily defeated the Republican nominee and became the first woman to be governor of Texas. Her administration, like her husband's, had a rocky two years, with her deposed spouse largely controlling it. In the face of continued complaints of political impropriety, she was defeated for a second term as governor in both the 1926 and 1930 elections, but she defeated the Republican nominee in the 1932 election.

FREDERICK BENJAMIN GIPSON

Frederick (Fred) Benjamin Gipson (1908–1973) was born near Mason, Texas, and entered the University of Texas in 1933. As a student he wrote for the *Daily Texan* and the *Ranger* but left school prior to graduation to take a job as a reporter in Corpus Christi. He later wrote for the *San Angelo Standard-Times*, then for the *Denver Post*. He soon began selling short stories and in 1946 published his first book, *The Fabulous Empire: Colonel Zack Miller's Story*. His next book, *Hound-Dog Man* (1949), established Gipson's reputation when it became a Book-of-the-Month Club selection and sold more than 250,000 copies in its first year of publication. In 1956 he published the classic Texas novel *Old Yeller*, which sold nearly three million copies by 1973. The novel was produced as a movie, and there is nary a Texas child who did not cry when Old Yeller died.

BAILEY HARDEMAN

Bailey Hardeman (1795–1836) led a colorful and adventuresome life as a soldier, a mountain man, and a founder of the Republic of Texas. Born in Tennessee, Hardeman fought in the War of 1812 in Louisiana. In 1821 he began a life of fur trapping and avoiding Indians. Hardeman was in the Meredith Miles Marmaduke Expedition to New Mexico in 1824–1825 and trapped beaver along the Colorado River.

In the fall of 1835 Hardeman and about twenty-four of his family members moved to Texas, where he immediately took up the cause of Texas independence. He was elected a representative from Matagorda to the convention at work on the Texas Declaration of Independence. He served on the five-member committee that drafted the declaration and helped write the constitution for the Republic of Texas. He served as both secretary of the treasury and secretary of state in the budding Republic. Hardeman County was named for Bailey and Thomas Jones Hardeman.

THOMAS JONES HARDEMAN

Thomas J. Hardeman (1788–1854) came to Texas with his brother Bailey and other family members in 1835. Hardeman served in the Congress of the Republic of Texas from Matagorda County in 1837–1839 and spent two terms in the state legislature from Bastrop and Travis counties (1847–1851). Thomas Hardeman is credited with suggesting the name of "Austin" for the Texas capital city. Hardeman County was named in honor of Thomas and Bailey Hardeman.

JAMES PINCKNEY HENDERSON

James Pinckney Henderson (1808–1858) was the first governor of Texas (1846). At the outbreak of the U.S.-Mexican War, he took command of the Texas Volunteers and led the Second Texas Regiment at the Battle of Monterrey. After the war he resumed his duties as governor but did not seek a second term. In 1857 he was elected to the U.S. Senate but died shortly thereafter. Henderson County was named in his honor.

JOHN REYNOLDS HUGHES

John Reynolds Hughes (1855–1947) was one of Texas' most famous Rangers. Hughes' daring began at an early age when he left home to trail cattle and then to live among the Choctaw and Osage Indians. After six years among the Indians and a brief stint trailing cattle on the Chisholm Trail, he moved to Travis County and began a horse ranch. In May 1886 he pursued a group of horse thieves, killed or captured all the outlaws, and returned the horses to their rightful owners. His exploits and daring resulted in his recruitment into the Texas Rangers in 1887. When he retired in January 1915, Hughes had served as a Ranger longer than any other man. John Hughes is a member of the Texas Ranger Hall of Fame.

JOHN IRELAND

John Ireland (1827–1896) came to Texas in 1853 and settled in Seguin. He served as mayor of Seguin and was a delegate to the Secession Convention. He served the Confederate army, rising to the rank of lieutenant colonel. After the war, he was elected to the Texas House or Representatives in the Thirteenth Legislature and to the Texas Senate in the Fourteenth. He was elected governor in 1882 and again in 1884.

ALBERT SIDNEY JOHNSTON

Albert Sidney Johnston (1803–1862) was educated at the U.S. Military Academy (1826) and came to Texas in 1836 after service in the Black Hawk War and the death of his wife. He enlisted in the Texas Army and was appointed adjutant general by Thomas J. Rusk. In January 1837 he replaced Felix Huston as senior brigadier general in command of the army. Huston apparently did not take the demotion well and challenged Johnston to a duel in which Johnston was seriously wounded, leaving him unable to assume command. After the Texas Revolution, Johnston served as secretary of war for the Republic of Texas.

Although Johnston served in the U.S.-Mexican War and returned to service in the U.S. Army, he is best remembered for his service to the Confederacy. As the Civil War erupted, Johnston resigned his commission in the federal army and was appointed as a general in the Confederate army with command of the Western Department. On April 6, 1862, he was killed while leading his forces at the Battle of Shiloh. Johnston was temporarily buried at New Orleans, but in 1867 his remains were brought back to Texas for burial in the Texas State Cemetery. Thirty-five years after his return to his adopted state, the acclaimed artist Elisabet Ney was commissioned to construct a monument for the legendary soldier. Ney's white-marble carving graces Johnston's gravesite and represents one of the most beautiful works of art to be found in Texas.

BARBARA CHARLINE JORDAN

Barbara Jordan (1936–1996) grew up in Houston and earned her undergraduate degree from Texas Southern University (1956) and a law degree from Boston University (1959). She became involved in politics by registering African American voters for the 1960 presidential campaign. After two unsuccessful campaigns for a seat in the Texas Senate, she was elected in 1967, making her the first African American woman elected to the Texas Senate. In 1972 she was unanimously elected president pro tempore of the Senate.

In 1973 Jordan successfully ran for the United States House of

Representatives from the Eighteenth Texas District. She gained national prominence during the 1974 Watergate hearings as a member of the House Judiciary Committee. The Democratic Party chose her to deliver the keynote address at the 1976 Democratic National Convention; she was the first woman to do so. In 1979, after three terms in Congress, Jordan retired from politics to teach public policy at the Lyndon Baines Johnson School of Public Affairs, University of Texas at Austin. Her class in political values and ethics was so highly sought by students that entry was gained by lottery. Those of us fortunate enough to have won a seat in her class were forever changed.

GIDEON LINCECUM

Gideon Lincecum (1793–1874) was a distinguished naturalist who contributed collections to the Philadelphia Academy of Science and the Smithsonian Institution. Lincecum's writings appeared in such national publications as *American Naturalist, American Sportsman,* and *Proceedings of the Academy of Natural Sciences,* and his views on a variety of subjects, including politics, appeared in the *Texas Almanac* and in newspapers. Charles Darwin sponsored the publication of Lincecum's paper on the agricultural ant in the *Journal of the Linnaean Society of London* in 1862.

JAMES MARION LOGAN

As a rifleman of an infantry company, James M. Logan (1920–1999) landed with the first wave of the assault troops on the beaches of the Gulf of Salerno, Italy, on July 5, 1944. For his conspicuous gallantry in removing enemy machine gun emplacements and his bravery in eliminating a sniper position, James Logan was awarded the Congressional Medal of Honor.

FRANCIS RICHARD LUBBOCK

Francis R. Lubbock (1815–1905) became active in Democratic politics in his home state of South Carolina. After a term as lieutenant governor (1857), Lubbock won the governorship of Texas in 1861 by only 124 votes. As governor he supported the Confederacy and worked to improve the military capabilities of Texas. When his term of office ended, Lubbock entered the service of the Confederacy as a lieutenant colonel and served as assistant adjutant general on the staff of Maj. Gen. John Bankhead Magruder. In August 1864, Lubbock was appointed aide-de-camp to Jefferson Davis. At the end of the war Lubbock fled Richmond with Davis but was captured in Georgia and imprisoned in solitary confinement at Fort Delaware for eight months. After his release, he returned to Texas and served as Texas state treasurer (1878–1891).

BENJAMIN McCULLOCH

Ben McCulloch (1811–1862) followed his friend and neighbor David Crockett to fight at the Alamo. A bout with the measles likely saved McCulloch's life, because it prevented him from reaching San Antonio before the Alamo fell to Mexican forces. McCulloch joined Houston's army as it retreated, and at the Battle of San Jacinto he commanded one of the Twin Sisters cannons.

McCulloch left the Texas Army, joined the Texas Rangers, and fought in the Battle of Plum Creek (1840). At the outbreak of the U.S.-Mexican War, he commanded a company of Texas Rangers as Zachary Taylor's chief of scouts. McCulloch fought with distinction at the Battle of Monterrey and at the Battle of Buena Vista, and his reconnaissance acumen saved Taylor's army from disaster. Thereafter he was promoted to the rank of major.

With the beginning of the Civil War, McCulloch was commissioned as a colonel and was the officer who demanded the surrender of all federal posts in the Military District of Texas. On May 11, 1861, Jefferson Davis appointed McCulloch a brigadier general, the second-ranking brigadier general in the Confederate army. On August 10, 1861, McCulloch won a victory over Union forces at Wilson's Creek, but on March 7, 1862, at the Battle of Pea Ridge, McCulloch was shot and killed as he scouted enemy positions.

DANIEL JAMES MOODY, JR.

Dan Moody (1893–1966) spent most of his life in public service, first as a military officer in World War I and then as county attorney of Williamson County (1920–1922). He served as district attorney of the Twenty-sixth Judicial District (1922–1925), attorney general of Texas (1925–1927), and as governor of Texas for two terms (1927–1931).

ROBERT RANKIN

Robert Rankin (1753–1837) is one of a handful of people buried in Texas who fought in the American Revolution. As a member of the Third Regiment of the Virginia line, he participated in the battles of Germantown, Brandywine, and Stony Point, as well as the Siege of Charleston, where he was captured. He remained a prisoner of war until exchanged, at which time he received a promotion to lieutenant. In 1832 Rankin moved to Texas as a member of Joseph Vehlein's colony.

STERLING CLACK ROBERTSON

Sterling Clack Robertson (1785–1842) established Robertson's colony in 1834 and 1835. As Texas moved toward independence from Mexico, Robertson represented the municipality of Milam at the Convention of 1836 at Washington-on-the-Brazos, where he signed the Texas Declaration of Independence and the Constitution of the Republic of Texas. He later served as senator from the district of Milam in the First and Second Congresses of the Republic of Texas (1836–1838). Robertson County was named in his honor.

HARDIN RICHARD RUNNELS

Hardin R. Runnels (1820–1873) came to Texas in 1842 and settled in Bowie County. From 1847 to 1855 he served as state representative in the Second through Fifth Legislatures. He was Speaker of the House during his final term. In 1855 he was elected lieutenant governor. In the spring of 1857 Runnels was nominated as the Democratic candidate for governor and ran against the venerable Sam Houston. Runnels won by a vote of 38,552 to 23,628 and thus became the only person ever to defeat Sam Houston in an election. However, when the two met again in the subsequent election, Houston defeated Runnels. Clearly, lightning was not going to strike Sam Houston twice.

EDWARD MUEGGE SCHIWETZ

E. M. (Buck) Schiwetz (1898–1984) was born in Cuero, and he apparently received from his artist-mother an artist's gift. His father, a banker, opposed Schiwetz's dream of pursuing art, and Buck graduated from Texas A&M in 1921 with an architecture degree. Still, Buck Schiwetz never gave up on his dream of being an artist, and by 1928 he had found a consistent market for his artwork. His popularity as an artist continued to flourish, and he was selected as the Texas State Artist for 1977–1978.

WILLIAM READ SCURRY

William R. Scurry (1821–1864) came to Texas in 1839 and was licensed to practice law soon after his arrival. Scurry represented Red River County in the Ninth Congress of the Republic of Texas (1844–

SCULPTOR CHARLES UMLAUF
CREATED THE BEAUTIFUL
STATUE THAT MARKS THE GRAVE
OF GOVERNOR ALLAN SHIVERS
IN THE TEXAS STATE CEMETERY,
AUSTIN.

1845) and served during the U.S.–Mexican War in Col. George T. Wood's Second Regiment, Texas Mounted Volunteers. After the war, he returned to his law practice and began newspaper publishing.

Scurry entered Confederate service in July 1861 as the lieutenant colonel of the Fourth Texas Cavalry. He was promoted to brigadier general in 1862 and was given command of the Third Brigade of Walker's Texas Division in October 1863. Scurry commanded the Third Brigade at the Battles of Mansfield and Pleasant Hill in April 1864. He was seriously wounded in the Battle of Jenkins Ferry, on April 30, 1864, but refused evacuation to the rear. When federal attack overran the place where he lay, his wound was unattended for over two hours. When his brigade regained the field he asked, "Have we whipped them?" On being told that the battle was won, Scurry replied, "Now take me to a house where I can be made comfortable and die easy." Scurry County is named in his honor.

ROBERT ALLAN SHIVERS

Allan Shivers (1907–1985) was born in Lufkin, Texas, and grew up in Port Arthur. He entered the University of Texas in 1924 but dropped out of school to work. In 1928 he returned to UT and was elected president of the Students' Association. He began the practice of law and in 1934 was elected as a Democrat to the Texas Senate, where, at age twenty-seven, he was the youngest member ever to sit in that body. In 1943 Shivers entered the U.S. Army and served in the European theater of operations until 1945.

After the war, he was elected lieutenant governor in 1946 and in 1948. As lieutenant governor, he was a major force in changing the face of the Texas Senate. Shivers began the practice of appointing senators to specific committees and setting the daily agenda. Upon the death of Governor Beauford Jester in 1949, Shivers became governor and served effectively for the next seven years. During his tenure he pushed through significant legislation, as well as reforms of state government. One of the most beautiful statues to be found anywhere in Texas graces Shivers' gravesite in the Texas State Cemetery. The statue is the creation of sculptor Charles Umlauf, and its detail and grace are magnificent.

JAMES AUSTIN SYLVESTER

On December 18, 1835, James A. Sylvester (1807–1882) joined Capt. Sidney Sherman to fight for Texas independence. On April 21, 1836, during the Battle of San Jacinto, Sylvester carried the flag of the Kentucky volunteers into battle. The day after the victory, as the Texans searched for stragglers, Sylvester found a Mexican soldier dressed in a private's uniform. Sylvester had no way of knowing at the time that he had captured the president of Mexico, General Santa Anna.

JOANNA TROUTMAN

Joanna (or Johanna) Troutman (1818–1879) was born and raised in Georgia. In 1835, in response to a plea for volunteers to serve the cause of Texas independence, the Georgia Battalion answered that call. Joanna Troutman designed and made a flag of white silk, bearing a blue, five-pointed star and two inscriptions: "Texas and Liberty" on one side, and on the opposite side, in Latin, "Where Liberty dwells there is my country." She presented the flag to the battalion, and it was unfurled at Velasco on January 8, 1836. It was carried to Goliad, where James W. Fannin, Jr., raised it as the national flag when he heard of the Texas Declaration of Independence.

Joanna Troutman was originally buried in her native state, and in 1913 Texas governor Oscar B. Colquitt had her remains brought to Texas for burial in the Texas State Cemetery. A bronze statue sculpted by Pompeo Coppini marks her grave, and her portrait hangs in the State Capitol.

WILLIAM ALEXANDER ANDERSON WALLACE

William A. A. (Bigfoot) Wallace (1817–1899) is one of Texas' most colorful historical figures. Born in Virginia, he came to Texas in 1836 upon learning that a brother and a cousin had been slain in the Goliad Massacre. By all accounts, Bigfoot Wallace was a huge man with exceptional strength and resolve. After farming for a period near La Grange, he moved to San Antonio and was among the Texans who fought Gen. Adrián Woll's invading Mexican army near San Antonio in 1842. Wallace then volunteered for the Somervell and Mier expeditions and was imprisoned in Perote Prison after the men of Mier were captured.

Wallace joined the Texas Rangers under John Coffee (Jack) Hays and was with the Rangers in the U.S.-Mexican War. He commanded a Ranger company in the 1850s and drove a mail wagon from San Antonio to El Paso. During the Civil War he helped guard the frontier against the Comanche Indians. In his later years he became a cultural icon in Texas as he spun tales of early Texas, and time has made Bigfoot Wallace a true Texas folk hero.

WALTER PRESCOTT WEBB

Walter Prescott Webb (1888–1963) was born in Panola County and graduated from the University of Texas in 1915. After a stint as a schoolteacher, he was invited to serve on the history faculty at the university. His master's thesis was a study of the Texas Rangers, and in 1931 his book *The Great Plains* was published. The book was recognized by the Social Science Research Council in 1939 as the most outstanding contribution to American history since World War I and was the winner of Columbia University's Loubat Prize. Webb received a Ph.D. from the University of Texas in 1932. In all, he wrote or edited more than twenty books, including his classic study, *The Texas Rangers: A Century of Frontier Defense*.

JOHN AUSTIN WHARTON

John A. Wharton (1828–1865) was a successful lawyer and landowner when the Civil War erupted. He was elected captain of Company B, Eighth Texas Cavalry (Terry's Texas Rangers). He rose to command the regiment after the deaths of Col. Benjamin F. Terry and Lt. Col. Thomas S. Lubbock, serving with distinction at the Battle of Shiloh. Wharton was promoted to the rank of brigadier general in November 1862 and major general in 1863. On April 6, 1865, while Wharton was visiting Gen. John B. Magruder's headquarters at the Fannin Hotel in Houston, fellow officer George W. Baylor, angered during a personal quarrel, killed him.

JOSIAH PUGH WILBARGER

Talk about having a bad hair day. Josiah P. Wilbarger (1801–1844) was a member of a surveying party that was attacked by Indians near Pecan Springs, about four miles east of the site of present Austin (1833). Wilbarger was wounded, scalped, and left for dead. When Reuben Hornsby found him the next day, Wilbarger was alive, if just barely. Josiah Wilbarger had appeared to Hornsby's wife in a vivid dream, and she urged her husband, Reuben, to go to him, although the unfortunate settler was believed to be dead. Hornsby located the scalp of his severely wounded neighbor and returned with him to his home, where Wilbarger was nursed back to health. He never completely recovered from the scalping, although he lived for eleven more years. Wilbarger County was named in honor of Josiah Wilbarger and his brother, Mathias.

GRAVESITE AND LIKENESS OF GEN. JOHN WHARTON, KILLED BY A FELLOW OFFI-
CER. TEXAS STATE CEMETERY, AUSTIN.

RALPH WEBSTER YARBOROUGH

Ralph Webster (Smilin' Ralph) Yarborough (1903–1996) had practiced law and served in the U.S. Army when he returned to Austin in 1946 to resume his law practice. He had made an unsuccessful bid for state attorney general in 1938 and then lost the 1952 and 1954 Democratic primary races for governor. Yarborough made another unsuccessful gubernatorial bid in 1956 but was elected to the U.S. Senate in 1957 when M. Price Daniel, Sr., vacated his Senate seat.

In the Senate, Yarborough was a champion of liberal causes and was one of only five southern senators to vote for the Civil Rights Act of 1957. He won a full term in the U.S. Senate in 1958 and defeated future president George H. W. Bush in the race of 1964. A vigilant supporter of human rights issues, Yarborough voted for the Civil Rights Act of 1964 and was one of only three southerners to support the Voting Rights Act of 1965.

Yarborough had an excellent environmental record. He cowrote the Endangered Species Act of 1969 and sponsored the legislation establishing three national wildlife sanctuaries in Texas: Padre Island National Seashore (1962), Guadalupe Mountains National Park (1966), and Big Thicket National Preserve (1971).

Evergreen Cemetery
3400 E. Twelfth St.
N 30 16.630, W 097 41.950

CONNIE YERWOOD CONNOR

Connie Connor (ca. 1908–1991) was the first African American physician named to the Texas Public Health Service (now the Texas Department of Health). She was the daughter of a physician and, as a young woman, often accompanied her father on his rounds. She received a B.A. degree from Samuel Huston College (now Huston-Tillotson College), and in 1933 she graduated cum laude from Meharry Medical School.

Connie Connor began as a pediatric doctor but soon became interested in public health and earned a scholarship to study public health at the University of Michigan. Upon returning to Texas in 1937, she joined the Texas Public Health Service and spent a lifetime working to improve health conditions and prenatal care for the rural poor of Texas. She was a recognized leader in development of early periodic screening, diagnosis, treatment, and chronic diseases of pregnancy and pediatrics. When she retired on August 31, 1977, she was director of health services.

JOHN W. HARGIS

John W. Hargis (1935–1986) was born in Austin and was valedictorian of his class at Anderson High School in 1953. After entering college to study medicine, he changed course and decided to pursue engineering. He was admitted to the University of Texas in 1955 and graduated in 1959, the first African American to receive a chemical engineering degree from the university. In 1961 he went to work for Ampex Corporation, and his innovative design capability resulted in a patent for magnetic recording tape. After Capitol Records purchased Ampex, Hargis became a vice president of manufacturing for Capitol. John Hargis was a man whose life speaks to education and achievement.

WILLIE WELLS *(Reinterred Texas State Cemetery, Austin, 2004)*

Willie (Devil) Wells (1905–1989) was a slick-fielding shortstop and one of the premier hitters in the Negro Leagues. Born in Austin, Wells was discovered in 1925 when he became a player for the St. Louis Stars. Wells had a reputation as a fierce competitor, a clutch hitter, and was such an extraordinary fielder at his position that he was called the "Shakespeare of Shortstops."

Wells played on three pennant-winning teams with the St. Louis Stars, one with the Chicago American Giants, and one with the Newark Eagles. In 1930 he led the league with a .403 batting average. Wells was a player-manager for the Chicago American Giants in the early 1930s and became famous as the player-manager of the Newark Eagles in the 1940s. Although Willie Wells was once considered the greatest player not in the Baseball Hall of Fame, his achievements were finally recognized when he was inducted into the Baseball Hall of Fame in 1997.

Bastrop

Fairview Cemetery
U.S. Highway 95 at Cedar St.
N 30 06.886, W 097 18.448

Fairview Cemetery is one of Texas' most historic and unusual cemeteries. Located on a hill just east of the center of the city of Bastrop, its pinnacle indeed provides a "fair view" of the surrounding country-side. Fairview Cemetery is unusual in its layout, largely because it is on a hillside such that some vantage points in the cemetery are upwards of one hundred feet above the lower gravesites.

ELIJAH P. PETTY

As one walks westward through Fairview Cemetery, only a few yards from Joseph Sayers' gravesite, there is a large granite stone under a towering obelisk with the name "Petty" on its base. The headstone has this inscription:

E. P. PETTY
OF BASTROP TEXAS
CAPTAIN OF
CO.F.17TH VOL. INF.
SCURRY'S BRIGADE
KILLED AT THE BATTLE OF PLEASANT HILL, LOUISIANA
APRIL 9, 1864
ERECTED BY HIS SONS

The Red River campaign had taken the life of many Texans, including Capt. Bird Holland (buried in Oakwood Cemetery, Austin), William R. Scurry (buried in the Texas State Cemetery, Austin), and Sayers' commanding officer, Gen. Tom Green (also buried in Oakwood Cemetery, Austin). In the spring of 1864, federal troops under Gen. Nathaniel Banks initiated a military campaign to acquire Texas cotton, stimulate Unionism, disrupt Confederate trade with Mexico, and protect French activities in Mexico. Moving into Louisiana, Union troops were bitterly defeated by Confederate forces at Mansfield, Louisiana, on April 8, 1864. Falling back to the hamlet of Pleasant Hill, the federal troops prepared to meet the oncoming Confederates.

On the afternoon of April 9, 1864, the Confederate army, including units of Walker's Texas Division and Tom Green's Texas Cavalry, engaged a large federal force at Pleasant Hill. Here the Union troops repulsed their attackers, and the Confederate soldiers withdrew from the battlefield. Walker's division had suffered gravely, listing 69 killed, 404 wounded, and 141 missing. The Seventeenth Texas, part of Scurry's brigade, reported 16 dead, 35 wounded, and 60 missing. Captain Petty was among the 16 killed.

Elijah P. Petty had been an attorney, practicing law and living in Bastrop with his wife, Margaret, and their children when the Civil War erupted. He immediately volunteered, telling Margaret that he would write to her at every opportunity. After an appeal to arms, among the companies responding was the Bastrop Lubbock Guards, organized on September 28, 1861. The men elected Petty to the rank of first lieutenant. From the fall of 1861, Petty began writing letters home to his family, and the flow of news from the war was certain if irregular. His last letter was dated April 2, 1864; one week later, Petty lay dead. He had been shot in the chest and carried to the nearby Childers House in Pleasant Hill, where he died and was buried.

For twenty-five years, the exact location of Petty's burial was unknown, but in 1889 family members visited Pleasant Hill and located his gravesite, with the intention of moving his remains back to Bastrop. But they did not. The Petty family eventually bought the land where Elijah Petty was buried and marked his grave with a gray granite monument. It is said to be the only monument on the field of battle.

Although Petty's remains apparently were not brought home to Bastrop, his wife lived for forty-seven years after his death and is buried in the family plot in Fairview Cemetery. Petty's letters remained boxed for more than one hundred years, until publication in a fine volume, *Journey to Pleasant Hill: The Civil War Letters of Captain Elijah P. Petty, Walker's Texas Division* (edited by Norman Brown).

Joseph Draper Sayers

Joseph Sayers (1841–1929) was governor of Texas at the turn of the century and witnessed his share of calamity. He had served during the Civil War as an aide to Texas legend Gen. Tom Green during the Red River campaign of 1864 and was governor during the Galveston hurricane of 1900. A prominent flagpole marks his gravesite in the far northeastern area of the cemetery.

Beaumont

Forest Lawn Memorial Park
4955 Pine St.
N 30 07.636, W 094 06.023

Jiles Perry Richardson

J. P. (the Big Bopper) Richardson (1930–1959) is known for his music hit, "Chantilly Lace," which reached number one on the charts in 1958, and for his presence on the tragic plane flight that took the lives of two of popular music's most promising artists. On February 2,

1959, Richardson, Buddy Holly, and Ritchie Valens had finished a performance in Clear Lake, Iowa, and were scheduled to play in Moorehead Armory, Minnesota, the next day. After the show, Holly and Valens chartered a plane so that they could rest before their bands arrived. Richardson, who had the flu, was supposed to take the bus but at the last minute switched places with Holly's band member Waylon Jennings. The plane went down just after takeoff in Mason County, Iowa, killing the pilot and all three musicians.

MILDRED ELLA DIDRIKSON ZAHARIAS

Mildred E. (Babe) Didrikson Zaharias (1911–1956) was arguably the most talented female athlete of the twentieth century. Born in Port Arthur, she and her family moved to Beaumont in 1915. Mildred was nicknamed "Babe" during sandlot baseball games with the neighborhood boys, who thought she hit like Babe Ruth. A gifted natural athlete, she excelled in basketball and track-and-field as a young woman. In the 1932 Olympic Games, Babe Didrikson won gold medals in the javelin and hurdles and a silver medal in the high jump.

In the early 1930s, Didrikson took up golf, became a championship amateur player, and was the first American to win the British Amateur. She turned professional in 1947 and helped found the Ladies Professional Golf Association (LPGA) in 1949. She was the LPGA's leading money winner between 1949 and 1951. In 1950 the Associated Press voted her Woman Athlete of the Half-Century. In 1953 she was stricken with cancer and died three years later.

The Associated Press voted her Athlete of the Year six times during her career. Between 1940 and 1950 she won every women's golf title, including the world championship (four times), the U.S. Women's Open (three times), and a total of fifty-five tournaments. She is a member of the National Women's Hall of Fame, was voted as one of the top fifty athletes (male or female) by ESPN, and was one of the first four women voted into the LPGA Hall of Fame (1951).

Bigfoot

Brummett Cemetery
Frio County, on Whitley Rd. east of Highway 173 S.
N 29 04.278, W 098 48.736

The first grave placed in the Brummett Cemetery is that of Elijah Ross, a two-year-old buried in 1860. The cemetery is neat and reasonably well kept, although grass burrs covered every exposed inch of my shoes and socks within minutes of entering its confines.

Buried here are the members of the Nixon, Winters, and Brummett families. Many of the graves are covered in concrete, and the relationship of the person to other family members is recorded on top of the domed graves. One of the most interesting gravesites in the Brummett Cemetery is that of Big Grannie McCray (1796–1901), one of a handful of Texans who lived in three centuries.

JAMES WASHINGTON WINTERS, JR.

James W. Winters (1817–1903) served in Capt. William Ware's company of independent volunteers, which became the Second Company of Col. Sidney Sherman's Second Regiment, Texas Volunteers. Winters and his two brothers participated in the Battle of San Jacinto. In 1842 James Winters participated in the Somervell Expedition but did not continue into Mexico with the Mier Expedition. In 1901 he was instrumental in aiding the Daughters of the Republic of Texas in placing historical markers at the San Jacinto battlefield. At his death in 1903, James W. Winters was one of the last survivors of the Battle of San Jacinto.

Blessing

Old Hawley Cemetery
FM 459, north of intersection with Highway 35
N 28 53.924, W 096 10.472

ABEL HEAD PIERCE

Abel Head (Shanghai) Pierce (1834–1900) was one of Texas' most colorful and successful cattlemen. Born in Rhode Island, Pierce came to Texas in 1854 as a stowaway headed for Indianola. After landing in Texas, he began splitting rails for a living and accumulating cattle of his own. Along with his brother, Jonathan, Abel Pierce established his ranch, named Rancho Grande, in Wharton County. Eventually, his landholdings exceeded 250,000 acres and formed the Pierce-Sullivan Pasture Company.

Pierce was larger than life, and in the early 1890s he commissioned sculptor Frank Teich to create a marble statue of himself, stating that the monument should be "as high as for any Confederate general and a fair likeness" of himself. Teich's statue stands at Pierce's grave in the Old Hawley Cemetery, having been hauled there by a team of six oxen.

Bonham

Willow Wild Cemetery
1220 W. Seventh St.
N 33 34.821, W 096 11.666

SAMUEL TALIAFERRO RAYBURN

Sam Rayburn (1882–1961) came to Texas in 1887, when his family moved to Fannin County from Tennessee. At the age of eighteen he entered East Texas Normal College; he alternately attended college and taught school and still completed in two years the three-year normal-school course leading to the B.S. degree. Rayburn began his political career when he was elected to the Texas House of Representatives in 1906. He attended the University of Texas Law School between sessions and was admitted to the State Bar of Texas in 1908. He was reelected to the Texas Legislature in 1908 and 1910; in his third term he served as Speaker of the House.

In 1912 Rayburn was elected to the U.S. Congress as a Democrat

SAM RAYBURN, LEGENDARY TEXAS CONGRESSMAN AND SPEAKER OF THE U.S. HOUSE OF REPRESENTATIVES, LIES AT REST IN HIS HOME OF BONHAM. WILLOW WILD CEMETERY.

from the Fourth Texas District. After the 1912 election, Rayburn had no Republican opponent at any time during his congressional career. Rayburn took his oath of office in 1913 and served in Congress for forty-eight years, the longest continuous record of service in the House (at the time of his death in 1961). He was elected Speaker of the House in 1940 and served in that position in every Democratic-controlled Congress from the Seventy-sixth through the Eighty-seventh (1940–1961).

Brackettville

Seminole-Negro Indian Scout Cemetery
FM 3348, 3 miles south of Brackettville
N 29 16.400, W 100 26.581

In 1870, Maj. Zenas R. Bliss enlisted a special detachment of thirteen Black Seminole scouts from a group of approximately one hundred who were stationed at Fort Duncan, Texas. These men were part of the mixed-blood Seminole and black population that had migrated to northeastern Mexico during 1849 and 1850 to escape American slave hunters. The first group of scouts proved to be outstanding trackers, and in July 1872, Lt. Col. Wesley Merritt asked Bliss to transfer some of the scouts to Fort Clark. At Fort Clark, Lt. John Lapham Bullis took command of the scouts, and they quickly played an important role in military operations involving hostile Indians.

Between 1875 and 1881 the scouts spent much time on the trail of small Indian raiding parties. On April 25, 1875, scouts under the command of Lieutenant Bullis were pursuing a band of Comanche Indians as they crossed the Pecos River. After engaging the Indians for forty-five minutes, and in danger of being surrounded, they mounted their horses to escape capture. Bullis' horse had broken away, however, leaving him stranded.

The Comanches laid down a steady stream of fire on the scouts. A bullet sliced the carbine sling of Sgt. John Ward (1848–1911), but he turned back into harm's way and swung Bullis onto his mount behind him. As Bullis mounted, another bullet smashed the stock of Ward's rifle. Troopers Isaac Payne (1854–1904) and Pompey Factor (1849–1928) alternately carried the lieutenant to safety. All three of the troopers were awarded the Congressional Medal of Honor and are buried in the Seminole-Negro Indian Scout Cemetery.

Brenham

Prairie Lea Cemetery
Prairie Lea at W. Fifth St.
N 30 09.390, W 096 24.493

A first impression of Prairie Lea Cemetery was that it should have been named the Cemetery of Angels. Some of Texas' most beautiful angel statuary is to be found in the Prairie Lea Cemetery, particularly in the Tristram family plot. This cemetery is truly beautiful, full of mature oak trees and glorious old magnolias, and is exceptionally well maintained.

An inviting white house stands in the middle of the cemetery, with a number to call if you need to find a gravesite on a weekend. I called and it worked, although I transposed two digits in the phone number and spoke to a woman who was polite if not quite skeptical that anyone could dial the same incorrect number twice. Sections of the cemetery are well marked so if you know the location of a specific gravesite, you should have no trouble finding it.

The main entrance to Prairie Lea Cemetery is lined with markers commemorating Texas soldiers who perished in World War I and are buried there. I was struck by the realization that so many of the young American men who died in a war with Germany were of German descent themselves, an irony repeated in other cemeteries throughout south central Texas.

NOEL MOSES BLAINE

Moses Baine (1800–1864) came to Texas in 1830 as a colonist of Stephen F. Austin's. In 1836 Baine enlisted in the Texas Army and fought at the Battle of San Jacinto. In 1842 he served as a member of the Somervell Expedition. He eventually settled in Washington County and became a successful planter.

PHILIP HOUSTON COE

Western legend has it that this unfortunate gambler was the last person who met his fate at the end of a pistol wielded by Wild Bill Hickok. Philip Coe (1839–1871) was a contemporary of John Wesley Hardin and Bill Longley, as well as a friend of Austin gunman and lawman Ben Thompson. Coe's demise came as a result of his interest in a woman who also held Hickok's interest. Apparently, Coe was the winner of her affection, and Hickok evidently did not take the news

well. Wild Bill shot and wounded Coe on October 5, 1871. Coe died a few days later, and his body was returned to his hometown for burial. Hickok still did not get the girl.

Joe Routt

Buried in Prairie Lea Cemetery is World War II hero and Texas A&M athlete Joe Routt (1914–1944). Routt played football during his years at A&M and became that university's first All-American player (1937 and 1938). After graduation from A&M, Routt was commissioned as a second lieutenant in the U.S. Army. On December 2, 1944, Capt. Joe Routt was killed in action in Holland and buried there. He was reinterred at Brenham in 1949. Routt was later named to the National Football Foundation Hall of Fame and to the Texas Sports Hall of Fame.

Brownsville

Old Brownsville City Cemetery
E. Fifth St. at E. Madison
N 25 54. 51, W 097 29.99

The Old Brownsville City Cemetery is surrounded by a tall white wall, dotted along its entire length by fully blooming bougainvillea. As I entered the cemetery, the Spanish and French influences in the history of Brownsville fully engulfed me. This old cemetery is reminiscent of the cemeteries of Louisiana, as whitewashed stucco aboveground mausoleums, proximal and seemingly stacked like a pueblo of tombs, lined both sides of the gravel road along the cemetery's main passage. There are brick sidewalks throughout the oldest part of the cemetery, and the diversity of materials used in construction of the mausoleums and gravestones is unique.

The cemetery was deeded to the city of Brownsville in 1868, but several of the headstones bear inscriptions dating from the late 1850s. Like many of the old cemeteries along the Texas coast, this one is replete with headstones of local citizens who fell victim to yellow fever epidemics in 1858 and again in 1868.

Santiago Brito

Santiago Brito (1851–1892) served as both sheriff and city marshal in Brownsville and as a special Texas Ranger. In January 1891 Brito set out to apprehend train robbers who had relieved the Rio Grande Railroad of several thousands of dollars and some government mail. In a matter of just a few days the crime was solved. The ingenious lawman began his search by examining the railroad tracks for the tool used to pull the spikes. He quickly located the blacksmith who made the tool, and that information led him to the leader of the outlaws, Jose Mosqueda. Mosqueda was found guilty and sentenced to jail, where he eventually died. Brito's own life ended violently and shortly after his apprehension of the train robbers, when he was shot and killed in an unrelated incident in 1892.

Hiram Chamberlain

Hiram Chamberlain (1797–1866) moved to Brownsville in 1850, where on February 23 he established the first Protestant church on the lower Rio Grande: the First Presbyterian Church of Brownsville. Chamberlain was an ardent secessionist and served as chaplain of the Third Texas Infantry throughout the Civil War. He was the father of Henrietta Chamberlain King, wife of Richard King, with whom she founded the famous King Ranch.

Brownwood

Greenleaf Cemetery
Center St. at Texas St.
N 31 42.286, W 098 59.842

Mollie Wright Armstrong

Mollie Wright Armstrong (1875–1964) was born in Bell County and studied optometry after attending Baylor Female College. When she began her practice in Brownwood in 1899, she was the first female optometrist in the state and only the second in the United States. She actively supported the first optometry law in Texas, became a member of the Texas Board of Examiners in Optometry, and served as vice president and president of the board. She was president of the Texas Optometric Association from 1923 to 1925.

Greenleaf Fisk

Greenleaf Fisk (1807–1888) moved to Texas in 1834 and settled near what is now Bastrop. Fisk served under Capt. Jesse Billingsley at the Battle of San Jacinto. After the war, he returned to Bastrop, where he served as clerk of the district court (1827) prior to his election to the Texas House of Representatives (1838–1839).

DEPUTY SHERIFF C. M. WEBB WAS THE LAST MAN TO DIE AT THE HAND OF GUN-MAN JOHN WESLEY HARDIN. GREENLEAF CEMETERY, BROWNWOOD.

In 1860 Fisk moved his family to Brown County, where he had been granted title to 1,280 acres of land for his service to the Republic of Texas. In Brown County, between 1862 and the mid-1870s, Fisk held a variety of positions, including county judge, justice of the peace, county surveyor, district clerk, county clerk, and county treasurer. Fisk founded the city of Brownwood (incorporated in 1877).

ROBERT E. HOWARD

Robert E. Howard (1906–1936) was born in Peaster and lived most of his life in Cross Plains. Cross Plains did not have a high school, so Howard attended Brownwood High School, and in 1925 he entered Howard Payne College. During his year at Howard Payne he began writing short stories and, after modest success, decided to support himself by writing fiction. He began to produce volumes of work at the price of one cent per word. He became an almost instant success, making as much as $500 a month, a huge sum during the Depression. Although he created many characters, he is most noted for his character Conan the Barbarian. Howard was the subject of a 1996 movie, *The Whole Wide World*.

CHARLES M. WEBB

Deputy sheriff of Brown County, Charles M. Webb (1848–1874) was a victim of killer John Wesley Hardin. Webb's death resulted in a three-year manhunt for Hardin, who was eventually captured in Pensacola, Florida, and then tried and sent to prison for Webb's death.

Burton

Mount Zion Baptist Church Cemetery
FM 1948 at FM 390, north of Burton
N 30 12.838, W 096 34.558

A wonderful example of a Texas country church cemetery is located just north of Burton. On maps the cemetery is listed as the Hall Cemetery, but markers on the site show the name as Mount Zion Baptist Church Cemetery. The five-acre cemetery lies on the site of an original 1831 grant to Robert Clokey, who received a league of land as a member of Stephen F. Austin's second colony. The oldest grave in the cemetery is dated 1852. The site is full of old oak trees, which surround the small white Baptist church and provide shade on the hottest of Texas afternoons. The cemetery is not enclosed in any fashion and is easily accessible by automobile.

Near the entrance to the church is the family plot of the Hons family. An iron fence surrounds it, but the gate is not secured, and I walked into this small area without difficulty. Many of the gravesites in the plot are decorated with seashells, as is often the case in southern cemeteries. The gravesite of Corine Knittel, who died in 1900 at age six, is marked by a perfect sculpture of an angel, and its viewing is well worth the few seconds it takes to open the gate and walk into the enclosure for a closer look. There are many unmarked graves in the cemetery, and most are thought to be the burial site of victims who succumbed to yellow fever in the 1867 epidemic that swept much of Washington County. The area's rich Civil War legacy is exemplified by the grave of R. T. Matson (1826–1863), killed at the Battle of Pine Bluff, Arkansas, and buried near the east wall of the church.

If you decide to visit this cemetery, be sure to take the scenic drive from Burton to Independence along FM 390 through Washington County. Making the drive on a spring morning when the countryside was resplendent in bluebonnets, I realized why Texans from the time of Sam Houston still find this historic county to be one of the most beautiful in Texas.

LEANDER H. MCNELLY

In the cemetery's farthest northeast corner lies one of Texas' most famous (or infamous) Texas Rangers, Leander H. McNelly (1844–1877). McNelly came to Texas in 1860 with his parents and entered the service of the Confederacy as a private in Col. Thomas Green's Fifth Texas Cavalry. Serving in the Red River campaign, he was seriously wounded at the Battle of Mansfield in April 1864, recovered from his wounds, and served gallantly for the remainder of the war.

Transferred to Washington County, Texas, to arrest deserters after the war, McNelly served as one of four captains of the Texas State Police from 1870 to 1873. In 1874 the seventh company of the Frontier Battalion of the Texas Rangers was formed in the county, and McNelly was appointed as its captain. He was quickly sent to DeWitt County to calm the outbreak of the Sutton-Taylor feud, and there he and his Rangers maintained law and order for the next four months.

In early 1875 McNelly was dispatched to raise a new Ranger company for service along the Texas-Mexico border in the Nueces Strip, an area between the Nueces River and the Rio Grande. The Nueces

Strip had been a haven for outlaws and cattle rustlers for years, and the bravado of these outlaws was such that cattle were often stolen in broad daylight. The unquestioned ruler of the area was John King Fisher, a Uvalde cattle rustler who so intimidated the local citizenry that, upon McNelly's capture of him in April 1876, the people of Eagle Pass released him soon after his arrival in town.

Though McNelly's idea of frontier justice was often questionable and his law enforcement strategies often bordered on brutality, his company of Texas Rangers provided badly needed protection from cattle rustlers and raiders for ranchers and settlers in South Texas. The company served from 1875 to 1876, but McNelly's frequent forays into Mexico resulted in his removal as captain, and his failing health required his departure from the Rangers altogether. In 1877 he died of tuberculosis at Burton, at the age of only thirty-three, and was buried in this quiet church cemetery.

Canyon

Dreamland Cemetery
187 Dreamland Rd.
N 34 56.493, W 101 55.313

LINCOLN GUY CONNER

Lincoln Guy Conner (1860–1920) came to Texas with his family after the Civil War. By 1887 he had married and established a small cattle herd in Randall County. After purchasing a large block of land in 1888, he constructed a half-dugout from logs hauled from nearby Palo Duro Canyon. Conner established a general store and post office, and in the spring of 1889 he laid out the town site of Canyon City. Conner donated town lots to those willing to build there and donated thirty acres to the Santa Fe Railroad for a depot and cattle pens. He also donated land for a county courthouse, schools, and churches. Conner expanded his ranching and real estate ventures steadily over the next two decades and became one of Canyon City's most prosperous citizens. A generous philanthropist, he donated forty acres near his residence and $2,000 to establish West Texas State Normal College (now West Texas A&M University) in 1910.

DORRANCE WILHELM FUNK

Dorrance Wilhelm (Dory) Funk (1919–1973) was Indiana state high school wrestling champion for three years and Indiana Amateur Athletic Union champion for a year. He continued wrestling at Indiana University, where during his senior year he was elected to the Amateur Wrestling Hall of Fame.

In 1949 Funk moved to Amarillo, and though he was a terror inside the wrestling ring, outside the ring he was a true humanitarian. In 1950 Funk began his stint as superintendent at Cal Farley's Boys Ranch after a group of rebellious teenagers had threatened to toss the previous superintendent into the Canadian River. Cal Farley asked Funk to assist him for a period, and the wrestler began working with the young men by demonstrating wrestling techniques to them. Funk served three years at the Boys Ranch, and although he left the Boys Ranch in 1953, he continued his work with young boys for much of the rest of his life.

MARGARET PEASE HARPER

Margaret Pease Harper (1911–1991) came to Texas in 1946 to accept the position of chairperson of the modern language department at West Texas State Teachers College (now West Texas A&M University) in Canyon. Margaret Harper fell in love with the Texas Panhandle and saw Palo Duro Canyon as a potential site for an outdoor musical. From her vision came the musical production *Texas*, which opened in 1966. Her many honors include induction into the National Cowboy Hall of Fame, the National Cowgirl Hall of Fame, and the Texas Hall of Fame for Women.

Chappell Hill

Masonic Cemetery

Cemetery Rd., 0.75 mile northwest of Chappell Hill off FM 2447
N 30 09.189, W 096 15.678

WILLIAM JONES ELLIOTT HEARD

William J. E. Heard (1801–1874) came to Texas in December 1830 and was granted land six miles from Texana in Stephen F. Austin's colony. In 1835 he moved to Egypt (Wharton County), where he operated a sugar and cotton plantation. On February 1, 1836, Heard was elected first lieutenant of Capt. Thomas J. Rabb's company of volunteers, and later he was elected captain of Company F of Col. Edward Burleson's First Regiment, Texas Volunteers. At the Battle of San Jacinto, Heard's company occupied the middle of the Texan line opposite the Mexican artillery and overran and captured the enemy cannons.

CHARLES EDWARD AND SUSAN ISABELLA TRAVIS (GRISSETT)

Charles Edward Travis (1829–1860) and Susan Isabella Travis (?–?) were the son and daughter of Alamo legend William Barrett Travis. Young Charles lived in New Orleans with his mother and stepfather, Dr. Samuel B. Cloud, after the death of his father, but later he moved to Brenham to live with his sister, Mrs. John (Susan Isabella) Grissett. Charles became a member of the Texas bar and served in the Texas Legislature in 1853–1854. He served in the Texas Rangers at Fort Clark and then was commissioned a captain in the Second U.S. Cav-

CHARLES E. TRAVIS, SON OF ALAMO HERO WILLIAM TRAVIS, LIES NEXT TO HIS SISTER IN THE MASONIC CEMETERY, CHAPPELL HILL.

alry in 1855. His period of service was short, and after enduring a court martial, he was released from service in 1856. Although he fought to have his named cleared, he was unsuccessful. He returned to the home of his sister and died of tuberculosis. Both Charles and his sister, Susan, are buried in the Masonic Cemetery.

Cherry Springs

Marschall-Meusebach Cemetery
Cherry Springs Rd.
N 30 28.944, W 099 00.258

This tiny country cemetery is one of the simplest and most elegant cemeteries in Texas. It is east of Cherry Springs, and the road that leads to the cemetery is on the north side of Cherry Springs Road and well marked. A black wrought iron fence and a gate that is a marvel to German engineering guard the entrance to the cemetery. The road winds a few hundred yards north and then abruptly turns east to the cemetery.

The cemetery is surrounded by a stone wall, assembled without mortar and yet perfectly symmetrical. Thin stones are set all along the top of the wall, each held in place by the other. To my knowledge, there exists in Texas no wall that is more perfectly engineered, cut, and assembled. It is simply gorgeous.

Inset in the wall is a white picket gate that allows entrance to the cemetery. In addition to the Meusebach gravesite and its unique surrounding wall, there is another treasure to be found in this cemetery. But I will leave its discovery to you.

John O. Meusebach

Buried in this cemetery is the founder of Fredericksburg, John O. Meusebach (1812–1897). Born in Germany and educated there in law, Meusebach was appointed in 1845 as commissioner general in Texas of the Society for the Protection of German Immigrants in Texas (the Adelsverein). In that post he was successor to Prince Carl of Solms-Braunfel, founder of New Braunfels. Soon after arriving in Texas, Meusebach left New Braunfels to survey lands for a second settlement in the Fisher-Miller Land Grant, which the Republic of Texas had awarded for the settlement of European immigrants. A town was surveyed and named Fredericksburg, in honor of Prince Frederick of Prussia.

Meusebach was interested in expanding settlement in the Fisher-Miller land, but one significant impediment stood in his way. These lands, located between the Colorado and Llano Rivers, were hunting grounds of the Comanche Indians, warriors who have been described as the "finest light cavalry ever to roam North America." In December 1846, Meusebach and interpreter Jim Shaw arranged a spring meeting with ten Comanche chiefs, and in March 1847 a treaty was struck with head chiefs Buffalo Hump, Santa Anna, and "Old Owl." The treaty allowed settlers to go unharmed by the Indians and allowed Indians into the European settlements. More than three million acres of land was opened to settlement by the Meusebach-Comanche Treaty, and folks in Fredericksburg will claim to this day that it is the only treaty ever made with the Comanche Indians that was not violated. After the Adelsverein folded, Meusebach continued to serve the German community in Gillespie County for many years, as a botanist and as a state legislator.

Claude

Claude Cemetery
FM 207, north of Claude
N 35 09.956, W 101 22.821

WILLIAM ARTHUR WARNER

William Arthur (Pop) Warner (1864–1934) came to the Texas Panhandle after finishing medical school at Northwestern University. In 1897 Warner began his medical practice in the tiny town of Claude. For many years, Warner was the only doctor in Armstrong County and often traveled in his horse-drawn buggy to visit patients.

Warner was the organizer of Lone Star Troop No. 17, the first Boy Scout troop west of the Mississippi (1912). At the outbreak of World War I, he joined an army medical unit and spent much of the war aiding the sick and wounded on the battlefields of Europe. After the war, he returned to his medical practice, continued his work with the Boy Scouts as a scoutmaster for twenty years, and was a recipient of the Boy Scouts of America's Silver Beaver, the highest award bestowed by the organization.

College Station

College Station Cemetery
Highway 6, 2 miles south of Texas A&M University
N 30 36.305, W 096 18.382

HARRY WARREN COLLINS

Harry Warren (Rip) Collins (1896–1968) was born in Weatherford, and after his family moved to Austin he developed into an exceptional athlete. His Austin High football team won two consecutive state championships in 1913 and 1914, and after graduation, Collins hoped to enroll at the University of Texas. However, his athletic ability did not impress the head coach at UT, so Collins enrolled at Texas A&M University and became one of America's premier kickers.

In the 1915 Aggie and Longhorn game, Collins punted the ball twenty-three times, averaging fifty-five yards per kick. Collins could impart an unusual spin to the football when he punted, and the Texas punt returners fumbled thirteen times. One fumble set up the only touchdown scored in the game, ironically scored by Collins. The final score was a 13–0 upset of the heavily favored Longhorns.

By the end of his college career, Collins was a legend and is still regarded as the best punter in Southwest Conference history. Collins was also an excellent baseball player and in 1920 joined the New York Yankees. He later pitched for Boston, Detroit, and St. Louis, with a lifetime record of 108 wins and 82 losses. After retiring from baseball, he joined the Texas Rangers and began a career in law enforcement that lasted until his retirement in 1950.

JAMES EARL RUDDER

On D-Day—June 6, 1944—Lt. Col. James Earl Rudder (1910–1970) and the members of his Second Ranger Battalion faced one of the most difficult missions of the Normandy invasion. Located four miles west of Omaha Beach, a battery of six German 155-mm howitzers, encased in massive concrete fortifications, represented the strongest defensive position on the Normandy front. Destruction of this fortified gun emplacement was critical to the success of the landings of American troops on Omaha and Utah beach. Bombing had been ineffective in removing the guns; only an attack by ground forces could ensure the full disablement of the German firepower. The location of the battery (on a plateau with a sheer drop of at least one hundred feet) convinced Allied commanders that only a special force could accomplish the mission.

The special force chosen for this mission was to be the American Second and Fifth Rangers. Under Rudder's command, three companies of the Second Rangers would execute a landing simultaneously with the forces on Omaha Beach. A fourth company would land at the westernmost point of the beach to attack another German defense at Pointe de la Percee. The Fifth Rangers, along with the remaining two companies from the Second, would form the second wave.

On the approach to the beach at Pointe du Hoc, crosscurrents carried Rudder's men away from their assigned landing site, and it took them forty minutes to correct the position. The second wave assumed that the landing had failed and were commanded to land at Omaha Beach and to attack the position from this point. All 225 of "Rudder's Rangers" were now on the very small beach at Pointe du Hoc, and the only thing between them and the guns were hundred-foot cliffs and firmly entrenched German troops. More than 50 percent of Rudder's Rangers were casualties, and Rudder himself was twice wounded.

Rudder and his men inched to the top, succeeded in their mission, and played a critical part in helping Allied forces secure the beach. Six months later Rudder was assigned to command the 109th Infantry Regiment that played a key role in the Battle of the Bulge. By the end of the war, he was a full colonel and was promoted to brigadier general of the U.S. Army Reserves in 1954 and major general in 1957. Rudder was one of the most decorated soldiers of the war, with honors that included the Distinguished Service Cross, Legion of Merit, Silver Star, French Legion of Honor with croix de guerre and palm, and others.

Rudder returned to his home in Brady, where he served as mayor (1946–1952), and in 1955 he assumed the office of land commissioner of the Texas General Land Office. Rudder won the election for land commissioner in 1956 and served until February 1, 1958, when he became vice president of Texas A&M University. Rudder became president of the University in 1959 and president of the A&M system in 1965. In 1967 Rudder was awarded the Distinguished Service Medal, America's highest peacetime service award.

ELI L. WHITELEY

Eli L. Whiteley (1913–1986) was born in Georgetown and graduated from Texas A&M in 1941. Drafted into the army in April 1942 and commissioned as a second lieutenant, he was assigned to duty in France. As a first lieutenant, he was a member of Company L, Fifteenth Infantry, Third Infantry Division. While leading his platoon on December 27, 1944, Whiteley was engaged in house-to-house fighting through the town of Sigolsheim, France. He was hit and severely wounded in the arm and shoulder, but he stormed an enemy-held house, killing its two defenders.

Reaching the next enemy position, he attacked, killing two enemy soldiers and taking eleven prisoners. He continued leading his platoon in the task of clearing hostile troops until he reached another enemy stronghold. The series of wounds he had received left his left arm useless, but he advanced on the house, used a bazooka to blast out a wall, and entered the building. Wedging his machine gun under his uninjured arm, he rushed into the house, killed five of the enemy, and forced the remaining twelve to surrender. As he emerged, he was again wounded but shouted for his men to follow him to the next house. Whiteley remained at the head of his platoon until forcibly evacuated. For his leadership and gallantry in action, 1st Lt. Eli Whiteley was awarded the Congressional Medal of Honor.

Colorado City

Colorado City Cemetery
Highway 208 at intersection with I-20J
N 32 23.576, W 100 50.459

RICHARD CLAYTON WARE

Richard C. Ware (1851–1902) came to Texas from Georgia in 1870 and settled near Dallas. In 1876 Ware joined the Frontier Battalion of the Texas Rangers and in July 1878 was one of the Rangers accompanying Maj. John B. Jones to intercept Sam Bass and his gang of bank robbers in Round Rock.

Ware was in a barbershop being shaved when the outlaws entered the town. Shortly after their arrival, the Bass Gang shot and killed Deputy Sheriff A. W. "High" Grimes. Ware jumped from the barber's chair, his face still covered in shaving cream, and began firing at the outlaws. One of Ware's bullets found its mark in Bass' accomplice, Seaborn Barnes. Although there is some question regarding who actually fired the shot that mortally wounded Bass, eyewitnesses (and Bass himself) assert that it was a man with lather on his face. Ware resigned from the Rangers in 1881 to become Mitchell County's first sheriff and in 1893 was appointed by President Grover Cleveland as U.S. marshal for the Western District of Texas.

Columbus

Old Columbus Cemetery

1300 Walnut St. (Highway 90)
N 29 42.372, W 096 33.130

Columbus is one of Texas' oldest settlements. Members of Stephen F. Austin's Old Three Hundred began arriving in the area in 1821, and by 1823 a small town had sprung up at the site of Beeson's Ferry (named for Benjamin Beeson) on the Colorado River. The name of the town was changed to Columbus in the early 1830s. The Old Columbus Cemetery reflects the history of Colorado County and the many difficulties of life on the Texas frontier. Columbus was the site of frequent attacks from Indians, and many of the graves in this old cemetery are the final resting places of residents who died during one of the frequent plagues of yellow fever that struck the area, and of at least one person who drowned in the nearby river.

The Old Columbus Cemetery is home to some of the most majestic and stately live oak trees in all of Texas. The soil in this cemetery is very sandy, and if you choose to drive through it after rainfall, be prepared to bog down in the sand with little chance of self-extrication.

Along the east fence of the cemetery is perhaps the most exquisite marble monument to be found in any Texas cemetery. Elegant and noble in its shape and intricacies, the monument marks the grave of William Jasper Anderson, and the signature on the base indicates that a stonecutter in Houston carved it. A beautifully rendered angel stands inside a steeplelike structure, tending to the specific needs of Mr. Anderson and to all those who rest in the cemetery. The monument was assembled in sections, but the workmanship is flawless and the carvings in the marble are in a class by themselves.

DILUE ROSE HARRIS

Dilue Rose Harris (1825–1914) came to Texas in April 1833 and settled at Stafford's Point in December of that year. She was involved in the Texas Revolution, and among her efforts in support of independence she molded bullets for men going to the Alamo. Her reminiscences about the leaders of the Texas Revolution and of the Republic of Texas were compiled when she was in her seventies and served as an important source of history of early Texas.

Cool

Holders Chapel Cemetery
Holders Chapel Rd.
N 32 48.533, W 098 00.379

JACK L. KNIGHT

Jack L. Knight (1917–1945) was born in Garner and graduated from Weatherford Junior College in 1938. Jack and his two brothers, Curtis and Loyd, enlisted in Troop F, 124th Cavalry, Texas National Guard—one of the last cavalry regiments in the army. Knight's unit was called to service in 1940 and posted to India, where it was charged with opening the Burma Road between India and China.

On February 2, 1945, near Loi-Kang, Burma, Lt. Jack Knight was leading his men against intense enemy fire. Preceding his men, Knight was wounded by a grenade. Jack's brother Curtis rushed to his aid but was himself wounded. Jack Knight ordered his men to his brother's aid, while he continued to lead the assault until he was mortally

FIRST LIEUTENANT JACK L. KNIGHT WAS POSTHUMOUSLY AWARDED THE CONGRESSIONAL MEDAL OF HONOR. HOLDERS CHAPEL CEMETERY, COOL.

wounded. His gallantry was responsible for the elimination of most of the enemy opposition. Louis Mountbatten, supreme Allied commander in Southeast Asia, later dedicated the area as Knight's Hill. For his courage and service to country, Lt. Jack Knight was awarded the Congressional Medal of Honor.

Corpus Christi

Old Bayview Cemetery
Waco St. at W. Broadway St.
N 27 48.062, W 097 23.951

This scenic little plot is the oldest federal cemetery in Texas, established by Zachary Taylor in 1845 after a steamship explosion took the life of seven of his cavalrymen. Taylor acquired a parcel of land overlooking Corpus Christi Bay and had a cemetery laid out for burial of his men. A Colonel Hitchcock, who served with Taylor, wrote, "On September 14, a military funeral took place at the burial ground that I selected. It is on the brow of a hill northwest of camp, and commands a view of Nueces and Corpus Christi Bays. It is a beautiful spot."

Soon after, Taylor's troops left Corpus Christi for the Rio Grande Valley and made their place in American history, as with him rode men whose names would become synonymous with the Civil War: Braxton Bragg, Ulysses S. Grant, Kirby Smith, and James Longstreet, to name but a few. When Taylor's cavalrymen departed Corpus Christi, this small knoll became the community cemetery.

Old Bayview Cemetery now lies in an older part of downtown Corpus Christi. The grounds are strewn with broken and uplifted markers and monuments, many of which had guarded the graves of cavalrymen since the 1840s. It's surrounded by oleanders and punctuated with palms and a mesquite tree or two. A wrought iron fence encompasses the cemetery, and although there are no posted hours, the gate through which I entered did have a padlock secured to a rail. One can see Corpus Christi Bay from the cemetery, but the view of Nueces Bay has fallen victim to the progress of steel and granite, much as Taylor's men fell to the progress of iron and steam.

Many of the graves in the cemetery are unmarked and the result of the crushing yellow fever epidemic that swept the area in 1867 and is commemorated by a marker on the south side of the cemetery. This

SERGEANT J. W.
PARSONS WAS
KILLED IN A
STEAMSHIP
EXPLOSION IN
CORPUS CHRISTI
BAY. A CAVALRY-
MAN IN THE
TROOPS LED BY
ZACHARY TAY-
LOR, HE IS
BURIED IN THE
OLD BAYVIEW
CEMETERY, COR-
PUS CHRISTI.

small cemetery, in the heart of the city, was peaceful and cool at sun-set. Colonel Hitchcock's description of Old Bayview Cemetery is as true today as it was on that September day 150-plus years ago: a beautiful spot, indeed.

GEORGE WASHINGTON HOCKLEY

George W. Hockley (1802–1854) served as chief of staff of the Texas Army during the Texas Revolution. He was commander of the artillery at the Battle of San Jacinto and in charge of the famous Twin Sisters cannons. Although a resident of Galveston, Hockley died in Corpus Christi (probably as a result of the yellow fever epidemic of 1854) and was buried in this cemetery. Hockley County is named in his honor.

Seaside Memorial Park
Robert Dr. at Ocean Dr.
N 27 43.976, W 097 21.887

SELENA QUINTANILLA PEREZ

Selena Quintanilla Perez (1971–1995), simply known as Selena, was a wildly popular recording artist. In 1982 her family moved from Lake Jackson to Corpus Christi, where she performed in her father's Tejano band. Selena became a star in Tejano music, winning the Tejano Music Award for Female Entertainer of the Year in 1987, and eight other awards soon followed. By the late 1980s Selena was widely regarded as the queen of Tejano music. On March 31, 1995, Selena was shot fatally by the founder of her first fan club and was laid to rest in Seaside Memorial Park. Her immense popularity among Texas' music lovers was well illustrated on the day I visited this cemetery. Her gravesite actually had a line of mourners waiting to pay their respects—four years after her death.

Corsicana

Oakwood Cemetery
19th St. at Hackberry St.
N 32 05.886, W 096 28.730

Corsicana's Oakwood Cemetery is a quiet old cemetery and perhaps one of the few cemeteries that has a stream coursing through the grounds. In talking to the local citizens of Corsicana, one hears many oddities related to those buried on the grounds of Oakwood. Perhaps the most unusual "cause of death" I found in my travels around the state was that which befell Eva Speed Donohoo (1877–1929): an attacking circus elephant killed her. Local legend tells the tale that the elephant and Eva Donohoo were actually acquaintances and that she had mistreated the elephant years before. The elephant ended up in Al G. Barnes' circus, and during a parade in Corsicana, the elephant is said to have seen Donohoo in the crowd, bolted from the parade, and killed her on the spot. Maybe elephants really do not ever forget.

JOSEF ARNOST BERGMANN

Josef Arnost Bergmann (1797–1877) was born in what is now the Czech Republic. He was ordained a minister in 1830, and after nine-

GRAVESITE OF EVA SPEED DONOHOO, KILLED BY A CIRCUS ELEPHANT. OAKWOOD CEMETERY, CORSICANA.

teen years of service to his congregations he decided to move to Texas, arriving in Galveston on March 2, 1850. Bergmann and his family settled in Cat Spring, where he preached and taught school in the German community. Soon after his arrival in 1850, he had written a letter home telling of the freedom and opportunity he had found in Texas. His letter, eventually published in the *Moravian News*, was the catalyst for the immigration of Czech families in the early 1850s, and he has been called the Father of the Czechs in Texas.

BEAUFORD HALBERT JESTER

Beauford H. Jester (1893–1949) was born in Corsicana. His father was lieutenant governor of Texas for two terms (1894–1898) under Governor Charles A. Culberson. After service in World War I, Jester entered law school at the University of Texas and graduated in 1920. From 1942 to 1947 he served on the Texas Railroad Commission. Jester was a member of the University of Texas Board of Regents from 1929 to 1935, and from 1933 to 1935 he was the youngest person ever to be chairman of that board.

In 1946 Jester was elected governor, and the popular states'-rights Democrat won a second term in 1948. As governor, he presided over the longest legislative session in the state's history to that time, the Fifty-first Legislature, which met from January 11 to June 6, 1949. Jester died of a heart attack on July 11, 1949.

CLINTON MCKAMY WINKLER

Clinton M. Winkler (1821–1882) came to Texas in July 1840. He soon became involved in frontier life as an Indian fighter and was instrumental in the development of Navarro County. He was elected to the Texas Legislature in 1847 after Navarro County was created by subdividing Robertson County. He is credited with sponsorship of the legislative act that made Corsicana the county seat.

With the election of President Lincoln, Winkler was an active leader in the secession movement in the county. Winkler volunteered for Confederate service as commander of the Navarro Rifles. The Rifles became Company I, Fourth Regiment, Hood's Texas Brigade, the only unit of Texas infantry to serve in Gen. Robert E. Lee's army of northern Virginia. Captain Winkler led the company until he was severely wounded at the Battle of Gettysburg. After the Civil War, he returned to Corsicana to practice law and was elected again in the Texas Legislature in 1872. Winkler County was named in his honor.

Cottondale

Cottondale Cemetery
Behind Cottondale Baptist Church
N 33 03.886, W 097 42.287

GEORGE KELLY BARNES

George (Machine Gun) Kelly (1895–1954) became a household name across much of America in the 1930s. He was born George Kelly Barnes in Memphis, Tennessee, the son of an insurance executive.

Legend also has it that Kelly's wife, Kathryn, created "Machine Gun" Kelly. She is said to have bought Kelly his first Thompson submachine gun in a pawnshop in Fort Worth. She had him practice firing it and then passed out the spent cartridges to her relatives and friends as souvenirs from Machine Gun Kelly, a desperate criminal wanted in three states for murder, kidnapping, and bank robbery.

Machine Gun Kelly began his life of crime as a bootlegger and graduated to bank robbery. But these activities apparently did not pay well enough, and he decided to try his hand at kidnapping. The Kellys (and their accomplice Harvey Bailey) selected Charles F. Urschel, a millionaire Oklahoma oilman, and took him hostage on July 22, 1933.

Urschel was taken to a ranch near Paradise, Texas, that was owned by "Boss" Shannon and his son. But Urschel proved to be an

GANGSTER GEORGE "MACHINE GUN" KELLY BARNES WAS BURIED IN THE
COTTONDALE CEMETERY, COTTONDALE, AFTER DYING IN PRISON.

alert prisoner, noting that twice daily an airplane passed overhead. He
would then wait about five minutes and ask his captors the time. The
plane flew over each day at about 9:45 A.M. and 5:45 P.M.—except for
one day when there was a severe thunderstorm. Urschel's ransom letter arrived about four days after his kidnapping, and in it was a
demand for $200,000 in $20 bills as ransom for Urschel's safe return.
The money was delivered near the LaSalle Hotel in Kansas City on
July 30. The following night Urschel was released near Norman,
Oklahoma.

Urschel's notations of the times of the airplane flights over the
ranch where he was held apparently proved to be a key piece of information regarding the location of his captors. American Airways
records showed that on the Sunday that Urschel was held captive, a
plane on the run from Fort Worth to Amarillo had been diverted to
avoid the storm. Furthermore, the morning flight on this route passed
over Paradise, Texas, at about 9:45 A.M., and the return flight passed
the town at 5:45 P.M.

On August 12 the Shannon ranch was raided. A party of FBI agents
and Dallas and Fort Worth officers arrested Boss Shannon and several
others. About $700 of the Urschel ransom money was taken from one
of those captured. Boss Shannon admitted guarding Urschel at the
ranch but claimed that Kelly had threatened to kill him if he refused.

Machine Gun Kelly and his wife eluded police until September 26, 1933, when Memphis police officers, accompanied by FBI agents, captured them. In what was likely a masterpiece of public relations propaganda, the FBI later circulated the story that at his capture, Kelly cried, "Don't shoot, G-men!" Supposedly, Kelly coined the term as an abbreviation for "government men."

In Oklahoma City the trial of the original defendants was drawing to a close. On October 7, Boss Shannon was sentenced to life, and his son Armon got ten years' probation. Flown to Oklahoma City under heavy guard, the Kellys were expected to plead guilty but surprised everyone by doing the opposite.

On October 12 both of the Kellys were convicted and sentenced to life imprisonment. Machine Gun Kelly was sent to Leavenworth, where he remained until October 1934, when he was transferred to Alcatraz.

He was returned to Leavenworth in 1951 and died there of a heart attack on July 18, 1954. Robert "Boss" Shannon had been pardoned by President Roosevelt in 1944, owing to ill health. When Boss Shannon heard of Kelly's death, he said he had two lots in the Cottondale Cemetery and that "they can use one if they want to." Ironically, the funeral services for Kelly typified his final move to obscurity. His name was misspelled on his grave marker. The original marker was stolen, and a small metal marker was put in its place.

Machine Gun Kelly is buried just a few steps away from Boss Shannon. Kelly's marker is inconspicuous—a flat marker—making it a bit hard to find. To locate that site, start at the marker of Boss Shannon and walk back due west to the concrete lane. Follow this lane to the center concrete lane that is to the left as you face west. Kelly's small marker is at the intersection of these two lanes.

Cuero

Hillside Cemetery
N. Valley St. at E. Prairie St.
N 29 05.666, W 097 16.867

Hillside Cemetery (much like Fairview Cemetery in Bastrop) is perfectly named. This large graveyard lies on a hillside that gently slopes up and away from Valley Street. It is easy to find, lying just west of the city water tower. The cemetery is replete with German surnames and is arranged and maintained in characteristic German fashion. It is perfectly laid out, and many, if not most, of the gravesites and plots at the lowest levels of the cemetery are covered in concrete and gravel. In its basic design and style of headstones and grave markers, it is reminiscent of the Fredericksburg City Cemetery. There must be a golf course nearby, because golf carts sporting clubs and rayon-clad operators putt along the cemetery roads.

Hillside Cemetery has an interesting assortment of trees. Catalpas, mimosas, mature junipers, and cedars are spread throughout the cemetery. It also appears to be home to a multitudinous flock of Inca doves, each calling *no hope* as if voicing their resignation to those who reside here permanently or predicting the fortunes of the itinerant golfers.

HENRY CLAY PLEASANTS

Cuero experienced a period of lawlessness during the Reconstruction period that was typified by a family feud. The Taylor-Sutton Feud (or Sutton-Taylor, depending on whose side you took) raged in and around Cuero for years in the 1870s and involved a series of murders and hangings that plagued both the town and DeWitt County.

The feud intermittently smoldered and burst into flame until district judge Henry Clay Pleasants (1828–1899) secured law enforcement from the Texas Rangers. Holding court with a shotgun across his lap, Pleasants presided over a series of trials that eventually brought the years-long feud to its conclusion. Judge Pleasants, who is given the lion's share of credit in bringing about the end to the feud, lies in Hillside Cemetery. His grave is in the central part of the cemetery and is marked by a state historical marker.

Dallas

Calvary Hill Cemetery
3235 Lombardy Ln.
N 32 52.039, W 096 52.215

THOMAS ELMER BRANIFF

Born in Salina, Kansas, Tom Braniff (1883–1954) began a career in his father's insurance business but soon struck out on his own. An astute businessman, Braniff built his company into one of the leading mortgage and insurance businesses in the Southwest. In 1928, Braniff and his brother Paul began operating an airline between Oklahoma City and Tulsa, which would become Braniff Airways. Moving his

THE GRAVESITE OF CONRAD HILTON, CALVARY HILLS CEMETERY, DALLAS, SEEMS TO BECKON PASSERSBY TO A GOOD NIGHT'S SLEEP.

operations to Dallas' Love Field in 1942, Tom Braniff built his airline into one of the premier air carriers in the country. Known for his generosity and philanthropy, Braniff was often honored for his contributions to education, science, and religion. He was killed in a private plane crash on January 10, 1954.

ADELAIDA CUELLAR

Adelaida Cuellar (1871–1969), founder of the El Chico restaurant chain, was born near Matehuala, Nuevo León, Mexico. Along with her family, Mrs. Cuellar eventually came to Texas and settled in Kaufman. In 1926, with twelve children to support, Mrs. Cuellar decided to supplement the family income by selling homemade tamales at the Kaufman County Fair. The success of this small tamale stand led to a series of restaurant ventures and to formation of the successful El Chico Corporation.

CONRAD HILTON

Born in New Mexico, Conrad Hilton (1887–1979) became one of America's premier hoteliers. He served as chairman of the Hilton Hotels Corporation and of Hilton International Company. In all,

Hilton eventually owned 188 hotels in 38 U.S. cities and 54 hotels abroad. He left the bulk of his estate, estimated at a half billion dollars, to charity through his Los Angeles–based Conrad N. Hilton Foundation. His headstone in Calvary Hills looks exactly like the polished stone entrance of a Hilton Hotel. You have to love a man who never abandons an effective advertising campaign.

FAUSTINA MARTINEZ

Faustina Martinez (1900–1990) was born in Chihuahua, Mexico, and her family moved to Dallas in 1914 during the Mexican Revolution. In 1915 she married, and by 1918 she had saved enough money to open the Martinez Restaurant in Dallas. This small restaurant was the seed of the El Fenix restaurant chain, and by 1990 the Martinez family operated restaurants throughout North Texas and Oklahoma.

Crown Hill Memorial Park
9700 Webb Chapel Rd.
N 32 51.942, W 096 51.806

BONNIE PARKER

Bonnie Parker (1910–1934) was born in Rowena, Texas, and moved to West Dallas as a child. Bonnie was a tiny woman, only four feet ten

GRAVESITE OF BONNIE PARKER, CROWN HILL MEMORIAL PARK, DALLAS.

inches tall and weighing eighty–five pounds, and had been an honor student in school. She met Clyde Barrow in January 1930, and by 1932 she had joined him in a life of crime. But their crime spree ended abruptly in Louisiana, on May 23, 1934.

A group of lawmen, led by former Texas Ranger Frank Hamer, ambushed and killed the duo. Bonnie Parker was initially buried in the Fish Trap Cemetery in Dallas, but after her gravestone was repeatedly stolen, her remains were moved to Crown Hill Memorial Park. Anyone who stumbled across her gravestone would be surprised at her criminal past, for her epitaph reads:

AS THE FLOWERS ARE ALL MADE SWEETER BY THE SUNSHINE AND THE DEW, SO THIS OLD WORLD IS MADE BRIGHTER BY THE LIVES OF FOLKS LIKE YOU.

Greenwood Cemetery

3020 Oak Grove Ave.
N 32 48.095, W 096 48.024

Greenwood Cemetery is one of Dallas' oldest cemeteries, and it has the historic feel that one finds in other cemeteries of its vintage. Greenwood has several interesting features, including large separate sites dedicated to both Union soldiers and Confederate soldiers. The trees in this old cemetery are mature and lovely. The cemetery office at Greenwood is just inside the main gate, and there is a full-time employee on-site. I found him to be very helpful in locating gravesites and in exploring the history of the cemetery. Do not visit Greenwood on a rainy day. The cemetery drains poorly and was largely afloat on a cold, rainy November morning.

JACOB BOLL

Jacob Boll (1828–1880) was one of America's finest naturalists. Although noted as an entomologist, between 1877 and 1880, he found thirty-two new, rare species of Permian vertebrates. Simultaneously he made an extensive collection of tiny butterflies and moths, as well as collections of Texas reptiles and fish.

JOHN A. SEEGAR

In the years before the name "Doc Holliday" became synonymous with the gunfight at the O.K. Corral, Holliday had been a practicing dentist. As a result of his active tuberculosis, he was advised to move to a drier climate. In 1875 he arrived in Dallas and found a position in the dental office of John Seegar (1831–1891). But Holliday's disease prevented him from continuing the practice of dentistry, and he turned to gambling as a livelihood. The rest, as they say, is history.

WILLIAM STEWART SIMKINS

It is quite possible that sixteen-year-old Pvt. William Stewart Simkins (1842–1929) fired the first shot of the Civil War. While serving under Gen. J. E. Jackson, he heard the federal gunboat *Star of the West* as it slipped into the harbor at Fort Sumter, South Carolina, in April 1861. Simkins immediately awakened his comrades and fired the first shot. He later became a professor of law at the University of Texas, from 1899 to 1929.

CHRISTOPHER COLUMBUS SLAUGHTER

Christopher Slaughter (1837–1919) was, along with other members of his family, one of the great cattlemen of Texas. Known as the "Cattle King of Texas," he at one time controlled more than a million acres of ranchland and held more than forty thousand head of cattle. He was founder of the Texas and Southwest Cattle Raisers Association, a founder of Baylor Hospital, and president of the United Confederate Veterans.

FRANCINA ALICE WRIGHT

Francina Wright (1850–1935) was the first female postmistress of Birdville, Texas (now Haltom City), and as a result of that appointment was the first postmistress in the United States.

Grove Hill Memorial Park
4118 Samuell Blvd.
N 32 47.530, W 096 39.518

TURNEY W. LEONARD

While serving as a weapons platoon commander near Kommerscheidt, Germany (November 4–6, 1944), 1st Lt. Turney Leonard (1921–1944) repeatedly braved overwhelming enemy fire in advance of his platoon in order to direct fire of his tank destroyer from exposed, dismounted positions. For his gallantry, he was awarded the Congressional Medal of Honor.

The Von Erich Family

The Von Erichs were among the most celebrated—and tragic— families of athletes in Texas. The father and his sons were a mainstay in the professional wrestling arena for decades. The patriarch, Fritz Von Erich (1929–1997; real name, Jack Adkisson), was an outstanding track athlete and received scholarship offers to Southern Methodist University in both track and music. He became an outstanding football player and played professionally for the American Football League's Dallas Texans. As his football career wound down, he considered his next career move and looked to professional wrestling.

After World War II, Adkisson came up with the idea of provoking wrestling fans into a frenzy by adopting a goose-stepping Nazi persona. He adopted the name Fritz Von Erich and immediately became one of the most successful—and disliked—wrestlers in the sport. During the decade of the 1950s, Fritz Von Erich became a wrestling icon.

After a dispute with the National Wrestling Association, Von Erich established World Class Championship Wrestling. He did not have to search far for talent, and his sons became wrestling luminaries—and tragedies—in their own right. Von Erich was the father of six boys. The oldest son, Jack, was killed at age seven when he came in contact with an electric fence on the family farm. David Von Erich (1958–1984), the most talented wrestler among the sons, died while touring in Japan from an acute inflammation of the intestines. The next year, Mike Von Erich (1964–1987) almost died after suffering from a toxic shock syndrome accident. Mike survived the illness, but his reprieve from death would be short, for he died from an overdose of tranquilizers on April 11, 1987.

Four years later, Chris (1969–1991), the smallest of the Von Erich boys, grew despondent over his chronic illnesses and lack of wrestling success. Chris committed suicide on the family's farm. Finally, Kerry Von Erich (1960–1993), handsome and destined for success in the ring, suffered a serious motorcycle accident that required amputation of his foot. Although he successfully wrestled for a number of years with a prosthetic foot, he had become dependent on painkillers. Facing a possible prison term for possession of narcotics and for forging a prescription, Kerry committed suicide on the family ranch on February 18, 1993. Fritz Von Erich and his wife divorced shortly after Kerry's death, and Von Erich himself died of brain cancer in 1997.

DALLAS POLICE OFFICER J. D. TIPPIT WAS THE SECOND VICTIM OF PRESIDENTIAL
ASSASSIN LEE HARVEY OSWALD. LAUREL LAND MEMORIAL PARK, DALLAS.

Laurel Land Memorial Park
6000 S. R. L. Thornton Freeway (I-35E)
N 32 40.500, W 096 49.163

J. D. TIPPIT

J. D. Tippit (1924–1963) joined the Dallas Police Department as a
patrolman in 1952. On November 22, 1963, he stopped a suspicious-
looking man walking down an Oak Cliff street. As Tippit approached
the man for questioning, Lee Harvey Oswald, the alleged assassin of
President John F. Kennedy, shot and killed the officer.

STEVIE RAY VAUGHAN

Stevie Ray Vaughan (1954–1990) was born in the Oak Cliff section of
Dallas. Vaughn grew interested in playing guitar after watching his
older brother, Jimmie, and was soon playing in Dallas nightclubs. In
1971 Stevie Ray Vaughn moved to Austin, where he played in obscu-
rity until the late 1970s when he formed the group Double Trouble.
Over the next few years, the band's following grew, and in 1983 he
released his debut album, *Texas Flood*. This album received the North
American Rock Radio Awards nomination for Favorite Debut
Album, and *Guitar Player Magazine*'s Reader's Poll voted him Best
New Talent and Best Electric Blues Guitarist for 1983. Stevie Ray

Vaughn had already established his place as a blues guitar legend and had won several Grammy Awards when he was killed in a helicopter crash in 1990.

Sparkman-Hillcrest Memorial Park
7403 Northwest Parkway
N 32 51.943, W 096 46.897

MAUREEN CATHERINE CONNOLLY BRINKER

Maureen (Little Mo) Catherine Connolly Brinker (1934–1969) was the dominant women's tennis player in the world from 1951 to 1954. In 1953 she became the first woman to win the grand slam of tennis, with victories at the national championship tournaments of Australia, France, Great Britain, and the United States. She was the Associated Press Female Athlete of the Year in 1952, 1953, and 1954.

GRACE NOLL CROWELL

Grace Crowell (1877–1969) published more than thirty-five books of poetry, stories for children, and poem and prose devotions. Her *Songs for Courage* went into twenty-five printings. In 1935 she was designated Poet Laureate of Texas.

SARAH T. HUGHES

Sarah T. Hughes (1896–1985) received her law degree in 1922 from the George Washington University Law School. That same year she moved to Dallas with her husband and practiced law until 1935, when Governor James Allred appointed her to the bench of the Fourteenth District Court in Dallas. She was the first woman to become a state district judge in Texas. In 1936 she was elected in her own right and was reelected on six subsequent occasions, the last in 1960. When President John F. Kennedy appointed her to the federal judgeship of the Northern District of Texas in October 1961, she became the first woman to serve as a federal district judge in Texas.

Although Judge Hughes was well respected in her judicial capacity, she became a national figure as a result of the assassination of John F. Kennedy in Dallas on November 22, 1963. Judge Hughes administered the oath of office to Lyndon Johnson aboard *Air Force One* at Love Field. The image of Judge Hughes, her back to the camera, administering the oath to the vice president as Mrs. Kennedy looked on, remains as one of the most powerful images of the twentieth century.

NEEL E. KEARBY

Neel Kearby (1911–1944) was commander of the 348th Fighter Group, Fifth Fighter Command of the U.S. Army Air Corps. Kearby was killed in combat on October 11, 1943, while in action over Wewak, New Guinea. For his sacrifice to his country, he was awarded the Congressional Medal of Honor.

FREDDIE KING

Freddie King (1934–1976) was born in Gilmer and began playing guitar with his mother and an uncle, Leon King. He moved to Chicago when he was sixteen and quickly absorbed the styles of the musicians around him there, including Lightnin' Hopkins, T-Bone Walker, and B. B. King. His recording career began in the 1950s, and over the years he recorded with many of the great blues legends. He toured with Eric Clapton and recorded the first major live album made at the Armadillo World Headquarters in Austin.

TOM LANDRY

Tom Landry (1924–2000) began coaching football after a five-year stint as a defensive back and punter with the New York Giants of the National Football League (1949–1955). He served with the Giants as an assistant coach and was given the head coaching job of the expansion Dallas Cowboys in 1960. The team went 0-13-1 in its first year, but by the end of the decade, Landry had laid the foundation of a football dynasty.

Tom Landry's innovations included his perfection of the flex defense, multiple offense schemes, and the revival of the spread, or "shotgun," offense. His twenty-nine-year tenure with one team tied the NFL record, and his career winning record was 270-178-6. Under Landry's leadership the Cowboys enjoyed twenty straight winning seasons, five NFC titles, and two Super Bowl wins.

MICKEY CHARLES MANTLE

Mickey Mantle (1931–1995) was born to play baseball. Named after Baseball Hall of Fame catcher Mickey Cochrane, Mantle starred in both baseball and football in high school. He began his professional baseball career as a shortstop for the New York Yankee farm team at Independence, Kansas, and during spring training in 1951 he so impressed Yankee manager Casey Stengel that Mantle opened the season as New York's right fielder.

GRAVESITE OF GOVERNOR W. LEE "PAPPY" O'DANIEL, SPARKMAN-HILLCREST
MEMORIAL PARK, DALLAS.

For all of those who grew up in the 1950s, Mickey Mantle was a
cultural icon. Handsome and unpretentious, he represented the all-
American boy. He was a tremendously gifted athlete and played center
field on perhaps the most dominant sports team in history. He was
elected to the Baseball Hall of Fame in 1974, his first year of eligibility.

WILBERT LEE O'DANIEL

Wilbert L. (Pappy) O'Daniel (1890–1969) represented the colorful
Texas political climate of the 1930s perhaps better than any other
Texan. In 1925 he moved to Fort Worth, where he became sales man-
ager of the Burrus Mills. He took over the company's radio advertis-
ing in 1928 and began writing songs and discussing religion on the air.
He hired a group of musicians and called them the Light Crust
Doughboys, and as a result of his radio presence, O'Daniel developed
a huge following in Depression-era Texas.

In 1938 he decided to run for governor and stumped the state on a
platform of flour, pensions, tax cuts, and the Bible. He ran again in
1940 and was reelected. While in office, O'Daniel was not a particularly successful leader, but he remained the consummate showman.

In 1941 O'Daniel ran for the U.S. Senate, defeating young Congressman Lyndon Johnson in an election that Johnson felt was stolen. As in his service as governor, O'Daniel was an ineffective senator and chose not to run again in 1948. He made unsuccessful attempts to regain the office of the governor of Texas in 1956 and 1958.

ELLA CARUTHERS PORTER

Ella C. Porter (1862–1939) pioneered child welfare issues in Texas. She had her first child when she was seventeen and maintained in her later years that a lack of preparation for motherhood was a driving force in her lifelong commitment to childcare issues. In 1909 she organized the Texas Congress of Mothers (now the Texas Congress of Mothers and Parent-Teacher Associations) and was elected its first president. The next year, she organized the first child welfare conference ever held in Texas. She was instrumental in persuading the Texas Legislature to form a state child welfare commission. Ella Porter devoted her entire life to issues related to the welfare of women and children in Texas.

JOHN GOODWIN TOWER

John Tower (1925–1991) was born on September 29, 1925, in Houston. In 1960 he challenged incumbent Senator Lyndon B. Johnson and was handily defeated. But Johnson was elected vice president in the election, and Tower was elected to the U.S. Senate in a special election. In his twenty-four years as a senator, Tower rose to positions of power on many of the most prestigious committees in that body, including service as chairman of the Senate Armed Services Committee. Tower retired from the Senate on January 3, 1985, and was appointed by President Ronald Reagan as chief U.S. negotiator at the Strategic Arms Reduction Talks in Geneva. Senator Tower and his daughter died in a commuter plane crash near New Brunswick, Georgia, on April 5, 1991.

EDITH EUNICE THERREL WILMANS

Edith E. T. Wilmans (1882–1966) was the first woman elected to the Texas Legislature. In 1914 she became active in the world of politics when she helped organize the Dallas Equal Suffrage Association. To improve her knowledge of women's issues, she studied law and was admitted to the State Bar of Texas in 1918. In 1922 she was elected to the Thirty-eighth Texas Legislature.

Restland Memorial Park
Valley View Ln. at Greenville Ave.
N 32 55.51, W 096 44.25

WILLIAM MADISON BELL

One of the most successful coaches in Southwest Conference history, William (Matty) Bell (1899–1983) coached five schools to winning records during his twenty-six-year career. Bell took up coaching at Haskell Institute in Kansas in 1920, planning to save money so he could go to law school. After two seasons there and one at Carroll College, he became head coach at Texas Christian in 1923. His teams won 33 games, lost 17, and tied 5 in six seasons. Bell coached at Texas A&M (1929–1933) and took the head coaching position at Southern Methodist in 1935 after a year out of football. His first team won all 12 of its regular season games before losing to Stanford, 7–0, in the Rose Bowl.

After naval service (1942–1944), Bell returned to SMU in 1945. Led by All-American Doak Walker, the school won 9 games and tied 1 in 1947 and had an 8-1-1 record in 1948. In two Cotton Bowl appearances, SMU tied Penn State, 13–13, and beat Oregon, 21–13. Bell retired from coaching after the 1949 season and served as SMU's athletic director until 1964. His overall coaching record was 154-87-17, including an 88-39-7 mark at SMU. He was president of the American Football Coaches Association in 1943–1944 and was inducted into the National Football Hall of Fame in 1955 and the Texas Sports Hall of Fame in 1960.

RUSSELL A. STEINDAM

Russell A. Steindam (1946–1970) was born in Austin and graduated from the University of Texas at Austin. First Lieutenant Steindam was a member of the Fourth Cavalry, Twenty-fifth Infantry Division, U.S. Army, in Tay Ninh Province, Vietnam, in action against enemy forces on February 1, 1970. While on a night ambush, his platoon came under heavy enemy fire. During the fight a fragmentation grenade was thrown into the site occupied by his command group. He immediately threw himself on the grenade and absorbed its full force, saving the lives of his comrades. For his gallantry, Lieutenant Steindam was awarded the Congressional Medal of Honor.

Western Heights Cemetery
1617 Fort Worth Ave.
N 32 45.891, W 096 50.724

THE BARROW GANG

Clyde Barrow (1909–1934) and Bonnie Parker (1910–1934) both grew up in and around Dallas. In the early months of 1932, "Bonnie and Clyde" began a string of murders and robberies that would engage national attention for two years. Like many gangsters of the 1930s, Clyde Barrow tended to operate on a "circuit" that led the gang throughout Kansas, Missouri, Texas, Oklahoma, New Mexico, Iowa, Illinois, and Arkansas. In late 1933 the Barrow Gang, including Marvin (Buck) Barrow (1905–1933), stopped in Platte City, Missouri. In a battle with police, Buck Barrow was mortally wounded. His body was returned to Dallas and buried in Western Heights Cemetery.

Returning to Texas in January 1934, Parker and Clyde Barrow aided Raymond Hamilton (1914–1935) in his escape from Eastham Prison Farm. During the escape a guard was killed and Texas governor James Ferguson apparently decided it was time to seek the services of one of Texas' most revered—and tough—lawmen, retired Texas Ranger captain Frank Hamer (1884–1955). Clearly, Governor Ferguson wanted something done, and Hamer was not a man to be denied.

CLYDE BARROW, OUTLAW PARTNER OF BONNIE PARKER, IS BURIED BESIDE HIS BROTHER MARVIN IN WESTERN HEIGHTS CEMETERY, DALLAS.

ACTIVIST KAREN SILKWOOD WAS THE SUBJECT OF THE 1983 MOVIE *SILKWOOD*. DANVILLE CEMETERY, DANVILLE.

On May 23, 1934, Bonnie and Clyde drove into a carefully laid trap set by the tenacious Frank Hamer. Hidden in the underbrush alongside a Louisiana back road, Hamer patiently waited with Robert Alcorn (1897–1964), Ted Hinton (1904–1977), and three other law officers. As the duo drifted to a stop, the lawmen opened fire.

Clyde Barrow was buried next to his brother Marvin in Western Heights Cemetery, Dallas. Frank Hamer retired to Austin, Texas, and his modest gravesite is in Austin Memorial Park. The simple gravesite of Bonnie Parker is in Crown Hill Memorial Park, Dallas. Raymond Hamilton died in 1935 and was buried in Elmwood Memorial Park, Dallas. Two of Hamer's fellow law officers from the ambush are also buried in Dallas: Bob Alcorn was laid to rest in Grove Hill Memorial Park, and Ted Hinton is buried in Sparkman-Hillcrest Memorial Park.

Danville

Danville Cemetery
Utzman Rd., west of intersection with FM 2276
N 32 23.808, W 094 48.649

KAREN GAY SILKWOOD

Union activist for the Oil, Chemical and Atomic Workers Union, Karen Silkwood (1946–1974) became the first female member of the union bargaining committee in the history of Kerr-McGee Corporation. She discovered evidence of missing plutonium at the Kerr-McGee plant in Oklahoma City and later testified before the Atomic Energy Commission regarding the radiation exposure she had experienced while an employee of the company. Silkwood was killed in an auto accident while on her way to meet with an AEC official and a newspaper reporter in November 1974. She was the subject of a motion picture entitled *Silkwood* that was released in 1983.

De Kalb

Woodman Cemetery
Highway 82, southeast of De Kalb
N 33 30.441, W 094 36.461

DAN BLOCKER

Dan Blocker (1928–1972) was the Texas-born actor who created the warm-hearted character Eric Haas (better known to fans as "Hoss"), the second of Ben Cartwright's three sons on NBC's hit *Bonanza*. A talented and intelligent actor, Blocker studied speech and drama while attending college at Hardin-Simmons University and Sul Ross State Teachers College. With a master of arts degree from Sul Ross, Blocker taught school in Sonora, Texas. Intending to work on a Ph.D. at UCLA, Blocker moved his family to California. It was while working as a substitute teacher in Glendale that he started acting in Hollywood. He landed the role of Hoss Cartwright in 1959, a part he played for thirteen seasons.

Del Rio

Whitehead Museum
1308 S. Main St.
N 29 21.121, W 100 53.894

ROY BEAN

Roy Bean (ca. 1825–1903) is one of the true legends of the Old West. Duels, quick exits, and a narrow escape from hanging marked his early years. He eventually drifted to San Antonio, where he set up business in an area of town that became known as Beanville as a result of his skill at dodging creditors, the law, and rival businessmen. In 1882 Roy Bean headed west and arrived at Vinegarroon, just west of the Pecos. The area was so lawless that the Texas Rangers were summoned to provide law enforcement in an area of which it was said, "West of the Pecos there is no law; west of El Paso, there is no God." Needing a local justice of the peace in order to eliminate the four-hundred-mile round-trip to the county seat at Fort Stockton, the Pecos County commissioners appointed Roy Bean to the position on August 2, 1882. He retained the post, with two short interruptions, until he retired voluntarily in 1902.

Bean's interpretation of frontier justice became part of the enduring folklore of the Old West. "Hanging Judge Roy Bean" held court sessions in his saloon along the Rio Grande. According to the myth, Roy Bean named his saloon (the Jersey Lilly) and town after the love of his life, Lillie Langtry, a British actress he'd never met. Calling himself the "Law West of the Pecos," he is reputed to have sentenced dozens to the gallows, saying, "Hang 'em first; try 'em later." In legend, Judge Roy Bean is a merciless dispenser of justice, and although Bean threatened to hang hundreds, there is no evidence that any of these sentences were ever carried out.

Judge Roy Bean became famous, however, as the result of a prizefight. In 1898, prizefighting had become illegal in most western states, as it was in Mexico. Promoters could not find a venue to hold the world championship title bout between Bob Fitzsimmons and Peter Maher. Bean had a novel solution. On February 22, Bean's saloon was packed with two hundred fight fans who, after a few rounds of drinks, followed Roy to a bridge he had built to a sandbar in the Rio Grande. While Texas Rangers watched the ring helplessly from atop the bluff, Fitzsimmons defeated Maher in only ninety-five seconds. The resulting newspaper stories began the myth of Roy Bean, and Bean himself contributed by fabricating stories for the dime novels that were prevalent in the era.

Eagle Lake

Lakeside Cemetery
Ranch Road 102, south of Eagle Lake
N 29 34.498, W 096 20.053

JOHNNIE DAVID HUTCHINS

Johnnie D. Hutchins (1922–1943) was born in Weimar and enlisted in the U.S. Navy in 1942. He was on board a landing ship during a landing assault on Lae, New Guinea, on September 4, 1943. During the attack, the landing craft helmsman had been dislodged by a bomb blast, and Hutchins was mortally wounded. As the torpedo bore down on this ship, Hutchins grasped the wheel and with his last strength maneuvered the vessel clear. Hutchins died while still clinging to the helm of his ship. A destroyer escort vessel, the USS *Johnnie Hutchins*, was launched in May 1944, and for his service and sacrifice, Johnnie David Hutchins was awarded the Congressional Medal of Honor.

Edinburg

Hillcrest Cemetery
Highway 281 at E. Schunior St.
N 26 18.414, W 098 08.513

ALFREDO CANTU GONZALEZ

Alfredo (Freddy) Cantu Gonzalez (1946–1968) holds the rare distinction of having twice been awarded the Congressional Medal of Honor. Born in Edinburg, he enlisted in the U.S. Marine Corps Reserve at San Antonio on June 3, 1965, under his mother's name, Gonzalez. He enlisted in the regular Marines on July 6, 1965, and then served a year as rifleman and squad leader with Company L, Third Battalion, Fourth Marines, Third Marine Division, in Vietnam. Gonzalez returned to the United States in January 1967 and served as rifleman with the Second Battalion, Sixth Marines, Second Marine Division, at Camp Lejeune, North Carolina.

On July 1, 1967, he returned to duty in Vietnam to serve his second tour of duty as a Marine and saw action against the Viet Cong near Thua Thein. On January 31, 1968, his unit was moving to relieve the city of Hue when the truck convoy transporting the soldiers came under heavy enemy fire. Gonzalez aggressively maneuvered his troops and directed their fire until the area was clear of snipers. A Marine on top of a tank was wounded and fell to the ground. Gonzalez ran though heavy fire and, although he too was wounded, rescued his comrade. On February 3 he was wounded again but refused medical treatment. The next day the enemy pinned his company down, inflicting heavy casualties with automatic weapons and rocket fire. Sergeant Gonzalez, using light antitank weapons, moved from place to place, successfully knocked out a rocket position, and suppressed much of the enemy fire before falling mortally wounded. Gonzalez was the only person at the Battle of Hue

City to be granted the Medal of Honor, which he was posthumously awarded in 1969. In May 2001, Gonzalez was awarded a second Congressional Medal of Honor.

In addition to the two Medals of Honor, Gonzalez was awarded the Purple Heart, the Presidential Unit Citation, the National Defense Service Medal, the Vietnamese Cross of Gallantry with Star, the Vietnamese Cross of Gallantry with Palm, the Military Merit Medal, and the Republic of Vietnam Campaign Medal. The Freddy Gonzalez Elementary School was named in his honor, as was the missile launcher *USS Alfredo Gonzalez*, the first ship named for a Hispanic Texan military man.

El Paso

Concordia Cemetery
E. Yandell at N. Boone St.
N 31 46.875, W 106 26.807

JOHN WESLEY HARDIN

John Wesley Hardin (1853–1895) was born May 26, 1853, in Bonham, and before his death was probably the most notorious gunman ever to live within the borders of Texas. Ironically, he was the son of James Hardin, a Methodist preacher, and was named after John Wesley, who founded the Methodist Church. Hardin's sociopathic tendencies surfaced at age fourteen when he stabbed a schoolmate. At age fifteen, he shot a man to death in Polk County, and while fleeing from the law following that murder, he killed at least one, and possibly four, Union soldiers who were attempting to apprehend him.

While herding cattle on the Chisholm Trail in 1871, Hardin killed seven people, and three more upon arriving in Abilene, Kansas. Back in Texas, following a run-in with the State Police in Gonzales County, Hardin married, settled down, and had three children. But he soon resumed his murder spree, killing four more times before surrendering to the Cherokee County sheriff in September 1872. He escaped jail after a couple of weeks, however. Hardin next killed Jack Helm, a former State Police captain, who had led the fight against the anti-Reconstructionist forces of Jim Taylor in the Sutton-Taylor feud.

In May 1874, Hardin killed Brown County deputy sheriff Charles Webb in Comanche. Fleeing to Florida with his family, Hardin was captured by Texas Rangers in Pensacola on July 23, 1877. During that flight, he killed at least one, and perhaps as many as five, more

NOTORIOUS GUNMAN JOHN WESLEY HARDIN DIED AS HE LIVED, BY THE GUN. CONCORDIA CEMETERY, EL PASO. PHOTO COURTESY OF DAVID LOTZ, COPYRIGHT © 2001.

victims. Brought back to Texas for trial by Texas Ranger John Barclay Armstrong, Hardin was sentenced to twenty-five years for the Brown County deputy's murder.

Having studied law while in prison, Hardin was admitted to the Texas bar soon after his release from prison on March 16, 1894. In 1895 he went to El Paso to testify for the defense in a murder trial, and following the trial, he stayed and established a law practice. Clearly a man who could not avoid trouble, Hardin began an affair with one of his married female clients. Her husband apparently discovered his wife's infidelity, and Hardin hired law officials to kill him. One of the hired gunmen, however, Constable John Selman, shot Hardin instead. Legend has it that his last words were, "Four sixes to beat, Henry."

Evergreen Cemetery
N. Boone at I-20
N 31 46.393, W 106 26.428

ALBERT BACON FALL

During the administration of Warren G. Harding, Albert Fall (1861–1944) served as secretary of the interior (1921–1923) and was a central figure in the Teapot Dome scandal that rocked the Warren G. Harding administration. In 1921, Fall persuaded Harding and Secretary of the Navy Edwin Denby to transfer control of three naval oil reserves from the Navy Department to the Department of the Interior. The reserves were in Teapot Dome, Wyoming, and Elk Hills, California. In 1922, Fall leased the reserves in Teapot Dome to oilman Harry F. Sinclair and those in Elk Hills to oilman Edward L. Doheny—without competitive bidding. Fall then resigned in 1923 and joined Sinclair's company. In 1924 a Senate investigation revealed that Fall had accepted a $100,000 "loan" from Doheny and more than $300,000 in other assets from Sinclair for helping secure the leases. Fall was convicted in 1929 of accepting a bribe for leasing government-owned oil reserves at Teapot Dome to private companies and was sentenced to a year in prison in 1931.

ESTHER NIETO MACHUCA

Esther Nieto Machuca (1895–1980) was born in Ojinaga, Chihuahua, Mexico. Both Esther and her husband, Juan, were prominent national leaders in the League of United Latin American Citizens (LULAC). In the years 1934–1937, Esther Machuca played an important leadership role in organizing women's LULAC chapters in El Paso. In 1938 she served as the official hostess for the LULAC national convention in El Paso. After LULAC president general Filemon T. Martínez took office at that convention, he appointed Esther Machuca as ladies' organizer general. This office first existed in 1934–1935, but it was Machuca's tenure in that office in 1938–1939 that made Ladies LULAC a national entity. She helped establish Ladies LULAC chapters in Las Vegas, New Mexico, and in Dallas. She devoted her life to LULAC and to the improvement of life for Latin American women.

Fort Bliss National Cemetery
5200 Fred Wilson Rd.
N 31 49.578, W 106 25.572

AMBROSIO GUILLEN

Staff Sergeant Ambrosio Guillen (?–1953) was a member of Company F, Second Battalion, Seventh Marines, First Marine Division, near Songuch-on, Korea, on July 25, 1953, when he and his platoon were participating in the defense of an outpost forward of the main line of resistance. When two battalions of enemy forces attacked, he exposed himself to heavy mortar and artillery fire in order to direct his men and direct the care and evacuation of wounded Marines. Guillen was seriously wounded during the battle but refused medical treatment and continued to direct his men until the enemy was defeated. He succumbed to his wounds a few hours later. For his service and valor, he was awarded the Congressional Medal of Honor.

SAMUEL LYMAN ATWOOD MARSHALL

Samuel Lyman Atwood (Slam) Marshall (1900–1977) was born in Catskill, New York, and his family came to Texas when he was fifteen. He enlisted in the Army and served in France during World War I. In 1922 he began his journalism career with the *El Paso Herald*, serving as reporter, sports editor, and city editor of the paper until 1927, when he joined the staff of the *Detroit News*. Over the course of his life, he would become an influential writer of military history. In his long career as a military commentator, Marshall wrote more than thirty books, dozens of journal articles, and innumerable newspaper, radio, and television pieces.

BENITO MARTINEZ

Benito Martinez (1932–1952) was born at Fort Hancock and entered military service there. Corporal Martinez was a machine gunner with the Twenty-fifth Infantry Division, near Satae-ri, Korea. On the night of September 6, 1952, enemy forces attacked his position. Despite the danger of his capture, he remained at his post and attempted to slow the enemy advance. Martinez remained in contact with his unit but told them that his situation was too dangerous to attempt his rescue. When he later withdrew, armed only with an automatic rifle and a handgun, he defended himself for six hours. Shortly before dawn, he stated that the enemy was closing in. That was the last contact with Martinez; during the night he was killed. His Medal of Honor was awarded posthumously to his mother by the secretary of the Army at the Pentagon in Washington.

Ennis

Myrtle Cemetery
W. Knox St. at Glasscock St.
N 32 19.455, W 096 38.439

KATIE LITTY DAFFAN

Katie Litty (Miss Katie) Daffan (1874–1951) was born in Brenham and attended public schools in Denison and Corsicana. She graduated

First Lieutenant Jack Lummus was one of two Texans awarded the Congressional Medal of Honor for their service on Iwo Jima. Myrtle Cemetery, Ennis.

from Hollins Institute in Virginia and was a history student at the University of Texas and the University of Chicago. Daffan taught elementary and high school and was first vice president of the Texas Teachers Association.

In 1911 Daffan was named to the position of superintendent of the Confederate Woman's Home in Austin and became the first woman in Texas to be appointed to head a state institution. She was the author of several books, including *Texas Heroes* (1924), a volume that was adopted as a Texas textbook. Her interest and lifelong pursuit of history led her to numerous positions of leadership within the Texas Division of the United Daughters of the Confederacy and the Texas Woman's Press Association (1908–1909); as state historian of the Daughters of the American Revolution (1909–1910); and as first vice president of the Texas State Historical Association (1912–1914). The Katie Daffan Chapter of the United Daughters of the Confederacy at Denton was named in her honor.

Jack Lummus

Jack Lummus (1915–1945) received the Congressional Medal of Honor for his gallantry in action on Iwo Jima. Born in Ellis County, and a graduate of Baylor University, he had played minor league baseball in Texas and professional football with the New York Giants.

On March 8, 1945, after having fought without rest for two days and nights, he was leading a rifle platoon attached to the Second Battalion, Twenty-seventh Marines, Fifth Marine Division. Advancing into the face of a concentration of hostile fire, Lummus was stunned by a grenade explosion. Recovering, he moved forward and single-handedly attacked and destroyed the occupied emplacement.

Under fire from a supporting enemy position, Lummus was struck by the impact of a second grenade and sustained shoulder wounds. Disregarding his injuries, he continued his one-man assault and charged another fortification, killing all the occupants. He then returned to his platoon position and encouraged his men to advance. While moving forward under fire, he rushed a third fortified installation and killed its defending troops. Jack Lummus was fatally injured when he triggered a land mine.

Fort Davis

Pioneer Cemetery
Highway 118 in Fort Davis
N 30 34.588, W 103 53.220

The Pioneer Cemetery was established in the early 1870s and was in use until 1914. This old cemetery is located just off Highway 118, south of Fort Davis, and is the resting place of many Jeff Davis County settlers. The cemetery entrance is at the end of a long sidewalk that is narrow and fenced along both sides. Small cottonwood trees, golden in fall, overhang the walk. The cemetery itself is in very poor condition. Many of the headstones are broken, and many more graves are unmarked. Dusty, foot-worn trails wind through the knee-high sagebrush that both shrouds the unmarked graves and adds a sense of desolation.

Low iron fences, reminiscent of the German cemeteries in the Texas Hill Country, surround many of the gravesites. The burials in Pioneer Cemetery are a lasting reminder of the harsh life of West Texas settlers. A single gravesite holds the remains of seven children—all from one family—who died within two days of each other during an 1891 diphtheria outbreak. Just inside the entrance to the Pioneer Cemetery, and marked by a flat metal sign, lie the graves of the Frier brothers. These two young men were the recipients of swift frontier justice, having been shot by a Ranger posse as horse thieves.

Lying at rest in Pioneer Cemetery is a woman, named Delores, who on the eve of her wedding is said to have lit a fire to guide her fiancé to safety. But he did not return. He was later found dead and scalped by Indians. She fell into mental illness and, until her death thirty years later, continued to light fires on a mountain near Fort Davis to guide the way home for her lost love.

Fort Worth

Dido Cemetery
FM 1220 at Dido Hicks Rd.
N 32 57.060, W 097 29.082

TOWNES VAN ZANDT

Born in Fort Worth, Townes Van Zandt (1944–1997) was a gifted and enigmatic songwriter. Although his own recordings were not particularly successful, his talents as a writer were enormous and fully appreciated by his peers. A scion of the historic Van Zandt family of Fort Worth, Townes struck out at an early age to become a troubadour. Over the course of his tumultuous and often tragic life, Van Zandt penned several of Texas' most enduring songs, including "Pancho and Lefty" (a number one hit) and served as an artistic inspiration for many renowned artists.

Greenwood Cemetery
3400 White Settlement Rd.
N 32 45.724, W 097 21.973

AMON G. CARTER

Amon G. Carter (1879–1955) merged the *Fort Worth Star* and the *Fort Worth Telegram* to form the *Fort Worth Star-Telegram* in 1908. In 1922 he started Fort Worth's first radio station, WBAP. Carter's interests in oil, transportation, and communications made him a millionaire, and he was a generous philanthropist. In many ways, Amon G. Carter characterized Fort Worth and was its leading business advocate. Upon his death, the terms of his will established the Amon Carter Museum, which is noted for its extensive western art collection, including many works by Charles M. Russell and Frederick Remington.

WILLIAM BEN HOGAN

Ben Hogan (1912–1997) was one of the greatest golfers to ever tee up a golf ball. He was four times the Professional Golfers' Association

(PGA) Player of the Year and one of only five players to win all four grand slam tournaments. He won four U.S. Opens, two Masters tournaments, two PGA championships, and one British Open between 1946–1953 and became the first player to win three of the four current majors in one year, when he won the Masters, U.S. Open, and British Open in 1953. Although critically injured in a 1949 car accident, he came back to win the U.S. Open in 1950. He is third on the all-time career win list, with sixty-three career wins.

William J. Marsh

William J. Marsh (1880–1971) was born in England and came to Texas in 1904. A naturalized U.S. citizen, he was a music professor at Texas Christian University. Although he composed many works, he is perhaps best known as the composer of the Texas state song, "Texas, Our Texas."

Lena H. Pope

Lena H. Pope (1881–1976) was founder of the Lena Pope Home for homeless children in Fort Worth. She came to Fort Worth around 1920 with her husband, a successful businessman. In 1930 Mrs. Pope founded a home to care for neglected and homeless children. She was unfaltering in her efforts to care for needy children, and the home eventually grew to a capacity of 250. Over the course of the next forty years, more than ten thousand children were housed and cared for in the Lena Pope Home.

Laureland Cemetery
7100 Crowley Rd.
N 32 38.667, W 097 21.069

Charles F. Pendleton

On July 16 and 17, 1953, Charles F. Pendleton (1931–1953) was a machine gunner with Company D, Fifteenth Infantry Regiment, Third Infantry Division, near Choo Gung-Dong, Korea. When a hostile force attacked his position, Corporal Pendleton's accurate fire into the enemy repulsed the attack as he held his machine gun on his knee to improve his field of fire. He reorganized before a second wave moved forward, and when a grenade landed nearby, Corporal Pendleton quickly retrieved it and lobbed it toward his attackers. Although wounded and burned, he refused to be evacuated until a grenade destroyed his machine gun. Undaunted, he grabbed a carbine and continued his heroic defense until mortally wounded by a mortar round. For his courage and sacrifice, Charles Pendleton was posthumously awarded the Congressional Medal of Honor.

Mount Olivet Cemetery

2301 N. Sylvania St.
N 32 47.567, W 097 18.505

ROBERT D. LAW

Specialist Fourth Class Robert D. Law (1944–1969) was a Ranger with the First Infantry Division, U.S. Army, on February 22, 1969, in Tinh Phuoc Thanh Province, Vietnam. He and five companions were on a long-range reconnaissance patrol when they made contact with a small enemy patrol. When an enemy grenade landed in his team's position, Law—instead of diving to safety—threw his body on the grenade and sacrificed his own life to save the lives of his comrades. He was posthumously awarded the Congressional Medal of Honor.

MARSHALL RATLIFF

Marshall Ratliff (? –1928) participated in one of Texas' weirdest bank robberies, known as "the Santa Claus Robbery." During a December 23, 1927, robbery attempt of the Cisco Bank, Ratliff dressed as Santa Claus to fool the bank employees and townspeople. As children followed "Santa" into the bank, his three confederates joined him in grabbing the money. Unfortunately for Ratliff and the other robbers, a mother in the bank with her child quickly realized that a robbery was in progress and sent her daughter to warn law enforcement and local citizens.

A shoot-out ensued in a nearby alley, and the local police chief and his deputy were mortally wounded. Ratliff was also hit, as was one of the other robbers. As Santa and his helpers began their getaway, they discovered that their getaway car was almost out of gas and its tires had been shot flat. Driving to the edge of town, with local citizens in hot pursuit, they attempted to take another car from fourteen-year-old Woody Harris. Harris gave them the car but took the car keys with him. After transferring the money and their wounded comrade to the stolen vehicle, they realized they could not start the car. Their unfortunate accomplice was now unconscious, so they left him in the stolen car and returned to the original car. They did not realize until later that they had left the money in the stolen car with their dying confederate.

Eventually, the three remaining robbers were captured. All three had numerous wounds, but all survived. Ratliff was first convicted of armed robbery on January 27, 1928, and sentenced to ninety-nine years in prison. But Ratliff had been acting insane for months, and his mother (acting on his behalf) filed for a lunacy hearing in Huntsville. Ratliff was extradited to Eastland County, where on November 18 he attempted to escape and managed to mortally wound a hospital orderly in the process. An angry mob of townspeople rushed into the hospital and dragged Ratliff outside, where they attempted to hang him from a power pole. Their first try failed because the rope slipped, but the second attempt proved Ratliff's undoing. Marshall Ratliff is buried in an unmarked plot in Mount Olivet Cemetery, but you can ask the cemetery staff for directions, and the plot is quite easily found.

Oakwood Cemetery
701 Grand at Gould Ave.
N 32 46.175, W 097 20.881

Fort Worth is Texas' quintessential "Cowtown," and Oakwood splendidly reflects the city's rich western heritage. Fort Worth's legacy as a center for the Texas cattle industry, a watering hole for rowdy trail drivers, the home of cattle barons, and a hideout for gunfighters is well represented in the list of citizens who now lay at rest in the Oakwood Cemetery.

The twenty-acre Oakwood site is actually a complex of three cemeteries; Oakwood, Trinity, and Calvary, all located on land donated in 1879 by mayor and philanthropist John Peter Smith. The chapel, located just inside the entrance, was built in 1914. Trinity Cemetery lies in the northwest corner of the complex, and Calvary, a Catholic cemetery, is located in the southwest corner. The Oakwood site lies on a hill overlooking the Trinity River, and the unobstructed view of downtown Fort Worth, particularly at sunrise and sunset, is both peaceful and beautiful. Tracts are dedicated to Union and Confederate soldiers. Oakwood is open daily from sunrise until 6:00 P.M., but a gatekeeper allowed me to stay until sunset after I offered a solemn promise to lock the gate when I left.

SAMUEL BURK BURNETT

Among the most impressive monuments in Oakwood is the mausoleum of cattleman Samuel Burk Burnett (1849–1922). Burk Burnett, whose friends included President Teddy Roosevelt and Native

American legend Quanah Parker, began trailing cattle in 1866. By 1871 Burnett had begun building what was to become one of the great cattle empires in Texas: the Four Sixes Ranch. Burnett is interred along with his second wife, Mary Couts-Burnett (1856–1924), the daughter of Weatherford cattleman and banker James R. Couts (whose own obelisk is the tallest monument in Weatherford's Greenwood Cemetery). After her husband's death, Mary donated much of his sizable estate to Texas Christian University. Today the Mary Couts-Burnett Library, located on the TCU campus, stands in her honor.

TIMOTHY ISAIAH COURTRIGHT

"Longhair Jim" Courtright (1845–1887) was a native of Iowa when he enlisted in the Union army at age seventeen. While fighting in the battles of Fort Donelson and Vicksburg, he was named Jim (a mistake for Tim). After the Civil War, he served as an army scout and was nicknamed "Longhair" after the style in which army scouts often wore their hair in those days.

Both Courtright and his wife, Sarah, were extraordinary marksmen and for a time demonstrated their skill by performing with Wild Bill Hickok in a Wild West show. Always carrying two six-guns, butts forward, Jim Courtright was generally considered to be one of the fastest guns in the West; faster than Hickok, Wyatt Earp, and Bat Masterson and every bit the equal of Robert Clay Allison.

Drifting to Fort Worth about 1873, Courtright failed at farming and later took a job as city jailer. But his natural gift with a six-gun made him a prime candidate for city marshal, and he was first elected in 1876. Expected by the citizens of Fort Worth to manage, if not quell, the violence in the frontier town, Courtright brawled and bullied his way through three terms before being defeated for a fourth.

Over the next few years, Courtright tried his hand at operating a detective agency, served as temporary marshal during the Great Southwest Strike of 1866, and was prosecuted and found not guilty of murder during a stint in New Mexico. He generally led a hard existence of gambling and drinking. On February 8, 1887, his life ended abruptly when friend and fellow gambler Luke Short (1854–1893) shot him dead in one of the few actual face-to-face gunfights that ever occurred in Texas. His funeral procession was reputed to have stretched for six blocks, the longest Fort Worth had ever seen.

Jim Courtright's gravesite is a true and lasting testament to the Old West. It lies a few yards inside the entrance to Oakwood on the south

CIVIL WAR VETERAN, SHERIFF, AND GUNFIGHTER JIM COURTRIGHT WAS KILLED
IN ONE OF THE FEW FACE-TO-FACE GUNFIGHTS IN TEXAS HISTORY. OAKWOOD
CEMETERY, FORT WORTH.

side of the cemetery's main artery. Luke Short died soon after and is
also buried in Oakwood Cemetery, just northeast of Courtright's
gravesite.

CHARLES A. CULBERSON

Charles A. Culberson (1855–1925) was elected as governor of Texas
in 1894, and in 1899 he was elected by the Texas Legislature to succeed Roger Mills as U.S. Senator.

WILLIAM M. McDONALD

One of Texas' most prominent African American citizens, William M.
(Gooseneck Bill) McDonald (1866–1950) is buried in Trinity, a sub-
section of Oakwood Cemetery. The son of a former slave, McDonald
attended college in Tennessee and returned to Texas, where he was
elected to the Republican Party's state executive committee in 1892. A
prominent figure in the Texas Republican Party for more than thirty
years, McDonald founded the Fraternal Bank and Trust Company,
which became the chief depository for the state's black Masonic
lodges. An impressive obelisk marks McDonald's gravesite in Trinity
Cemetery.

JOHN BUNYAN SLAUGHTER

Directly across a paved avenue and only a lariat toss away from the resting place of Samuel Burk Burnett stands the mausoleum of Texas cattle baron John Bunyan Slaughter (1848–1928). Slaughter spent his youth riding cow ponies and began trailing cattle up the Chisholm Trail around 1866. A survivor of numerous scrapes with the Indians, including one in which he was seriously injured, Slaughter eventually amassed vast land and cattle holdings in several Texas counties.

THOMAS NEVILLE WAUL

Thomas Neville Waul (1813–1903) had practiced law in Mississippi before coming to Texas in 1850. After an unsuccessful run for a U.S. Congressional seat, Waul recruited soldiers for the Confederacy in what was to become Waul's Legion. Waul was captured at Vicksburg (July 4, 1863) but was soon exchanged and then promoted to brigadier general on September 18, 1863. Waul led the first brigade of the Texas Division in the Red River campaign, and after the battles of Mansfield (April 8, 1864) and Pleasant Hill (April 9, 1864), Waul and his brigade were transferred to Arkansas. At the Battle of Jenkins' Ferry on April 30, 1864, Waul was wounded in action. After the war, Waul returned to the practice of law.

Pioneer's Rest Cemetery
600 block of Samuels Ave.
N 32 45.943, W 097 19.734

Pioneer's Rest Cemetery is a small cemetery tucked into one of Fort Worth's oldest neighborhoods. Dr. Adolphus Gouhenant donated the original three-acre site. In 1871 Baldwin Samuels gave three adjoining acres to the cemetery association for expansion of Pioneer's Rest Cemetery. Many of Fort Worth's early settlers and numerous Civil War veterans are buried here.

A private association maintains Pioneer's Rest, and the cemetery is open weekdays only, from 9:00 A.M. to 5:00 P.M. There is no authorized access on weekends. I found Pioneer's Rest early on a Saturday afternoon and, having traveled several hours to see the cemetery, decided to scale its surrounding low, iron fence near a padlocked gate. I spent much of that late Saturday afternoon begging mercy and forgiveness from an unamused yet benevolent Fort Worth police officer.

Visit Pioneer's Rest Cemetery on a weekday, just in case Officer Mc-Kinney no longer patrols Samuels Avenue.

RIPLEY A. ARNOLD

The cemetery was established in 1850 when Ripley A. Arnold (1817–1853) buried his children Sophie and Willis Arnold there. A West Point graduate, Arnold had been ordered to establish a military camp near the confluence of the Clear Fork and West Fork of the Trinity River. As commander of the Second Dragoons (mounted riflemen), Arnold scouted the site in May 1849 and established Camp Worth in June 1849, naming the site for his former commander Gen. William Worth. Eventually the site was renamed Fort Worth.

Rip Arnold was killed in 1853 by Josephus Murray Steiner (1823–1873, buried in Oakwood Cemetery, Austin), the fort surgeon at Fort Graham. Arnold and Steiner enjoyed a profound distaste for each other. In 1853 Steiner aided the post inspector general in an investigation of the sale of government horses for which Arnold had not turned in the cash. Unfortunately, Arnold was not present during the investigation, and upon his return, he swore that Steiner would not live to "give evidence against me."

On September 5, 1853, Arnold ordered Steiner's arrest. When the orders were delivered the next day, the surgeon threw them on the floor, bolted to Arnold's quarters, and demanded an explanation of the charges against him. Arnold replied, "Drunkenness and falsifying."

Steiner demanded an apology, and both men drew their guns. Arnold fired first and missed Steiner with two shots. Steiner then shot Arnold four times, and the major died within a matter of minutes. Steiner was tried for murder and acquitted. Arnold was buried at Fort Graham, but his remains were later moved to Pioneer's Rest Cemetery, where his gravesite is marked by a huge uncut stone.

Shannon Rose Hill Cemetery
7301 E. Lancaster Ave.
N 32 43.992, W 097 12.075

LEE HARVEY OSWALD

Lee Harvey Oswald (1939–1963) was the alleged assassin of President John F. Kennedy. He was arrested on November 22, 1962, and charged with the assassination of President Kennedy and with the murder of Dallas police officer J. D. Tippit. Two days later, Oswald was shot and killed by Dallas businessman Jack Ruby. Oswald's grave is difficult to find, and cemetery employees are reluctant to give its location. But Oswald was laid to rest here; I visited the gravesite myself in 1968.

Franklin

Mount Pleasant Cemetery
FR 2446 at intersection with CR 314
N 31 01.349, W 096 26.769

WALTER WASHINGTON WILLIAMS

Walter W. Williams (1842–1959) is likely to have been the last surviving soldier of the Civil War (1861–1865). During the conflict, he was a forage master for Hood's Texas Brigade. Soon after the war, he moved to Texas, to a farm near Franklin. He lived rather anonymously, until in extreme old age he gained recognition as one of a very few remaining Civil War veterans. After all other men who had fought in the Civil War had passed, President Dwight D. Eisenhower awarded him the honorary rank of general. When General Williams died, President Eisenhower proclaimed a period of national mourning.

Fredericksburg

Fredericksburg City Cemetery
N. Lee St. and Schubert St.
N 30 16.293, W 098 51.717

The Fredericksburg City Cemetery is the classic example of a German ethnic cemetery, a model of order and precision. If you visit in the summer, bring an umbrella because the cemetery, although immaculately kept, is (like many German cemeteries) almost devoid of trees. Laid out in perfect German precision (on an unusual southwest-to-northeast diagonal), the cemetery is bounded on the southwest by Barons Creek and a nice mortared stone wall.

The northwest quadrant of the cemetery appears to hold its oldest gravesites. Ornate metal fences surround many of the plots in this cemetery; several of these fences were produced by the Stewart Fence Company of Cincinnati, Ohio. There is a prominent windmill in the cemetery and a beautiful cut-limestone storage building. Virtually all of the gravesites are surrounded by concrete borders, and many of the plots have been completely cemented or covered with gravel. There is

SCULPTURE BY ELIZABET NEY, FREDERICKSBURG CEMETERY, FREDERICKSBURG.

just not a whole lot of lawn mowing taking place in this cemetery—
even in wet years.

Many of the concrete gravesites are constructed with small recep-
tacles to allow placement of clay flowerpots on the individual graves.
In almost every case the pots are very small, preventing any ostenta-
tious placement of flowers. The oldest part of the cemetery contains a
large number of limestone headstones that have become weathered
and in some cases almost unreadable, but several were clearly
painstakingly carved. There is a remarkable diversity of markers in
the Fredericksburg City Cemetery, including plain metal crosses and
carved marble and limestone markers, as well as the more typical
granite markers. Most of the inscriptions in the older parts of the
cemetery are in German.

The cemetery is attractive in a Spartan sense, pragmatic, perfectly
surveyed, and straight to the point. There is little statuary, but two
angels play prominent roles here. The first appears to be praying to
the windmill that stands in the middle of the cemetery and is a rather
interesting sculpture. But the second angel, a small cherubic figure, is
magnificent. Created by one of Texas' most famous sculptors, Elizabet Ney, the figure—an angel resting her chin on her arms and pen-
sively looking skyward—adorns the grave of Elizabeth Emma Schnei-

der Schnerr (1827–1903). The cherub is based on a figure in Raphael's painting *Sistine Madonna*. This statue has been reported to be Ney's last statue and the only one she ever created for a nonpublic figure. It is worth a trip to the cemetery just to see this statue. Mrs. Schnerr's gravesite is just to the east of the entrance road into the cemetery and is quite easily located. Note Ney's signature on the lower left-hand side (facing the statue) of the figure.

Galveston

Lakeview Cemetery
3015 Fifty-seventh St.
N 29 16.293, W 094 49.515

CORA CLINE

As the morning light crept through the windows of her second-floor bedroom, Cora Cline (?–1900) began to awaken. Reaching for the hand of her husband, Isaac, she found herself alone. Yet, she was unalarmed, for he often arose early to walk the streets and beaches of the city. The cool morning air that hung over the city on the morning of September 8, 1900, was a welcome relief from the past weeks. It had been a dreadfully hot summer in Galveston and in the rest of the United States. A *Western World* magazine correspondent wrote, "The summer of 1900 will be long remembered as one of the most remarkable for sustained high temperatures that has been experienced for almost a generation."

Although ill and enduring the discomforts of a difficult fourth pregnancy, she drifted back to sleep, comforted in the assurance that her husband, chief of the local Weather Bureau Office, would soon return to her side. She could not know that a few miles away, a massive tropical cyclone was driving across the Gulf of Mexico and directly toward Galveston. As evening fell on the island, the great storm struck the city. Although her children and husband would survive the storm, Cora Cline—and more than eight thousand of her friends and neighbors—had been swallowed by its fury.

The hurricane that crashed the shores of Galveston on that Saturday morning in September was the worst natural disaster ever to strike the continental United States. For days after the storm, survivors searched for missing family members and friends. On September 30 a demolition gang unearthed the body of a woman captured in a tangle of debris. Isaac Cline recognized the rings on her left hand as those of his beloved wife. On October 4, 1900, Cora Cline was buried in Block 47, Lot E, in Lakeview Cemetery.

In 1904 a bronze statue commemorating those who lost their lives in the hurricane was erected in Lakeview Cemetery. Sculpted by Pompeo Coppini and funded by the Order of the Woodmen of the World and private donations, the figure looks out to sea as if protecting the city from future storms.

MAUD CUNEY-HARE

Maud Cuney-Hare (1874–1936), an African American musician and writer, studied piano at the New England Conservatory of Music. As a folklorist and music historian, she was especially interested in African and early American music. She was the author of *Creole Songs* (1921); *The Message of the Trees* (1918), a collection of poetry; and *Norris Wright Cuney: A Tribune of the Black People* (1913), a biography of her father. Her most memorable work is *Negro Musicians and Their Music* (1936).

SIDNEY SHERMAN

Sidney Sherman (1805–1873) came to Texas in 1835 with a volunteer company from Kentucky. In that company was the only battle flag carried by Texans during the Battle of San Jacinto. Sherman was appointed to the rank of lieutenant colonel in March 1836 and at the San Jacinto battle, he commanded the left wing of the Texas Army. Sidney Sherman is credited with the battle cry "Remember the Alamo!" The flag now hangs in the House Chambers in the Texas Capitol. Sherman spent his last years in Galveston. Sidney Sherman is the namesake of Sherman County and the city of Sherman in Grayson County.

DAVID G. BURNET

David Burnet (1788–1870) was the first president of the Republic of Texas and was vice president under the presidency of Mirabeau Lamar. He also served as secretary of state in the administration of Governor James P. Henderson. In 1866 the Texas Legislature named Burnet and Oran M. Roberts to the U.S. Senate, but they were not seated. Burnet is the namesake of Burnet County.

A TOWERING OBELISK MARKS
THE GRAVESITE OF TEXAS
HEROES DAVID BURNET AND
SIDNEY SHERMAN AT LAKE-
SIDE CEMETERY, GALVESTON.

GALVESTON CITY CEMETERIES

Prior to the 1900 hurricane, Galveston was the most prosperous city in Texas. It was the jewel of the coast, a busy seaport and a center of both culture and commerce. Its history, including the aftermath of the hurricane and the yellow fever epidemics, is well catalogued in the cluster of cemeteries located along Broadway Street between Fortieth and Forty-third Streets.

Within this rectangle are the Trinity Episcopal Cemetery, Old City Cemetery, Oleander Cemetery, Old Catholic Cemetery, New City Cemetery (Yellow Fever Yard), Evergreen Cemetery (or Cahill Ground), New Cahill Yard, and the Hebrew Benevolent Society.

Evergreen Cemetery (Cahill Ground)
Avenue K at Forty-third Street
N 29 17.593, W 094 48.867

ANGELINA DICKINSON

Angelina Dickinson (1834–1869) was the daughter of Almaron and Susanna (Wilkerson) Dickinson and was but two years old when the forces of Gen. Antonio López de Santa Anna moved into the city of San Antonio on February 23, 1836. Her father was one of the "Old Eighteen" patriots who had held the Mexican forces at bay in Gonzales, and he had brought his wife and baby daughter with him to the Alamo. Although Almaron perished in the battle, his wife and daughter survived. Legend has it Santa Anna wanted to adopt Angelina, but after her mother's refusal, mother and child were released to carry the message of defeat—and the fate of the Alamo combatants—to Gen. Sam Houston.

Angelina's life proved to be a string of broken marriages and broken homes. At seventeen she married a Montgomery County farmer, but after six years and three children she apparently abandoned her family and drifted to New Orleans. Angelina died of a "uterine hemorrhage" in Galveston, where she lived under the assumed name of "Em Britton" and may have worked as a courtesan. She apparently never could accept the notoriety of being "the Babe of the Alamo," and her life ended in sadness. Burial records from Galveston place her burial in the "Cahill Ground," but her burial site is unmarked.

Trinity Episcopal Cemetery
Avenue K at Fortieth St.
N 29 17.619, W 094 48.658

WILLIAM S. FISHER

William S. Fisher (?–1845) led Company I, First Regiment of Texas Volunteers, at the Battle of San Jacinto. Fisher also served as Texas secretary of war in 1836–1837. Fisher joined the Somervell Expedition in 1842 and was elected to lead the members of the expedition who chose to continue into Mexico in what was later called the Meir Expedition. Captured with his army, Fisher was imprisoned in Mexico and released in 1843.

JOHN BANKHEAD MAGRUDER

A graduate of West Point, John B. Magruder (1807–1871) served with Winfield Scott in Mexico during the U.S.-Mexican War. Resigning his commission in the U.S. Army, he was commissioned as a brigadier general in the Confederate army. Magruder was assigned to the District of Texas in 1862 and headquartered in Houston. His greatest military success was the recapture of Galveston from federal forces in January 1863.

JEAN COVENTREE SCRIMGEOUR MORGAN

Jean Coventree Scrimgeour Morgan (1868–1938) was a native of Galveston, and throughout her life she was dedicated to public service there, held firm by her belief that "Christian social service is the church at work: it is Christ in action through us." In 1901 the Women's Health Protective Association was founded by a group of sixty-six women with a goal of clearing the debris and reburying the dead from the Galveston hurricane of 1900. Morgan served in several positions within the association, including its presidency. She was active in almost every phase of civic life in Galveston, including the Galveston Anti-Tuberculosis Association, the Galveston chapter of the Red Cross, the Galveston Orphan's Home, and the Galveston YWCA.

ALEXANDER MAY SHANNON

A facile and shrewd cavalryman, Alexander Shannon (1839–1906) served with both Gen. John B. Hood and Gen. Nathan Bedford Forest. He voted against Texas' secession from the Union but joined Gen. H. H. Sibley's brigade soon after Texas entered the Confederacy. He also served with Terry's Texas Rangers.

After the fall of Richmond, Shannon was selected to escort President Jefferson Davis, but Davis was captured before Shannon could reach him. After the war, Shannon prospered as a private businessman. In 1886 he proposed the building of a seawall in Galveston, but the proposal apparently failed. Four years later the city was destroyed by the great hurricane of 1900.

Louis Trezevant Wigfall

Hot-tempered and quarrelsome, Louis T. Wigfall (1816–1874) was an ardent secessionist. He served in the Texas House of Representatives, where he labeled U.S. Senator Sam Houston as a traitor to Texas and the South. An exceptional orator, Wigfall was a leader in the Southern "fire-eaters" and was elected to the U.S. Senate in 1859. After Texas seceded from the Union, he stayed in the Senate until he was expelled in 1861. Wigfall was present at the opening of the Civil War, rowing out to Fort Sumter to deliver his own terms for surrender. He later served in the Confederacy, but his fractious nature resulted in problems at every turn. Contentious to the end, he fled to England in 1866 and tried to gather support for a war between the United States and Britain. He returned to the United States in 1872 and to Texas in 1874, where he died shortly thereafter.

Old Catholic Cemetery
Avenue K at Forty-first St.
N 29 17.609, W 094 48.731

Frank and Tony Perucini

In early November 1942 the USS *New Orleans* (CA-32) set sail from Pearl Harbor as an escort for the USS *Saratoga* (CV-3). *Saratoga* had been torpedoed on August 31 during action near Guadalcanal, and both ships were now returning to action in the Solomon Islands. Onboard the *New Orleans* were two brothers, Frank (1919–1944) and Tony Perucini (1922–1944), but their presence onboard was hardly routine. The two brothers had been brought together by coincidences beyond imagination.

First, Frank and Tony shared the same birthday, July 23, although Frank was three years older. They had joined the Navy on the same day; however, they were totally unaware of that fact, as each joined in different states and had no idea that the other had enlisted.

On the night of November 30, 1944, they were in the same gun turret aboard the *New Orleans* as she steamed with four other cruis-

BROTHERS FRANK AND TONY PERUCINI PERISHED DURING WORLD WAR II ON THE SAME DAY, ON THE SAME SHIP, IN THE SAME GUN TURRET. OLD CATHOLIC CEMETERY, GALVESTON.

ers and six destroyers to engage forces of the Imperial Japanese Navy at the Battle of Tassafaronga. When flagship *USS Minneapolis* (CA-36) was struck by two torpedoes, the *New Orleans*—next astern—was forced to sheer away to avoid collision. In doing so, the ship ran into the track of a torpedo that ripped off her bow. Bumping down the ship's port side, the severed bow punched several holes in *New Orleans*' hull. Though badly damaged, the *New Orleans* stayed afloat and limped into Tulagi Harbor on December 1, but the two Perucini brothers had perished in the same gun turret. Frank and Tony Perucini are buried in the Old Catholic Cemetery, their faces—young and handsome—preserved in porcelain on the stone that marks the graves where they stay on station, side by side, shipmates for eternity.

Goliad

Oak Hill Cemetery
W. Franklin at San Patricio
N 28 40.039, W 097 23.982

It was warm for an early spring morning, muggy even, and the western horizon promised rain. As the Sunday morning sun rose over the sleepy town of Goliad, its 1,200 citizens began to stir, and many prepared for church. The newly constructed Baptist church began to fill with parishioners on that morning of May 18, 1902, but skies were threatening and rapidly darkening. Perhaps the members of a nearby

African American Methodist church noticed the pelting rain against the windows of their church and questioned each other about the intensity of the coming storm.

The massive tornado that engulfed Goliad on that Sunday morning struck without warning and destroyed much of the western section of the town. Within four minutes a strip roughly two blocks wide and a mile long, including about one hundred houses, a Baptist church, and a Methodist church—filled with worshipers—were reduced to rubble. Several hundred residents of Goliad were injured, and 114 lost their lives.

The toll of this storm is well recorded in Oak Hill Cemetery. Walking among the stones, one finds the graves of Margaret Pope and Mary E. Johnson, buried next to each other, their lives carved into a single white marble stone. Nearby, in the middle of the cemetery, stands a pink granite obelisk with the name "Maddux" carved into its base. Next to the obelisk are the graves of three Maddux children, Ellen, Edna, and Ruby—all killed in the storm of May 18. The obelisk marks the graves of William Maddux, who died on May 29, and Phinney Flores Maddux, who died two days later. An entire family lost in a matter of seconds.

MARY JOHNSON AND MARGARET POPE WERE LAID TO REST IN OAK HILL CEMETERY, GOLIAD, AFTER A TORNADO DEVASTATED MUCH OF THE TOWN ON MAY 18, 1902.

Fannin Memorial
Highway 183, south of the Guadalupe River
N 28 38.804, W 097 22.931

JAMES WALKER FANNIN, JR.

Jim Fannin (1804–1836) came to Texas in 1834. He was raised in Georgia and attended West Point for two years, but he withdrew before graduating. In Texas, Fannin became an advocate of the Texas Revolution and in September 1835 became active in the volunteer army. General Sam Houston commissioned Fannin as a colonel in the regular army on December 7. Fannin was elected colonel of the Provisional Regiment of Volunteers at Goliad on February 7, 1836, and from February 12 to March 12 he acted as commander in chief of the army.

When he was notified that Mexican forces had occupied Matamoros, Mexico, Fannin set to the defense of Goliad. On March 14, Fannin's command was ordered to retreat to Victoria. On March 19 he began his retreat, but he and his men were surrounded by Mexican troops and forced to surrender at the Battle of Coleto. On Palm Sunday, March 27, 1836, Fannin and about 340 of his men were executed by order of Gen. Antonio López de Santa Anna.

The remains of Fannin and the men in his command were burned and left exposed to the elements. On June 3, 1836, Thomas Rusk gathered their remains and buried them in a common grave. A large monument now stands at their gravesite, a testament to the lives of Texans whose deaths would mark one of the most infamous and critical events of the Texas Revolution.

Gonzales

Old City Cemetery (Gonzales Memorial Cemetery)
N. College St. at Wells St.
N 29 30.711, W 097 27.123

This old cemetery lies in the heart of Gonzales and is one of several historically significant cemeteries in the city. The history of Gonzales and its place in Texas lore are well represented by the Texans buried here. The cemetery itself is reasonably well kept, but like many urban cemeteries, it has been subject to vandalism. The first time I visited the Old City Cemetery, I noted in my journal that the western part of the cemetery was well shaded. But I did not realize until a subsequent visit that the source of the shade was the tallest and most luxuriant crape myrtle bushes I have ever seen. The cemetery has been renamed, but it remains a true treasure in the history of Gonzales—and in all of Texas.

GEORGE W. BARNETT

George Barnett (1793–1848) represented Washington at the Convention of 1836 and signed the Texas Declaration of Independence. Barnett participated in the Siege of Bexar and later served several terms as a senator in the Republic of Texas. Lipan Apache Indians killed Barnett while he was deer hunting west of Gonzales.

VALENTINE BENNET, JOHN SOWELL, AND THE "OLD EIGHTEEN"

Valentine Bennet (1780–1843) was born in Massachusetts and participated in the War of 1812. He came to Texas after the death of his wife in 1825 and settled at Velasco in November of that year. In 1832 he took a leading part in the Battle of Velasco, in which he was severely wounded. Bennet moved to Gonzales in 1834 and then stepped directly into Texas history.

In 1825 impresario Green B. DeWitt had honored the spirit of cooperation between Mexico and its colony in Texas by naming the capital of his colony after Rafael Gonzales, the governor of Coahuila and Texas. Also in the spirit of cooperation, the Mexican government provided a six-pound cannon to the settlers in Gonzales as a means of protection from Indian raids. Although the citizens of Gonzales had been strong supporters of the Mexican government, in September 1835, a hundred Mexican army dragoons under the command of Lt. Francisco de Casteñada were ordered to Gonzales to reclaim the small brass cannon. But the Texians were unwilling to return it as tensions began to mount between Mexico and its Texian colonists.

When Casteñada's men reached the banks of the Guadalupe River, they found their progress blocked by Bennett, John Sowell (also buried in this cemetery), and sixteen other Gonzales militiamen. The "Old Eighteen" had removed the ferry, and the Mexican soldiers could not cross the swollen river.

The Texians stalled for time by telling Casteñada that Alcalde Andrew Ponton was out of town and that, until he returned, the Mexican officer would have to wait on the other side of the river. Immediately, the Gonzales militiamen began to seek reinforcement from nearby settlements, many of whom arrived September 29.

On October 2, with both sides now in a defensive position across

Mathew Caldwell, nicknamed Old Paint, signed the Texas Declaration of Independence and was a renowned Texas Ranger. Old City Cemetery, Gonzales.

the river from each other, Casteñada requested that the gun be returned to the Mexican government (a condition of its original loan). In response and emboldened by the arrival of their comrades in arms, the Texians were ready to fight. They had raised a white banner upon which they had scrawled in black, "Come and Take It." With the first shots of the conflict, the Mexican soldiers withdrew.

The cannon remained in the hands of Texians. Mounted on cartwheels in the blacksmith shop of John Sowell, the "Come and Take It" cannon soon was on its way to San Antonio, to become part of the city's artillery defense. Within a matter of days, members of the "Old Eighteen"—Jacob Darst, Thomas Jackson, Albert Martin, Thomas Miller and Almaron Dickinson—would achieve immortality: all fell while defending the Alamo.

Mathew Caldwell

Mathew Caldwell (1798–1842) was born in Kentucky and came to Texas as part of the DeWitt colony in 1831. Nicknamed "Old Paint" for his spotted moustache, Mathew Caldwell is often called the Paul

Revere of the Texas Revolution, because he rode from Gonzales to Bastrop to call men to arms before the Battle of Gonzales in October 1835.

Caldwell was one of the delegates from Gonzales at the Convention of 1836 and signed the Texas Declaration of Independence. In 1839 he was appointed as a Texas Ranger, taking part in the Council House Fight, and he participated in the Battle of Plum Creek in August 1840. In 1842 Caldwell led a force of about two hundred men in defeating Mexican army general Adrian Woll at the Battle of Salado Creek. Caldwell County was named in honor of this military hero.

Masonic Cemetery

Highway 183, south of intersection with U.S. Highway 90
N 29 30.513, W 097 27.356

Like the Old City Cemetery, the Masonic Cemetery is a wonderfully historic cemetery. The role of the citizens in Gonzales in the Texas Revolution is well represented in those Texians who are buried here, including Margaret Darst (1781–1846; widow of Alamo hero Jacob Darst) and Eli Mitchell, a member of the Old Eighteen and upon whose farm the first shots of the Texas Revolution were fired. Also buried here are San Jacinto veterans Jesse K. Davis, William Mathews, and Thomas Polk.

ANDREW PONTON

Andrew Ponton (1804–1850) arrived in Texas in 1829. Ponton was the last alcalde of Gonzales, elected to that position in 1835. In September 1835, when Domingo de Ugartechea demanded that the Gonzales "Come and Take It" cannon be surrendered to Mexican soldiers or that Ponton be brought to San Antonio as a hostage, Ponton put off the Mexicans with excuses. He then immediately sent calls for help to the surrounding settlements and participated in the Battle of Gonzales on October 2, 1835. On February 23, 1836, William B. Travis sent Ponton a short dispatch, asking for men and provisions for the relief of the Alamo. The Gonzales Ranging Company of Mounted Volunteers responded, and these thirty-two men from Gonzales rode into history. All perished in the Alamo.

AMASA TURNER

Amasa Turner (1800–1877) came to Texas in 1835 to regain his health after a bout with yellow fever. Turner joined the Texan forces that were defending Gonzales in September 1835 and fought with

Capt. Robert M. Coleman's Bastrop Company in the Siege of Bexar. As a recruiting officer for the revolutionary army, he traveled to New Orleans in January 1836 and raised ninety-nine volunteers. Turner's volunteers joined Sam Houston's army and fought at the Battle of San Jacinto on April 21, 1836. Turner was twice elected to the Texas House of Representatives (1851–1853; 1853–1854).

NINA ELOISE WHITTINGTON VANCE

Nina Vance (1914–1980) was the founder and artistic director of the Alley Theatre in Houston. Under her guidance the Alley Theatre grew into one of the most prestigious theaters in the United States. In 1960 the theater received one of the first Ford Foundation grants to support a resident acting company.

In 1961 Vance helped found the Theatre Communications Group (an organization for professional regional theaters), and in that year President John F. Kennedy invited her to serve on the advisory committee of the proposed National Culture Center. Over the course of her life Vance was a dominant force in American theater and was oft honored for her contributions.

Goodnight

Goodnight Cemetery
From Goodnight, north on FM 294 to first right-hand turn; left turn at next intersection to end of road
N 35 02.785, W 101 10.444

CHARLES GOODNIGHT

Charles Goodnight (1836–1929) came to Milam County, Texas, in 1845. As a young man growing up in the Brazos River bottomlands, he learned the backwoods of Texas, as well as learning to ride horses and to work in the backbreaking profession of freighting. In 1857 Goodnight trailed a herd of cattle up the Brazos River and settled near Black Springs. During his years there, he met and befriended Oliver Loving, who was also herding cattle in that area. When the Colorado gold rush started, Goodnight and Loving began providing beef to the Rocky Mountain mining operations.

Goodnight became involved in the Indian hostilities in northwest Texas and was helped in the recapture of Cynthia Ann Parker. During the Civil War years he gained an excellent knowledge of the Texas high plains as a member of the Frontier Regiment of the Texas

LEGENDARY
CATTLEMAN
CHARLES
GOODNIGHT WAS
BURIED OVER-
LOOKING THE
TEXAS PLAINS.
GOODNIGHT
CEMETERY,
GOODNIGHT.

Rangers. In 1864 he returned to Palo Pinto County and began his cattle business in earnest.

In 1866, Goodnight and Loving directed a trail drive that would begin at Fort Belknap and reach a terminus at Fort Sumner, New Mexico. Among the cowboys who made this historic trip were Bose Ikard and famous gunman Robert Clay Allison. This route became known as the Goodnight-Loving Trail. Charles Goodnight would eventually build an immense cattle empire in the Texas Panhandle, near the present site of Goodnight. He is buried in a small cemetery that is the high point of the area and looks out across the Texas plains that he so dearly loved.

Greenville

East Mound Cemetery
Morse St. at Pine St.
N 33 08.177, W 096 05.978

LALLIE P. CARLISLE

Lallie P. Carlisle (1866–1949) was the first woman in Texas to hold an elective public office. Upon the death of her first husband, E. W. Briscoe, she was appointed, on April 17, 1902, by the Commissioners Court to complete his term as clerk of Hunt County. At that time, women could not vote in Texas, and her appointment was challenged. However, a ruling by the Texas attorney general upheld the appointment.

Grit

Grit Cemetery
Highway 29, approximately 4 miles southeast of Grit
(Mason County)
N 30 46.657, W 099 18.164

JOHN BATE BERRY

John Bate Berry (1813–1891) came to Texas with his father, John Berry, and two brothers in 1826. Bate and his brother Andrew Jackson Berry joined the Texas Army in 1835. Andrew fought in the Battle of San Jacinto. Bate had been detailed to guard the baggage train and the camp of the sick opposite Harrisburg and did not take part in the battle. Bate and Andrew Berry both fought with Col. Edward Burleson in the Battle of Plum Creek on August 12, 1840.

After Gen. Adrián Woll captured the city of San Antonio in September 1842, Bate and his brother joined the Somervell Expedition and decided to continue as members of the Mier Expedition in December of that year. Joseph was killed in the Battle of Mier, and Bate was captured and imprisoned in Mexico until September 16, 1844. During the U.S.-Mexican War he served as a scout (under Capt. Creed Taylor) for Gen. Zachary Taylor in northern Mexico. Berry eventually settled in Mason County where he farmed and ranched.

Harlingen

Marine Military Academy
320 Iwo Jima Blvd.
N 26 13.430, W 097 40.214

HARLON BLOCK

As he stood with the other seniors from his 1942 Weslaco High School football team, Harlon Block (1924–1945) could not know that the oath of military service he was about to take would assure his place in American history. Although his face would be unknown, the image of his straining figure would be captured in a moment that was to become perhaps the most dramatic image of the twentieth century.

He was raised in the rural Rio Grande Valley, born into a family that religiously believed in the commandment "Thou shalt not kill." A gifted natural athlete, Block starred on the unbeaten 1942 Panther football team and was named to the All South Texas team. He and the other senior members of the team had decided to join the service as a group and were accelerated through their senior year. In January

MARINE CORPS CORPORAL HARLON BLOCK WAS A CENTRAL FIGURE IN THE MOST FAMOUS PHOTOGRAPH OF WORLD WAR II, THE FLAG RAISING ON IWO JIMA. MARINE MILITARY ACADEMY, HARLINGEN. PHOTO COURTESY OF DAVID LOTZ, COPYRIGHT © 2001.

1943 these thirteen teammates took their oath together, and on February 18, Harlon Block entered the U.S. Marine Corps.

First trained as a Marine paratrooper, Harlon Block saw his first combat on the island of Bougainville, arriving December 21, 1943, as the battle drew to a close. Already on the island were two other Marines, Mike Strank and Ira Hayes, whose destinies were inextricably intertwined with that of this young Marine from Texas.

After Bougainville, Block's parachute division was disbanded, and he was assigned to Company E, Second Battalion, Twenty-eight Marines, Fifth Marine Division. On February 19, 1945, Company E hit the beaches on a distant volcanic atoll whose translated name is Sulfur Island. To the twenty-two thousand Japanese soldiers entrenched there, it was known as Iwo Jima.

By midmorning on February 23, Marine riflemen had reached the summit of Mount Suribachi, the volcanic cone that towers above the island. After a small American flag had been raised on the summit, five Marines and a Navy hospital corpsman were ordered to raise a second, larger flag in place of the first one. Harlon Block grabbed the base of the makeshift flagpole and strained to jam it into the rocks as his five countrymen, including Mike Strank and Ira Hayes, raised it to its full height. In that instant, Associated Press reporter Al Rosenthal snapped what is perhaps the most powerful photo ever taken in wartime. Corporal Harlon Block never saw the photograph. He was killed in action on May 1, 1945.

The photo was an instant sensation back home in the States. Everyone wanted to know the identities of the Marines in the picture, but Harlon Block's back was to the camera, and he was misidentified as another Marine who had also lost his life on the island. For two years, the Marine holding the base of the pole was thought to be Henry Hansen. But in May 1946 a small, quiet man appeared at the home of Ed Block, Harlon's father. Having hitchhiked 1,300 miles in three days, Ira Hayes—who had fought on Iwo Jima and survived the battle—walked out into the cotton field where Mr. Block was working. There the native Pima Indian told him that the image in the picture was actually that of his son, Harlon.

After only a few minutes of conversation, Hayes turned away and hitchhiked 1,300 miles back home to Arizona, his last service to his fellow Marine completed. After an inquiry, Harlon Block was correctly identified as the young Marine in the picture and took his honored place in history.

After interment in the 5th Marine Division Cemetery on Iwo Jima,

Harlon's remains were brought home to Weslaco and later were relocated to the Marine Military Academy in Harlingen. Ira Hayes and Mike Strank now rest in Arlington National Cemetery.

Hempstead

Hempstead City Cemetery
At the terminus of Groce St.
N 30 05.098, W 096 04.038

LILLIE ELIZABETH MCGEE DRENNAN

Lillie Drennan (1897–1974) was the first licensed female truck driver and trucking-firm owner in Texas and, likely, in the United States. She and her husband began a trucking business in March 1928, and when the enterprise began to thrive, they purchased a second truck. Lillie was soon behind the wheel. She received her commercial truck driver's license in 1929, but not without some bureaucratic wrestling. Commission examiners were reluctant to grant her a license, contending that her poor hearing (she wore a hearing aid most of her life) would make her a safety risk. But Lillie argued that she was fully capable of operating a vehicle and pointed out her driving record: "If any man can beat my record, I'll just get out of here." By any measure, Lillie Drennan was a colorful character.

Profane, tough, and self-sufficient, she carried a loaded revolver by her side when she drove, and she successfully operated her company for many years. A stickler for safety, she personally trained all her drivers and received numerous safety awards during her trucking career.

Hillsboro

Park Ridge Cemetery
Julatka St. at Mulford St.
N 32 01.246, W 097 07.488

JAMES L. HARRIS

James L. Harris (1916–1944) was born in Hillsboro, drafted into military service, and assigned to the 756th Tank Battalion. In 1944 Harris earned a battlefield commission to the rank of second lieutenant. On the night of October 7, 1944, near the village of Vagney, France, a German raiding party, comprising a tank and two platoons of infantry, attacked his tank command. Realizing the need for immediate action, Lieutenant Harris ordered his tank to halt while he proceeded on foot, armed only with a service pistol, to probe the darkness for the enemy.

Although mortally wounded by machine gun fire, he crawled back to his tank and issued firing orders while lying on the road. The tank he commanded was destroyed in the course of the exchange, but Harris stood the enemy off until friendly armor turned the course of battle. Suffering a second wound in the course of this tank duel, Lieutenant Harris refused aid until after a wounded member of his crew had been carried to safety. He died before he could be given medical attention. For his valor he was awarded the Congressional Medal of Honor.

Houston

Forest Park Lawndale Cemetery
6900 Lawndale St.
N 29 43.278, W 095 18.187

RICHARD ANDERSON

Lance Cpl. Richard Anderson (1948–1969) was a member of Company E, Third Reconnaissance Battalion, Third Marine Division. In the early morning of August 24, 1969, in Quang Tri Province, Anderson's reconnaissance team came under a heavy attack, and Anderson was hit in both legs during the initial moments of the attack. Though painfully wounded, he continued to return fire at the enemy. Observing an enemy grenade land between him and the other Marine, Anderson immediately rolled over and covered it with his body. He gallantly gave his life in the service of his country and for that sacrifice was awarded the Congressional Medal of Honor.

SAM HOPKINS

Sam (Lightnin') Hopkins (1912–1982) was born in Centerville, Texas. He was a Texas country bluesman whose career began in the 1920s and stretched into the 1980s. In 1946 a talent scout discovered Hopkins playing music in Houston's Third Ward. Hopkins was paired with pianist Wilson "Thunder" Smith, and Hopkins was christened "Lightnin'." Hopkins recorded for Aladdin Records into 1948, scoring a national rhythm and blues hit with his "Shotgun Blues."

But the advent of 1950s rock and roll relegated Hopkins to obscurity until he enjoyed a rebirth in the 1960s folk-blues music revival. His recording career once again blossomed as he recorded for several genre-related record labels. Sam "Lightnin'" Hopkins' lifestyle was captured in the acclaimed 1967 documentary *The Blues Accordin' to Lightnin' Hopkins.*

Richard H. Kerr

Richard "Dickey" Kerr (1893–1963) must have wondered what was happening around him as his teammates on the American League champion Chicago White Sox faced the Cincinnati Reds in the 1919 World Series. Kerr did not know that many of his teammates had sold out to gamblers and had agreed to throw the series. Of the White Sox starting rotation, Kerr was the only starter not involved in the "Black Sox" scandal. He won his two starts against the Reds, one by shutout, while the star pitchers, Ed Cicotte and Lefty Williams, each lost their first two games. Kerr's record was 21-9 in 1920 and, after the guilty players were purged, went 19-17 for the decimated 1921 White Sox. Kerr went on to have a long career as a minor league manager.

Glenwood Cemetery
2525 Washington Ave.
N 29 46.088, W 095 23.060

Glenwood Cemetery, incorporated in 1871, is one of Houston's oldest and best maintained cemeteries. Immaculately kept and permanently endowed, Glenwood is much more a park than a final resting place for its many prominent Texans. On the grounds of the cemetery is a multitude of beautiful Texas live oak trees (some of the most beautiful I have ever seen), and one, appropriately called the Cemetery Oak, is reputed to be among the largest in Harris County.

Two gravesites in Glenwood Cemetery are not the resting places of notable Texans but are worthy of visiting for the wonderful statuary. The first marks the grave of Capt. William Dunovant. A jealous partner, who suspected Dunovant of making advances toward his wife, apparently murdered him. Dunovant's sister had erected a statue of an angel that is unlike any other. This angel, dubbed the Avenging Angel, clearly is not a vision of kindness and mercy but rather a specter bent on revenge. It is a remarkable statue, although a bit unnerving to those of us who see angels in a more benevolent light.

The second may well be one of the most unique and touching markers in all of Texas. At the gravesite of Aaron and Christopher

HEADSTONE OF OVETA CULP HOBBY, FIRST SECRETARY OF THE DEPARTMENT OF
HEALTH, EDUCATION AND WELFARE. GLENWOOD CEMETERY, HOUSTON.

Robbins is a serene, almost ethereal windmill. Its gentle motions and
eclectic design imbue the structure with elegance, gentility, and a
peace that speaks to eternal rest and grace. Standing at this site and
watching the gentle motion of the windmill, one imagines that these
boys were themselves as gentle as the summer breezes.

MARY JANE HARRIS BRISCOE

Mary Jane Harris Briscoe (1819–1903) founded the Daughters of the
Republic of Texas. She was an acquaintance of Sam Houston and
other Texas leaders. She married Andrew Briscoe, one of the signers
of the Texas Declaration of Independence. The Daughters of the
Republic of Texas was organized at the Briscoe home in 1891, and
she served as vice president of the organization until 1897.

OVETA CULP HOBBY

Oveta Culp Hobby (1905–1995; wife of William P. Hobby) was the
first secretary of the U.S. Department of Health, Education, and Welfare, a position she held from 1953 to 1955. She organized and
directed the Women's Auxiliary Army Corps (later known as the
WAC) during World War II. She became the first woman to receive the
Distinguished Service Medal.

WILLIAM P. HOBBY

William Hobby (1878–1964) was lieutenant governor of Texas (1914–1917) and became the twenty-sixth governor of Texas (1917–1921) when Governor James Edward "Pa" Ferguson was removed from office. At thirty nine years of age, he was the youngest man to hold the office of governor. He was also the owner and publisher of the *Houston Post* newspaper, and Houston Hobby Airport was named in his honor.

HOWARD R. HUGHES, JR.

Howard Hughes (1905–1976) was born in Houston and grew up in the elite of the city's society. At his father's death in 1924, Howard Hughes gained control of his father's business, Hughes Tool Company. In 1925 he headed to Hollywood to make movies and in 1928 produced *Two Arabian Nights*, which won an Academy Award. Hughes then embarked on writing and directing the classic movie *Hell's Angels*, a story about air warfare in World War I. During the filming of the movie, Hughes earned his pilot's license and survived a serious plane crash.

In 1932 Hughes entered the aviation industry and began racing aircraft. By 1935 he had set a land speed record of 352 miles per hour

THE GRAVESITE OF RECLUSIVE INDUSTRIALIST HOWARD HUGHES, JR., IS BEHIND LOCKED GATES IN GLENWOOD CEMETERY, HOUSTON.

and in 1936 set the transcontinental record. He next converted a Lockheed 14 for an around-the-world flight and circled the globe in three days, nineteen hours, and seventeen minutes.

Hughes decided to enter production of military aircraft, but these efforts were not particularly successful. He suffered his fourth airplane crash in 1946 and dallied in a series of different military, filmmaking, and airline enterprises well into the 1950s, eventually selling his stock in Trans-World Airlines for $546 million in 1966. By the early 1970s he was becoming increasingly reclusive. He had been obsessed with his health since his boyhood, and his last days in a Las Vegas hotel have become the basis for several movies and legends. His health rapidly deteriorated, and he died on route to a Houston hospital in 1976.

Anson Jones

Anson Jones (1798–1858) was the last president of the Republic of Texas. He had come to Texas in 1833 and was involved in the San Jacinto campaign, serving in Robert Calder's company as judge advocate and surgeon. During the First Congress of the Republic, Jones' interests drifted to public policies, and Sam Houston appointed him minister to the United States. Jones was recalled by President Mirabeau B. Lamar in May 1839 and, upon his return, finished the senatorial term of William Wharton.

Sam Houston appointed Jones to the post of secretary of state, and from December 13, 1841, until February 19, 1846, Jones guided the foreign affairs of Texas as the state faced several crises. Jones was elected president of Texas in September 1844 and served until February 19, 1846. At the ceremony that declared Texas as a state in the Union, Jones announced, "The Republic of Texas is no more."

Ross Shaw Sterling

Ross S. Sterling (1875–1949) was born near Anahuac and attended school and farmed until 1896. After operating a series of businesses, Sterling bought two oil wells in 1910 that evolved into the Humble Oil and Refining Company. He went on to real estate development and into the newspaper business, where he merged the *Houston Dispatch* and the *Houston Post*. Sterling was elected governor of Texas in 1930 but was defeated for a second term by Miriam A. Ferguson. Sterling returned to Houston, where he accumulated another fortune as an oilman.

Benjamin Franklin Terry

Benjamin Franklin (Frank) Terry (1821–1861) organized and commanded the Eighth Texas Cavalry (Terry's Texas Rangers) in the Civil War. In June 1861, Terry and several others traveled to Richmond, Virginia, to offer their services to the Confederacy. An aide to Gen. James Longstreet, Terry served with distinction in the Battle of First Manassas. On August 12, 1861, Terry and Francis Lubbock issued a call for volunteers, and 1,170 men answered. In November 1861 they were officially designated the Eighth Texas Cavalry. Terry was killed in the first battle fought by the Rangers near Woodsonville, Kentucky, on December 17, 1861. Terry County was named in his honor.

Gene Tierney

Gene Tierney (1920–1991) began her theatrical career on Broadway in 1939. After being spotted by the movie mogul Darryl Zanuck during a stage performance, she was signed to a contract with Fox Studios. In 1944 Tierney was nominated for an Oscar for best actress, and during the 1950s she was one of the most popular actresses in Hollywood.

Hollywood Cemetery
3506 N. Main St.
N 29 47.642, W 095 22.061

Henry Philemon Attwater

Henry Attwater (1854–1931) was one of America's premier naturalist-conservationists. Though born in England, he came to Texas in 1884 to collect specimens and moved to Sherman in 1889. During the 1890s he collected throughout the state while lecturing and writing on natural history. Attwater was elected a director of the National Audubon Society about 1900 and served in that capacity until 1910. In 1907 he served on the game law committee, which recommended that a license be required for both resident and nonresident hunters and that revenue from licenses and fines be used for wildlife management and protection. Several vertebrate species, including the Attwater's greater prairie-chicken (*Tympanuchus cupido attwateri*), are named in his honor.

MOLLIE ARLINE KIRKLAND BAILEY

Mollie Bailey (1844–1918) began her long circus career when she and her husband formed the Bailey Family Troupe just prior to the Civil War. During the war, her husband Gus served as bandmaster for a company of Hood's Texas Brigade. Mollie traveled with the brigade as a nurse, and legend has it that she also served as a spy for Gen. John Bell Hood and Jubal A. Early.

The Bailey Family Troupe came to Texas in 1879, where it was renamed the Bailey Circus. The circus became the Mollie A. Bailey Show after her husband's failing health required his retirement. Mollie ran the very successful enterprise, which at its zenith had thirty-one wagons and about two hundred animals. She continued to operate the circus until her death and was known for her generosity to Civil War veterans, various church organizations, and children who could not afford the price of admission.

Houston National Cemetery
10410 Veterans Memorial Dr.
N 29 55.736, W 095 27.206

JAMES FIELDS

First Lieutenant James Fields (1921–1970) was assigned to the Tenth Armored Infantry, Fourth Armored Division. On September 27, 1944, at Rechicourt, France, 1st Lt. Fields led his platoon in a counterattack against enemy infantry and tank forces. After seeing one of his men wounded by enemy fire, Fields showed complete disregard for his personal safety as he leapt from his trench to attend to the wounded man and administer first aid. While returning to his slit trench, he was seriously wounded in his face and rendered speechless by his wounds.

Lt. Fields refused to be evacuated and continued to lead his platoon by the use of hand signals. Only when his objective had been taken and the enemy scattered did he consent to be evacuated to the battalion command post. At this point he refused to allow his platoon to move farther back until he had explained to his battalion commander—by drawing on paper—the position of his men and the disposition of the enemy forces. For his gallantry and self-sacrifice, 1st Lt. James Fields was awarded the Congressional Medal of Honor.

Marcario García

Army staff sergeant Marcario García (1920–1972) was assigned to Company B, Twenty-second Infantry, Fourth Infantry Division. On November 27, 1944, near Grosshau, Germany, he single-handedly assaulted two enemy machine gun emplacements. Although painfully wounded, he refused to be evacuated and on his own initiative crawled forward alone until he reached a position near an enemy emplacement. Tossing grenades, he overran the position, destroyed the gun, and with his rifle killed enemy soldiers. When he rejoined his company, a second machine gun opened fire. Sergeant García again took the lead, stormed the position and destroyed the gun, killing three more enemy soldiers and capturing four prisoners. For his courage he was awarded the Congressional Medal of Honor.

Raymond L. Knight

First Lieutenant Raymond Knight (1922–1945) was killed while piloting a fighter-bomber aircraft in a series of bombing raids on April 24–25, 1945. His daring and skillful flying had resulted in two successful raids on April 24. Early the next morning, during a second attack at Bergamo, Italy, he sighted an enemy plane on the runway. Again he led three other American pilots in a low-level sweep through heavy antiaircraft fire that damaged his plane so severely that it was virtually inoperable. Realizing the critical need for aircraft in his unit, he declined to parachute to safety over friendly territory and unhesitatingly attempted to return his shattered plane to his home field. As he flew homeward, his plane crashed and he was killed. First Lieutenant Knight was posthumously awarded the Congressional Medal of Honor.

Hubbard

Fairview Cemetery
N.W. Second St., west of Hubbard
N 31 50.260, W 096 48.358

Tristram Speaker

Tristram Speaker (1888–1958) began his major league baseball career with the Boston Red Sox in 1907. He was traded to Cleveland, where he won the American League batting title in 1916. He assumed the team's managerial reins at age thirty-one. A lifetime .344 hitter, "Tris"

Speaker was a great defense outfielder and recorded 139 double plays from the outfield. He batted more than .300 in eighteen of his nineteen seasons in the majors and set a major league record with 793 doubles. For the first half of the century, Tris Speaker was considered the best center fielder ever to have played the game, and he was elected to the Baseball Hall of Fame in 1939.

Huntsville

Oakwood Cemetery
Ninth St. at Avenue I
N 30 43.595, W 095 32.813

Huntsville's Oakwood Cemetery is one of Texas' most historic graveyards. The western half of the cemetery is shady and peaceful, resembling a forest rather than a cemetery. The ground smells of pine trees, and soft needles covering the ground make walking through the cemetery a pleasure. Oakwood has a single paved avenue that runs through the eastern section of the cemetery, but the western part is not readily accessible except on foot. Two additions to Oakwood Cemetery, the Mays and Addickes additions, lie at its far eastern boundary and across Avenue F.

Oakwood Cemetery, much like the Prairie Lea Cemetery in Brenham, serves as a vivid reminder of the yellow fever epidemic of 1867. Along the fence line in the northwestern section of the cemetery stand six identical white stones, which mark the graves of Union soldiers who died during the epidemic; each stone is marked "Unknown Soldier." Although the names of the deceased were apparently recorded, their exact burial locations were not. These federal soldiers had returned to Walker County to maintain order during Reconstruction, having been imprisoned in Huntsville during the war. In addition, several gravestones in the cemetery list yellow fever as the cause of death.

Of particular interest is a large section of the cemetery that lies just east of the graves marked as yellow fever victims. It is almost completely devoid of markers, suggesting that many of the people buried here also died in the epidemic and were placed in unmarked graves.

On the northern edge of the cemetery, tucked away among the trees and shrubbery, is one of the most beautiful statues to be found in any Texas cemetery. A larger-than-life statue titled *The Christ*, created by Danish sculptor Bertel Thorvaldsen, stands gracefully and magnificently over the gravesite of Judge Ben H. Powell (1881–1960). Cre-

THOMAS GOREE SERVED AS AIDE-DE-CAMP TO CONFEDERATE GENERAL JAMES LONGSTREET. OAKWOOD CEMETERY, HUNTSVILLE.

ated in memory of Powell's son, Rawley R. Powell, this reproduction is worth a trip to the cemetery on its own merit.

THOMAS J. GOREE

Civil War officer and prison director Thomas J. Goree (1835–1905) was an attorney prior to the Civil War and, while traveling east for service in the Confederate army, met Gen. James Longstreet. Goree would become Longstreet's aide-de-camp, serving in almost every battle of the war in which Longstreet's division saw action. After several years as a planter, businessman, and attorney, Goree became superintendent of the Texas State Penitentiary at Huntsville, a position he held for fourteen years.

JOSHUA HOUSTON

Although Sam Houston is arguably the most noteworthy person who lies at rest in Oakwood, the life, accomplishments, and character of another man buried here—another man named Houston—are every bit as impressive as those of the general. A few yards from the Houston gravesite lies Sam Houston's servant Joshua Houston (1822–1902). Joshua was raised in slavery in Alabama on the plantation of Temple Lea, the father of Margaret Lea Houston. After Lea's death, Joshua came to Texas when Margaret married Sam Houston.

Joshua served with Sam Houston during the days of the Republic of Texas, became a skilled blacksmith and craftsman, and helped build Houston's Huntsville home. The Houstons taught Joshua to read and write, and when in 1862 Joshua Houston was given his freedom, he chose to stay with the Houston family. After the Civil War, Joshua Houston became a successful businessman, church leader, and civic leader.

His life stands as a lasting reminder that character, ability, and kindness are not the product of one's race or station in life; rather these are the products of the person.

SAM HOUSTON

The oldest section of the cemetery is located on the western extremity, and in this area is the final resting place of Texas patriot and leader Gen. Sam Houston (1793–1863). Houston is perhaps the central figure in Texas history and was born on his family's plantation in sight of Timber Ridge Church, Rockbridge County, Virginia. After the death of his father, he moved to Tennessee in 1807 but left home in 1808 to live three years with the Cherokee Indians, who named him "the Raven." Throughout the rest of his life, Houston was a strong supporter of Native American people.

Houston served in the War of 1812, during which he was seriously wounded and won the attention of Andrew Jackson. He was first elected to the U.S. House of Representatives from the Ninth Tennessee District in 1823 and to the office of governor of Tennessee in 1827. After a short and disastrous marriage, Houston resigned as governor and returned to live with the Cherokee Indians for three additional years.

Houston came to Texas in 1832 because he saw the territory as his "land of promise." He quickly became embroiled in the Anglo-Texans' politics of rebellion. By 1835 he was sure that war between Texas and Mexico was inevitable. In March 1836, Houston served as a delegate from Refugio to the convention at Washington-on-the-Brazos, where the delegates adopted the Texas Declaration of Independence. Houston was immediately appointed major general of the army and instructed to begin organizing the Texas Army.

Sam Houston's service during the Texas Revolution culminated in the defeat of Gen. Santa Anna's forces at the decisive Battle of San Jacinto on April 21, 1836. During the battle, Houston was severely wounded, but the Texans had won independence from Mexico.

Houston became the first regularly elected president of the Republic of Texas and served two terms. Houston succeeded Mirabeau Lamar for a second term as president from December 12, 1841, to December 9, 1844.

When Texas joined the Union, Houston became one of its two U.S. senators, along with Thomas Jefferson Rusk, and served from 1846 to 1859. In 1857 he ran for governor of Texas but was defeated. Out of the Senate, Houston ran a second time for governor in 1859 and defeated Hardin Runnels. Houston was an ardent supporter of the Union and opposed secession. When he refused an oath of loyalty to the Confederacy, he was removed from office. He lived out his final days in Huntsville, succumbing to illness in 1863 at age seventy.

The native Texas granite sculpture that marks Houston's gravesite is the impressive creation of sculptor Pompeo Coppini. A historical marker at this gravesite is dedicated to his wife, Margaret Lea Houston (she died during a yellow fever epidemic and is buried in Independence, Texas). The Houston gravesite is one of only two gravesites I have visited that actually had a crowd of people stopping to pay their respects. Located just on the edge of the cemetery, it is also easily viewed from Avenue I.

John William Thomason, Jr.

John W. Thomason, Jr. (1893–1944), was born in Huntsville, Texas. His military career began when he entered the Marine Corps in 1917, and he served during many of the most important battles of World War I. Though he was an excellent soldier, Thomason's fame came as a result of his writing and artistic skills. In his lifetime he published more than sixty magazine articles and eleven illustrated books, including *The Adventures of Davy Crockett, Told Mostly by Himself.*

Colonel Thomason was awarded a multitude of military commendations, including the Silver Star. Thomason Park, a section of the Marine Corps Base at Quantico, Virginia, and the Navy destroyer *USS John W. Thomason* were named in his honor.

Henderson K. Yoakum

Henderson Yoakum (1810–1856) was a West Point graduate and came to Huntsville in 1845 to practice law. After service in the U.S.-Mexican War, Yoakum returned to practice law in Huntsville, where he became close friends with Sam Houston and later wrote a two-volume history of Texas. Yoakum County is named in his honor.

Independence

Old Independence Cemetery
CR 60, north of Old Baylor College
N 30 19.720, W 096 21.668

The town of Independence, founded in 1835, was an established religious and educational center in the Republic of Texas. In 1845 the Texas Baptist Educational Society acquired a charter to establish a university. Independence, at that time the most prosperous community in Texas, won the bid. The next year, Baylor University held its first classes with a total student population of twenty. In 1851 the school was divided into two universities, one to serve female students, the other to serve male students. In 1852, Independence was incorporated and the town's first mayor was T. T. Clay. When the city fathers failed to grant a right of way to the Santa Fe Railroad, the future decline of Independence was sealed.

The railroads largely bypassed the city, and since the Baylor students had difficulty getting to the universities in the absence of railroads, the officials decided to move the women's college to Belton (Mary Hardin Baylor) and the men's school to Waco (Baylor University). The decision to move the schools resulted in the slow decline of the town. Today only the four columns of the Old University still stand in Independence, just across FM 390 from the homesite of Sam Houston.

There are several false crypts in the cemetery, one of which is constructed of precisely cut native limestone. This old cemetery is well manicured, although many of the markers are broken and lying about the area. As in the Mount Zion Baptist Church Cemetery near Burton, many of the graves here are decorated with large seashells. Although the Clay family members (almost every male of the clan appears to have been named Tacitus Clay) are prominent among the burials in the cemetery, several prominent Texas pioneers and educators are also buried here, including Asa Hoxey (1800–1863), a signer of the Texas Declaration of Independence. The Old Independence Cemetery is a splendid country graveyard. It is replete with mature cedar trees, which were alive with the chipping of wintering yellow-rumped warblers when I visited. There is also a large oak motte in one corner of the cemetery. The cemetery has no set hours for visitation and in fact has no enclosure of any type along its boundary with County Road 60.

MOSES AUSTIN BRYAN

Moses Austin Bryan (1817–1895) was the nephew of Stephen F. Austin and served for a period as Austin's private secretary. Bryan enlisted and fought at the Battle of San Jacinto and was the interpreter between Sam Houston and Gen. Santa Anna. Bryan was a member of the Somervell expedition in 1842 and fought for the Confederacy during the Civil War.

SAM HOUSTON, JR.

The eldest son of Sam and Margaret Houston, Sam Houston, Jr. (1843–1894), was born at Washington-on-the-Brazos. He began service in the Confederacy in 1861 and was captured at the Battle of Shiloh. After the war, he studied medicine at the University of Pennsylvania but left the practice of medicine to pursue a career in writing.

Indianola

Old Town Cemetery
1 mile east of Highway 316
N 28 30.728, W 096 29.230

The port of Indianola was founded in August 1846 as Indian Point and served as a deep-water port on Matagorda Bay for more than thirty years. Indianola, as it was named in 1849, was the county seat of Calhoun County from 1852 to 1886, and at its peak the city had a population in excess of five thousand. But the port of Indianola stood in the way of two powerful hurricanes, one in 1875, which killed as many as 150–300 residents, and another in 1886 that obliterated the town. By 1887, Indianola had been abandoned.

Indianola was served over the years by three cemeteries, Old Town Cemetery, Indianola Cemetery, and the Zimmerman Cemetery. Although all three cemeteries are still in existence, the Zimmerman Cemetery lies on private property and is not readily accessible. Bring some insect repellent if you visit the other two cemeteries; they are adjacent to marshes, and the mosquitoes were atrocious when I visited. Old Town Cemetery lies on the north side of a gravel road that intersects Highway 316 in Calhoun County. The exit to the cemetery is clearly marked, but the cemetery road apparently crosses private property guarded by "No Trespassing" signs on the fence near the intersection. Taking a chance, I drove to the first house on the road, approached its front door in a heavy coastal downpour, and was told that I was welcome to visit the cemetery. If you carefully avoid the cattle on the road, you will find the cemetery about a mile from the house. It is surrounded by a low fence and has a historical marker at the entrance.

This tiny cemetery lies on a low hill surrounded by a coastal marsh, and periodic coastal floods and hurricanes (along with vandalism) have left this site almost devoid of markers and vegetation, save a patch or two of grass. A close inspection of the area reveals why this particular hill was chosen as a cemetery: it is the highest point in a low-lying marsh.

ANGELINA BELLE EBERLY

One of Texas' most unusual heroines, Angelina Belle Eberly (1798–1860) woke up one morning and secured her place in history. In December 1842, Mrs. Eberly realized that a company of Texas Rangers was secretly removing the state archives from the city of Austin. Legend suggests that she sounded an alarm by firing shot from a six-pound cannon the citizens of Austin kept loaded in the event of an Indian attack. Local citizens chased the Rangers, took back the state papers, and returned them to Austin during what came to be known as the Archive War. Mrs. Eberly, who ran a boardinghouse in Austin, moved to Indianola and operated a hotel there until her death. Sadly, her grave is now unmarked, its headstone carried away by one of Indianola's storms.

Jefferson

Oakwood Cemetery
E. Webster at N. Main St.
N 32 45.997, W 094 20.906

The weather had been dreadful in Jefferson for over a week, much worse than would be expected for even a January day in 1877. As the weather began to warm, Sarah King had wandered out into the countryside in search of firewood and instead found the body of a well-dressed woman near an old East Texas oak. Nearby were what appeared to be the remnants of a picnic lunch. The woman, Bessie Moore, had died from a gunshot wound to her head, and the body was devoid of any jewelry. The citizens of Jefferson took up a collection and buried her in Oakwood Cemetery.

GRAVESITE OF "DIA-
MOND BESSIE,"
WHOSE MURDER
BROUGHT ABOUT THE
FIRST HIGH-PROFILE
TRIAL IN TEXAS. OAK-
WOOD CEMETERY,
JEFFERSON.

Several days later Bessie Moore's traveling companion, Abraham
Rothschild (a traveling jewelry salesman), was arrested on a charge of
murder, and Texas' first high-profile trial was soon under way.

The prosecution was laden with powerful Texas lawyers, including
two assistant attorneys general. The defense was equally strong, as
Rothschild was represented by a future governor, Charles A. Culberson, and a U.S. senator, David B. Culberson. After three weeks of testimony the jury found Rothschild guilty of murder in the first degree
and sentenced him to death by hanging. The defense asked for a rever-
sal of the case on the grounds that the trial had been unfair. The first
trial was subsequently declared a mistrial.

Rothschild's second trial began on December 2, 1880, and this
time the defense was able to create a reasonable doubt in the minds of
the jurors. On December 30, 1880, the jury found Rothschild not
guilty. In the 1930s a headstone mysteriously appeared at the
gravesite of Bessie Moore. In 1941 a Mr. E. B. McDonald declared
that he had put the headstone on her grave because it did not seem
right for Diamond Bessie to sleep in an unmarked grave. A beautiful

iron fence surrounds her gravesite, and although her killer was never officially found, it is unlikely that he escaped death himself.

DAVID BROWNING CULBERSON

David Browning Culberson (1830–1900) came to Texas in 1856, where he practiced law in partnership with Gen. Hinche P. Mabry in Upshur County until 1861. Although Culberson opposed secession, when the Civil War began he aided in raising the Eighteenth Texas Infantry, of which he became lieutenant colonel. After service in the Vicksburg area (1862–1863), he was assigned to Austin as adjutant general of Texas. In the winter of 1864 he was elected to the Texas Legislature from Cass, Titus, and Bowie counties and resigned his military position to accept.

A prominent Jefferson lawyer, Culberson was one of the defense attorneys in the Diamond Bessie murder trial. He was elected in 1873 to the Texas Senate and resigned his seat upon election to the Forty-fourth Congress of the United States. Culberson served eleven terms in the U.S. House (1875–1897). Culberson County was named in his honor.

Kingsville

Chamberlain Cemetery
W. Caesar at S. Armstrong St.
N 27 30.381, W 097 52.745

RICHARD AND HENRIETTA KING

If any life story exemplifies the Texas legend of the 1800s, it would be that of Richard King (1824–1885) and his wife, Henrietta (1832–1925). Born in New York City, the son of poor Irish parents, Richard left a life of indenture by stowing away on a ship bound for Mobile, Alabama. Between 1835 and 1841 he pursued steamboating on Alabama rivers and was a pilot by age sixteen. In 1842 he enlisted for service in the Seminole War in Florida, where he met Mifflin Kenedy, who became his lifelong friend and business mentor.

King came to Texas in 1847, where he joined Kenedy during the U.S.-Mexican War. King remained on the Rio Grande after the war and began a steamboat operation that flourished. Soon after his arrival on the Rio Grande, King began speculating in Cameron County lands and in lots in the new town of Brownsville. The proceeds from his steamboat interests provided capital, and King bought

TEXAS CATTLE BARON AND RANCHING LEGEND RICHARD KING AND HIS VISION-
ARY WIFE, HENRIETTA, ARE AT REST IN THE CHAMBERLAIN CEMETERY IN THE
CITY NAMED FOR THEM, KINGSVILLE.

land as quickly as he could raise the cash. The year of 1854 was a
momentous year for King, as he married Henrietta Maria Morse
Chamberlain and purchased the fifty-three-thousand-acre Santa
Gertrudis de la Garza grant, the nucleus of the great King Ranch.

Henrietta King came to Texas with her parents when her father,
Hiram Chamberlain, organized the first Presbyterian mission in South
Texas at Brownsville in 1850. In 1854 she taught briefly at the Rio
Grande Female Institute before her marriage to Richard King. Upon
her husband's death in 1885, Mrs. King assumed full ownership of his
estate, consisting chiefly of five hundred thousand acres of ranchland
between Corpus Christi and Brownsville and $500,000 in debts.
Under Henrietta King's stewardship the King Ranch not only became
debt free but also increased in acreage.

Mrs. King proved to be a woman of remarkable vision. The Santa
Gertrudis cattle developed on the King Ranch became a mainstay of
the Texas cattle industry, and her offer of right-of-way allowed rail
service to stretch between Corpus Christi and Brownsville, opening
the area to economic growth and settlement. The cities of Kingsville
and Raymondville were built on town sites she provided, and her
investments furnished the economic stimulus for the town that would
become Kingsville. She constructed the First Presbyterian Church
building in Kingsville and also donated land for Baptist, Methodist,

Episcopal, and Catholic churches. Mrs. King constructed a public high school and presented it to the town.

Among her many charities were donations of land for the Texas-Mexican Industrial Institute and for the Spohn Sanitarium. In her last years she provided land and encouragement for the establishment of South Texas State Teachers College (now Texas A&I University).

RICHARD MIFFLIN KLEBERG

Richard M. Kleberg (1887–1955) was born on the King Ranch and graduated from law school at the University of Texas. Returning to the ranch, he actively managed the spread as foreman and part owner from 1913 to 1924. He was elected in November 1931 as a Democrat to the Seventy-second Congress and was reelected to six succeeding congresses before being defeated in 1944. Known as the "Cowboy Congressman," he had as his first administrative assistant Lyndon B. Johnson. Kleberg served on the Agriculture Committee during his entire tenure in Congress (1931–1945) and sponsored legislation that established the Farm Credit Administration, duck stamp programs, and migratory bird conservation. After retirement from Congress, he served as chairman of the board of the King Ranch and as a member of the Texas Game and Fish Commission (1951–1955).

La Grange

Old City Cemetery
N. Jackson at Highway 71 E.
N 29 54.488, W 096 52.361

La Grange is another of Texas' early settlements and is the site where La Bahía Road crossed the Colorado River. The first settlement in the vicinity was about 1819, and in 1826 John Henry Moore built a twin blockhouse within what are now the city limits. Named Moore's Fort, it served as a safe haven for those seeking shelter from Indian attacks. By 1831 a small community had developed around the fort, and the town was platted in 1837.

The Old City Cemetery in La Grange reflects the heritage, history, and tragedy of the city. Several of the Texans who participated in the "Dawson Massacre" (1842) and the Somervell and Mier expeditions were from La Grange, including Nathaniel Faison, who is buried in the cemetery. From August through December 1867, La Grange was ravaged by a yellow fever epidemic that took the lives of 240 citi-

zens—about 20 percent of its population at the time. Walking near the east end of the cemetery, one finds a clustering of gravesites of families virtually wiped out by the disease.

ASA HILL

Asa Hill (ca. 1788–1844) came to Texas about 1834 and moved his family to his new home in 1835. Hill joined the Texas Army in 1836. He was ordered by Gen. Sam Houston to spread the message of the impending movements of the Mexican army after the burning of the city of Gonzales and thereby did not participate in the Battle of San Jacinto.

In 1842 Hill and two of his sons, Jeffrey Barksdale Hill and John Christopher Columbus Hill, joined the Somervell expedition and continued as members of the Mier expedition. All three men were captured, and Gen. Santa Anna eventually adopted John Hill (a fourteen-year-old youth at the time of his capture). In the Black Bean Episode, Asa Hill drew a white bean and thus was spared execution. He and his son Jeffrey were held with the other Texan prisoners at Perote Prison until late in 1843. The physical toll of imprisonment proved to be Hill's undoing, and he died soon after his return to Texas.

JAMES SEATON LESTER

James S. Lester (1799–1879) was born in Virginia and came to Texas in 1834. In 1835 he represented the Mina, or Bastrop, District at the Consultation and was a member of a committee appointed to plan the organization of the provisional government. Lester was the recruiting agent at Bastrop for the army to attack Bexar in 1835, and he later fought in the Battle of San Jacinto. He served in the Texas Senate from Bastrop and Gonzales in the First and Second Congresses, in the House from Fayette County in the Third Congress, and as senator from Fayette, Bastrop, and Gonzales in the Fourth and Fifth Congresses. He was one of the first trustees of Baylor University.

Monument Hill State Historic Site
414 State Loop 92
N 29 53.304, W 096 52.633

On the morning of September 18, 1842, fifty-four Texans found themselves trapped by hostile Mexican military forces on the open prairie near San Antonio. Most were from Fayette County. They had set out to join forces with Mathew Caldwell as the Texans attempted to drive invading Mexican troops (under the command of Mexican general Adrian Woll) from the city of San Antonio. Now Nicholas Dawson and his fellow patriots found themselves confronted with an overwhelming force of Mexican troops. Dawson quickly withdrew to a small mesquite thicket (near the present site of Fort Sam Houston) and prepared for battle. In just over one hour, thirty-six men lay dead and fifteen had been captured in what became known as the Dawson Massacre; only three men escaped. The bodies of the Texans were buried in a shallow grave on the field where they had died.

Later that year, approximately 750 Texan soldiers under the command of Alexander Somervell set out from San Antonio on a punitive military operation that history has dubbed the Somervell expedition. Gen. Sam Houston ordered the expulsion of the invading Mexican army from Texas soil after the Dawson Massacre.

When the force reached the Rio Grande, Somervell realized that to continue the expedition would be foolhardy and gave the soldiers the option of ending the affair and returning home, or continuing into Mexico under different leadership. Of the 683 men gathered at the river, only 187 decided to return home. The others elected William S. Fisher as the new commander and crossed the river into Mexico as the Somervell expedition quickly evolved into what became known as the Mier expedition. On the morning of December 26, the Texans engaged the Mexican garrison at Mier, where they were soon defeated, captured, and marched away to imprisonment.

On February 11, 1843, a large band of the Texans tried to escape their captors and, in doing so, killed a handful of guards. Within days, 176 of the escapees were recaptured. As punishment, each had to reach into a jar that contained 159 white beans and 17 black beans. Each of those who drew a black bean was executed in what became known as the Black Bean Episode.

Most of the imprisoned were eventually released and returned home in 1844. In 1848 a public meeting was held at La Grange, at which it was decided that suitable arrangements should be made for the interment of the executed Mier prisoners and those killed in the Dawson Massacre. A small tomb was built overlooking the Colorado River, and on September 18, 1848, the remains were buried there with full military honors in a ceremony attended by Sam Houston and other dignitaries.

Laredo

Laredo Catholic Cemetery
3600 McPherson Ave.
N 27 31.725, W 099 29.071

THE BROTHERS BENAVIDES

José del Refugio Benavides (1821–1899), Santos Benavides (1823–1891), and Cristóbal Benavides (1839–1904) were all born in Laredo and were direct descendents of Tomás Sánchez de la Barrera y Garza, who had founded Laredo in 1755. The Benavides family played an important role in secession and the Civil War in South Texas.

During the war on the border, Refugio Benavides rose to the rank of captain and commanded a company in the Thirty-third Texas Cavalry. Santos Benavides became the highest-ranking Mexican American to serve the Confederacy. He was commissioned a captain in the Thirty-third Texas Cavalry (or Benavides' Regiment) and assigned to

CRISTÓBAL BENAVIDES
AND HIS BROTHERS,
SANTOS AND REFUGIO,
WERE CENTRAL FIGURES
IN THE TEXAS CONFED-
ERACY. LAREDO
CATHOLIC CEMETERY,
LAREDO.

the Rio Grande Military District, where he quickly won recognition as a fighter and a leader. In November 1863, Benavides was promoted to colonel and authorized to raise his own regiment of "Partisan Rangers," for which he used the remnants of the Thirty-third. In 1864 he was promoted to the rank of general.

The brothers served together in what was to become their greatest military triumph. On March 19, 1864, the brothers defended Laredo from a Union cotton raid in what became known as the Battle of Laredo. A federal expedition from the Lower Rio Grande Valley had pushed upriver to Laredo, hoping to burn the five thousand bales of cotton stacked in St. Augustine Plaza. After three hours of fighting, the federal force was defeated. Sparing the precious cotton store, Santos arranged for safe passage of Texas cotton along the Rio Grande to Matamoros during the Union occupation of Brownsville in 1864.

After the war the brothers returned to life in Laredo. Refugio was elected mayor in 1873 and served in that capacity until 1876. In 1874 he raised a company of Rangers at Laredo to combat the growing threats posed by bandits and Kickapoo Indians on the border. Santos returned to his mercantile and ranching activities with his brother Cristóbal and remained active in politics. Santos served three times in the Texas Legislature from 1879 to 1884 and twice as an alderman of Laredo. Cristóbal married Lamar Bee, daughter of Confederate general Hamilton P. Bee but, unlike his brothers, was not interested in politics; instead he concentrated his efforts in ranching and a mercantile business. At the time of his death, Cristóbal had become one of the wealthiest men in Webb County.

Allen Walker

Allen Walker (1866–1953) was a private in the U.S. Army during the Indian Wars. Walker was awarded the Medal of Honor for attacking a party of three armed men and securing papers valuable to the United States in Texas on December 30, 1891.

Livingston

Alabama-Coushatta Tribal Cemetery
Highway 190, east of intersection with FM 2500, Polk County
N 30 43.012, W 094 40.263

In 1805 approximately one thousand Alabama Indians came to Tyler County's Peach Tree Village. The Coushattas were already in East

Texas, having arrived in the Big Thicket area sometime after 1795. The intertribal friendship between these two peoples became even stronger as they roamed and hunted this new land together. In the early 1800s the Texas Congress granted each tribe two leagues of land along the Trinity River. This land was soon taken over by white settlers, leaving these Native Americans homeless. Sam Houston recommended that the state purchase 1,280 acres for the Alabamas and set aside 640 acres for the Coushattas. The land for the Coushattas was never plotted nor surveyed; and so, either through marriage or special permission, they came to live on the allotted land with the Alabamas—uniting the two to become the Alabama-Coushatta.

This cemetery is one of the most culturally interesting in all of Texas. Only white crosses mark many of the gravesites, and the plots are classic "scrape" plots, completely free of grass, mounded, and covered with rocks and shells. The graves are maintained by replacing sand washed away during rainstorms. The placement of shells on the sandy mound results in mushroom shaped towers that are formed

JOHN SCOTT, PRINCIPAL CHIEF OF THE ALABAMA-COUSHATTA TRIBE FOR MORE THAN FORTY YEARS, AT REST IN THE TRIBAL CEMETERY ON THE ALABAMA-COUSHATTA RESERVATION, NEAR LIVINGSTON.

when rainfall washes away the sand not protected by the shells. In some cases, such shell-clad mushrooms protrude several inches above the surrounding mound. The ground is completely carpeted in pine needles and cones and is lush and fragrant after the frequent East Texas rain showers. Four prominent tribal chiefs are at rest here: Colabe Cillistine (ca. 1780–ca. 1865), Bronson Cooper Sylestine (Tic-ca-Itche, 1879–1969), Charles Martin (Sun-Kee) Thompson (1860–1935), and John Scott (1805–1913).

John Scott

John Scott (1805–1913) was principal chief of the Alabama-Coushatta Indians of Texas from 1871 to 1913. He arrived at the reservation during the winter of 1854–1855, and in 1862 he was among nineteen Alabama-Coushattas who were recruited and sworn into service with Company G, Twenty-fourth Texas Cavalry (Second Lancers), Confederate States of America Army. After brief service at the Arkansas Post on the Arkansas River, the Indians were returned to Texas in December 1862. In an 1871 election of tribal leaders, the Alabama-Coushattas elected John Scott as principal chief. Scott lived 108 years and served as a historical record of the tribe.

Losoya

El Carmen Cemetery
18555 Leal Rd.
N 29 13.269, W 098 28.523

Numerous nineteenth-century journals and other written historical accounts trace the origin of this cemetery to the burial of casualties of the Battle of Medina. Fought on August 18, 1813, the battle was the result of a failed attempt by a republican army of the north—consisting of about 1,200 to 1,500 Mexicans, Anglo-Americans, and Indians—to free Mexico for royalist Spanish rule. The royalist army was victorious, and hundreds of men who died on the battlefield later were interred at this site between 1813 and 1817. The church of Nuestra Señora del Carmen traces its origin to a chapel built over the soldiers' burial crypt. The burial site became a community cemetery as pioneer settlers established homes in this area. Among those interred in the graveyard are the families of Domingo Losoya and Dionicio Martinez, who received Mexican land grants surrounding the cemetery property.

ENRIQUE ESPARZA

Enrique Esparza (1828–1917) survived the Battle of the Alamo, although his father, Gregorio Esparza, was killed in defense of the fortress. In a 1907 interview, Esparza claimed to be the last living survivor of the Alamo and provided a vivid account of the death of the Alamo defenders.

Lubbock

City of Lubbock Cemetery
2011 E. Thirty-fourth St.
N 33 33.812, W 101 48.932

JOSEPH ALVIN CHATMAN

Joseph Alvin Chatman (1901–1967) was born in Navasota. At age eighteen he was admitted to Prairie View Agricultural and Mechanical College (now Prairie View A&M University), where he played football and led an undefeated baseball team. Chatman then attended Fisk University in Nashville, Tennessee, pursuing a premed curriculum. In 1926 he received an M.D. from Meharry Medical College in Nashville, Tennessee. He began his medical career in Mexia, Texas, where he built the Chatman Hospital. He received a B.S. degree in 1927 from Samuel Huston College (now Huston-Tillotson College) in Austin.

Chatman moved to Lubbock in 1939 and there dedicated his life to public service. He founded the Chatman Medical and Surgical Clinic and Hospital, the first hospital for African Americans in Lubbock, which was completed in 1945, and he was elected Lubbock Man of the Year for six consecutive years. Governor Price Daniel appointed Chatman in 1960 to the President's White House Conference on Youth and in 1964 to the Conference on the Aged. In 1955 Chatman was awarded an honorary doctor of humanities degree by Paul Quinn College. On March 23, 1963, he was appointed by Governor John Connally to serve on the board of directors of Texas Southern University in Houston.

Chatman was the first African American to be an official in the Democratic Party in Lubbock County and served as a delegate to the state Democratic convention.

GEORGE ANDREW DAVIS, JR.

George A. Davis, Jr. (1920–1952), was born in Dublin, Texas. He joined the U.S. Army Air Corps as an aviation cadet at Lubbock on March 21, 1942. After completing flight training and fighter pilot training, Davis was assigned to the 342nd Fighter Squadron, 348th Fighter Group, Fifth Fighter Command, in the Southwest Pacific. While in the Pacific during World War II, Davis became an "ace" with seven victories and was awarded the Silver Star, the Distinguished Flying Cross with one oak leaf cluster, and the Air Medal with seven clusters.

During the Korean War, while leading a flight of four F-86 jet fighters near the Manchurian border, his element leader ran out of oxygen and, with his wingman, was forced to return to base. Major Davis and the other remaining F-86 fighters continued the mission. The pilots sighted approximately twelve MIG-15 aircraft about to attack friendly fighter-bombers conducting low-level ground operations. Davis attacked the MIG formation and shot down two planes. While attacking a third, his aircraft was destroyed by enemy fire. For his "conspicuous gallantry and intrepidity at the risk of his life above and beyond the call of duty," Davis received the Medal of Honor posthumously. On his sixtieth combat mission in Korea, his final mission, he scored his thirteenth and fourteenth aerial victories and became America's leading jet ace.

BUDDY HOLLY

Buddy Holly (1936–1959) (real name: Charles Hardin Holley) was born in Lubbock. Nicknamed "Buddy" because he was the youngest child, he was encouraged by his father to pursue music. In the mid-1950s, Buddy Holly and his band, the Crickets, were a national rock and roll sensation. The first Crickets single, "That'll Be the Day," backed with "I'm Looking for Someone to Love," was released on Brunswick Records on May 27, 1957, and began a string of hit records for Holly and his group.

Early in January 1959, Buddy headlined a show called "The Winter Dance Party," which also featured Ritchie Valens (whose recording of "Donna" was number 10 in the U.S charts), and Jiles "the Big Bopper" Richardson (whose "Chantilly Lace" had been a million-seller). On Monday, February 2, the tour had reached Clear Lake, Iowa, and was due to appear the next evening at the Moorehead Armory, Minnesota. Earlier Buddy had chartered a four-seat plane to

GRAVESITE OF ROCK AND ROLL LEGEND BUDDY HOLLY. CITY OF LUBBOCK
CEMETERY, LUBBOCK.

take two of his group, along with Waylon Jennings, Tommy Allsup, and himself to Moorehead. When the other performers on the tour heard of Buddy's arrangement, Jennings and Allsup got separate requests to give up their seats on the plane.

The Big Bopper approached Waylon Jennings asking that Jennings give up his airplane seat to him. Richardson was ill, and Waylon Jennings agreed to relinquish his seat on the plane. When Ritchie Valens learned of the planned flight, he persuaded Tommy Allsup to bet his seat on the plane on a coin toss. Valens won the coin toss and boarded the plane. The plane took off shortly before 1:00 A.M. but crashed within a few miles of the airport, killing all the passengers on board.

BESS BIGHAM HUBBARD

Bess Bigham Hubbard (1896–1977) was born in Fort Worth and began her college education at Texas Christian University. She married and moved to Lubbock in 1917. Bess Hubbard began her art career in 1925 as a hobby and over the next few years continued her art education at Colorado College, the University of New Mexico, Bradley University, and the Chicago Academy of Fine Arts.

RIGHT: THE GRAVESITE OF SCULPTOR BESS HUBBARD IS MARKED BY A LOVELY CREATION BY THE SCULPTOR. CITY OF LUBBOCK CEMETERY, LUBBOCK.

Hubbard soon won acclaim for her impressionist-style paintings, lithographs, and etchings, which featured local subjects and south-western regional motifs. By the mid-1950s she had earned international recognition for her art pieces. Her work is in the permanent collections of the Dallas Museum of Art, the Texas Fine Arts Association, the Elisabet Ney Museum, and the Colorado Springs Fine Arts Center.

ROBERT LAWRENCE LAYNE

Robert L. (Bobby) Layne (1926–1986) was born in Santa Anna. Layne was a gifted high school athlete, and in his senior year at Highland Park High School (Dallas) he was named to the All-State football team. He enrolled at the University of Texas in 1944 and almost became a sports legend. In the January 1946 Cotton Bowl, he led Texas to victory over Missouri, completing eleven of twelve passes for two touchdowns and scoring four times himself. Layne led the Longhorns to a 1948 win over Alabama in the Sugar Bowl and a ranking of fifth in the nation.

Layne was an All–Southwest Conference selection all four years he played at Texas and, after his senior season, was the consensus choice All-American quarterback. By the time he graduated, he held every major school passing record, including most attempts, most completions, most passing yards, most total yards, and most touchdowns.

Though in his years at the University of Texas he was an excellent baseball player, he decided to pursue professional football and starred in the National Football League for more than a decade. He was elected to the Texas Sports Hall of Fame in 1960, to the Longhorn Hall of Honor in 1963, and to the Pro Football Hall of Fame in 1967.

HERMAN C. WALLACE

Herman C. Wallace (?–1945) served with Company B, 301st Engineer Combat Battalion, Seventy-sixth Infantry Division, near Prumzurley, Germany. On February 27, 1945, he was helping clear enemy mines from a road when he stepped on an S-type antipersonnel mine. With two comrades directly behind him, he immediately placed his other foot on the mine in order to confine the blast to the ground, thereby saving the lives of his fellow soldiers. For his sacrifice, he was awarded the Congressional Medal of Honor.

Marfa

Marfa Cemetery
Highway 90 at S. Tenison St.
N 30 18.417, W 104 02.315

JAMES BUCHANAN GILLETT

James Buchanan Gillett (1856–1937) was born in Austin and reared in Lampasas. After a stint as a working cowboy, Gillett joined Company D, Frontier Battalion, of the Texas Rangers in 1875. As a Ranger, Gillett gained fame as an Indian fighter and as a man who could round up cattle thieves and outlaws. In December 1881, Gillett resigned from the Texas Rangers and was appointed assistant city marshal of El Paso; in June 1882 he was appointed marshal.

El Paso at that time was a tough border town, and Gillett was known as a man without fear, despite his relatively tender age. Arrow straight, he neither cursed nor drank, and he claimed that "no man will ever kill me drunk." On April 1, 1885, he left law enforcement and became a cattle manager for the Estado Land and Cattle Company. Six years later, he began ranching on his own and became a successful cattleman in his own right. His years with the Texas Rangers were chronicled in his book, *Six Years with the Texas Rangers* (1921).

Marshall

Greenwood Cemetery
Herndon St. at Carter St.
N 32 33.239, W 094 22.575

MATHEW DUNCAN ECTOR

Mathew Duncan Ector (1822–1879) moved to Texas from Georgia in 1850. In 1855 he was elected to represent Rusk County in the Sixth Texas Legislature. At the beginning of the Civil War he enlisted as a private in the Third Texas Cavalry, and after service in a series of major battles, including the Battle of Richmond, he was promoted to brigadier general on August 23, 1862. His military career ended at Atlanta, after wounds he received there forced the amputation of his left leg at the knee. He moved to Marshall in 1868 to practice law and was elected in 1875 to the Court of Appeals. Ector County was named in his honor.

Marshall Cemetery
Highway 80 at N. Columbus St.
N 32 32.944, W 094 21.893

EDWARD CLARK

Edward Clark (1815–1880) was the first Confederate governor of Texas. He was elected Texas secretary of state (1853–1857) and lieutenant governor in 1859. Clark was elected governor in 1861 upon removal of Governor Sam Houston (who opposed secession), but he lost the race for a full term to Francis Lubbock. In late 1861 Clark raised and became a colonel in the Fourteenth Texas Infantry Regiment. He was wounded at the Battle of Pleasant Hill in 1864 and discharged. After the war, he eventually returned to Marshall to practice law.

HORACE RANDAL

Horace Randal (1833–1864) came to Texas in 1839 from Tennessee. In 1849 Horace Randal and James B. McIntyre became the first Texas appointees to the U.S. Military Academy at West Point, and Randal graduated in 1854. Randal served in the U.S. Army until 1861, when he resigned and went into Confederate service.

Commissioned as a colonel of cavalry on February 12, 1862, he recruited the Twenty-eighth Texas Cavalry Regiment (Dismounted) in and around Marshall. Randal was appointed brigade commander on September 3, 1862, and served in Arkansas and Louisiana. He led the brigade at Milliken's Bend during the Vicksburg campaign in June 1863 and in repulsing Maj. Gen. Nathaniel P. Banks' Red River campaign in the spring of 1864. General E. Kirby Smith appointed him to the rank of general on April 8, 1864, but his promotion was never confirmed by the Confederate government. Horace Randal died of wounds received at the Battle of Jenkins' Ferry, Arkansas, on April 30, 1864. Randall County was named in his honor.

Old Powder Mill Cemetery
FM 1997, just south of intersection with Loop 390
N 32 34.069, W 094 22.433

Located on part of a site once occupied by a Confederate gunpowder factory, this cemetery originated with the burial of slaves on the Powder Mill acreage. After the factory was destroyed in 1865 with the collapse of the Confederacy, the acreage fell into private ownership.

One of the landowners, mortician M. M. Rains, began recording the burials here in 1880; however, the earliest known marked grave, that of Millie Abner, is dated 1878.

DAVID ABNER, SR.

David Abner, Sr. (1826–1902), was born in slavery in Alabama and brought to Upshur County, Texas, in 1843 by the daughter of his master. Abner remained there until after the Civil War. In 1866 he moved to Marshall. After settling in Harrison County, the former slave became a prosperous farmer and politician. He was appointed to the State Executive Committee of the Colored Men's Convention of 1873 and was later elected Harrison County treasurer. In 1874 he was elected to the Texas Legislature. He was also elected a member of the Constitutional Convention of 1875, and in 1876 he was a member and a vice president of the Republican State Convention.

MITCHELL KENDALL

Mitchell Kendall (Kendal) (ca. 1822–ca. 1885) was born a slave around 1822 in Georgia. He served as a voter registrar in 1867 and 1868 in Harrison County, where the population was predominantly African American. Kendall won election as a delegate to the Constitutional Convention of 1868–1869, and as a member of the Public Lands Committee, he voted to divide Texas into three states and signed the constitution produced by the convention. After Kendall's nomination by the Union League in Harrison County, he won a seat in the Texas House of Representatives, where he was one of fourteen African Americans who helped give the Republican Party a working majority in the Twelfth Legislature.

Matagorda

Matagorda Cemetery
Highway 60, north of intersection with N. Gulf Rd.
N 28 42.060, W 095 57.377

SAMUEL RHOADS FISHER

Samuel Rhoads Fisher (1794–1839) represented Matagorda Municipality in the Convention of 1836 at Washington-on-the-Brazos and there signed the Texas Declaration of Independence. The Texas Senate confirmed Fisher's nomination by President Sam Houston as secretary of the Texas Navy on October 28, 1836. In October 1837, Houston suspended Fisher from office, but the Senate resented the suspension and ordered Fisher's reinstatement on October 18, 1837. Fisher County was named in his honor.

ALBERT CLINTON HORTON

Albert Clinton Horton (1798–1865) was the first lieutenant governor of Texas. He arrived in Texas in April 1835 and became an early and active supporter of the Texas Revolution. Horton recruited a company of volunteers in Alabama that became known as the Mobile Grays, and these soldiers were outfitted at Horton's own expense. Colonel Horton's company joined Col. James Walker Fannin, Jr.'s command in South Texas in early March 1836. On March 19, Horton advanced with a small scouting party at Coleto Creek. When he found the remainder of Fannin's army surrounded by Mexican soldiers, Horton and his men escaped capture by fleeing the area.

From 1836 to 1838 Horton served as senator in the First and Second Congresses of the republic, representing Matagorda, Jackson, and Victoria counties. He campaigned unsuccessfully for the vice presidency in 1838.

Horton served as a delegate to the Convention of 1845 and subsequently consented to run for lieutenant governor and won the office. Horton served as governor pro tem in the absence of Governor Pinckney Henderson from May 19, 1846, until Henderson returned on November 13, 1846. Horton was never again elected to public office.

SETH INGRAM

Seth Ingram (1790–1857) served during the War of 1812 as a sergeant in the Eleventh Regiment, U.S. Infantry. In 1822 he and his brother Ira came to Texas. Seth Ingram was hired by Stephen F. Austin to survey his colony in August 1823, and he platted the town of San Felipe de Austin (1823–1824). Seth Ingram was one of Austin's Old Three Hundred colonists, receiving land in what became part of Wharton and Austin counties; six years later he obtained additional lands in southwestern Matagorda County.

In 1830 Ingram dueled San Felipe lawyer John G. Holtham, an action that resulted in Holtham's demise and a trip to jail for Ingram. Ingram spent the next sixteen months in prison and was eventually tried and found not guilty. By 1834 the Ingram brothers had moved to Matagorda, where Seth served, ironically, as a justice of the peace.

Mercury

Cowboy Cemetery
County Road 145 (Cowboy Rd.)
N 31 20.612, W 099 07.149

No one knew his name or from where he came. They found him under an oak tree, his horse grazing quietly nearby. This wandering cowboy had been shot once and now lay dead on the Texas prairie. He was buried under the tree where he was found; a simple rock headstone with no inscription would serve as the only evidence of his passing, yet the Cowboy Cemetery would be forever named in his remembrance.

Cowboy Cemetery, on the south side of Cowboy Road near Mercury, is one of the most pleasant and well-kept cemeteries in rural Texas. The large rock wall that forms the north-facing facade is built from local stone and is both sturdy and elegant in its simplicity. A small chapel is located inside the chain-link fence, which surrounds the cemetery, and a working windmill delivers a steady stream of water to an adjacent cistern. Oak and cedar trees have been planted along the front of the cemetery as a windbreak, and the view of the surrounding countryside is serene and inviting. Many of the gravestones in the cemetery are marked by luxuriant native Texas lantana bushes, which were in full summer bloom on the May morning I visited. One particular gravestone is home to the largest rat snake I have ever seen or hope ever to see. The cemetery is not locked and has no posted hours.

The names in the cemetery reflect settlement of the area, particularly the Powell, Foster, and Farris families. W. G. S. and Sarah Hughes donated the grounds, and the Hugheses and four of their children are buried here. The Hugheses' sons, Willie and Gilmer, both died before age three, but the two daughters, Alma Mater and Neacie, both lived into their late seventies. I was struck by the large number of infants and young children buried here, a reminder of the hard life of the West Texas prairie.

Also buried in Cowboy Cemetery is Texas Border Patrol agent Jefferson Barr (1962–1996), who was killed by drug smugglers on the Texas border in 1996. Attorney General Janet Reno and hundreds of fellow law officers attended the funeral of the young lawman.

The next time you travel near Brady, Brownwood, or San Saba, take the short detour to Cowboy Cemetery. It is well worth the trip.

Mexia

City Cemetery
Rock St. at N. Red River St.
N 31 41.599, W 096 28.699

PETER WILLIS CAWTHON

Peter W. (Pete) Cawthon (1898–1962) was born in Houston and, after graduating from high school in 1917, enrolled at Southwestern University in Georgetown. As a freshman he lettered in football, basketball, and baseball and coached the baseball team. Cawthon earned four athletic letters his sophomore year and was selected as an All-State halfback.

After a series of coaching positions between 1919 and 1930, Cawthon was hired as head football coach and athletic director at Texas Technological College (now Texas Tech University). During his tenure, Cawthon led the Raiders to a record seventy-nine wins, twenty-seven losses, and six ties, and an appearance in the Sun Bowl in 1938.

In 1939 he led the Tech team through its first undefeated season and an appearance in the Cotton Bowl. In 1943 he began coaching professional football with the Brooklyn Dodgers (1943–1944) and then served three years as associate coach and head scout for the Detroit Lions. He returned to college football when he became athletic director for the University of Alabama (1952–1953).

ALFONSO STEELE

Alfonso (Alphonso) Steele (1817–1911) was born in Hardin County, Kentucky, and came to Texas in 1834 to fight in the Texas Revolution. When Texas declared independence, Steele joined a company of men traveling to San Antonio to join William B. Travis at the Alamo, but the mission garrison was defeated before they arrived. Steele and his comrades joined Gen. Sam Houston's army, and at the Battle of San Jacinto, Steele served as a private in Sidney Sherman's regiment. He was severely wounded in the first minutes of the battle but continued to fight throughout its entirety. Houston rode Steele's gray horse through much of the battle, until the animal was shot from beneath him.

After months of recuperation, Steele was discharged and made his way to Montgomery County, where he farmed and raised cattle. On February 10, 1909, the Thirty-first Texas Legislature honored him as

ALFONSO STEELE FOUGHT AT THE BATTLE OF SAN JACINTO AND WAS THE LAST
SURVIVING PARTICIPANT AT THE TIME OF HIS DEATH. CITY CEMETERY, MEXIA.

one of two living survivors of the Battle of San Jacinto, and when
Steele died on July 8, 1911, he was the last Texas survivor of the Battle of San Jacinto.

Mountain Home

Sunset Cemetery
West of Highway 27 in Kerr County
N 30 09.320, W 099 21.032

This hardscrabble cemetery is located along the banks of Johnson
Creek, and the road to the cemetery is just north of the entrance to the
Texas Parks and Wildlife Department Fisheries Research Center.

The first marked graves in this cemetery are those of James and
Susan Dowdy's four children—Alice, Martha, Susan, and James. The
Dowdy family had settled near Johnson Creek after migrating from
Goliad. On October 5, 1878, the four Dowdy children were tending
sheep near their home about 3.5 miles northwest of Ingram. Without
warning, they were attacked and killed by Indians in one of the last
raids in Kerr County. The four small graves were placed side by side,
and there the Dowdy children were laid to rest. The small graves were

each adorned with seashells, and small stones bearing the initials of each child were placed at the feet of the children.

Nacogdoches

Oak Grove Cemetery
E. Hospital St. at W. Lanana St.
N 31 36.196, W 094 38.991

WILLIAM CLARK, JR.

William Clark, Jr. (1798–1871), represented Sabine Municipality at the Convention of 1836 and signed the Texas Declaration of Independence. He was elected to represent Sabine County in the House of the Second Congress in September 1837, but he resigned in April 1838 because of illness. Clark later purchased the Planter Hotel in Nacogdoches, which he operated until his death in 1871.

JOHN S. ROBERTS

John S. Roberts (1796–1871) came to Texas after having participated in the War of 1812 and in the Battle of New Orleans. In 1826 he came to Texas, where he became a wealthy landowner. Roberts enlisted in the Nacogdoches Independent Volunteers on October 4, 1835, and participated in the Siege of Bexar (November 25–December 5). He was elected a delegate to the Convention of 1836 at Washington-on-the-Brazos and signed the Texas Declaration of Independence.

THOMAS JEFFERSON RUSK

Thomas Jefferson Rusk (1803–1857) came to Texas from Georgia in 1834, in pursuit of business partners who had embezzled money from him. He never retrieved the money but did decide to stay in Texas. Rusk almost immediately became involved in the independence movement, organized volunteers from Nacogdoches, and hastened to Gonzales, where his men joined Stephen F. Austin's army in preventing the Mexicans from seizing the "Come and Take It" cannon. As a delegate from Nacogdoches to the Convention of 1836, Rusk not only signed the Texas Declaration of Independence but also chaired the committee to revise the Constitution. The ad interim government appointed Rusk to the office of secretary of war.

Rusk participated in the Battle of San Jacinto and from May 4 to October 31, 1836, served as commander in chief of the Army of the Republic of Texas, with the rank of brigadier general. In the first regularly elected administration, President Houston appointed Rusk as secretary of war, but Rusk resigned shortly after his appointment. On December 12, 1838, Congress elected Rusk as chief justice of the Supreme Court. He served until June 30, 1840, when he resigned to resume his law practice, and later headed the bar of the Republic of Texas.

Rusk supported the annexation of Texas by the United States and served as president of the Convention of 1845, which accepted the annexation terms. The first state legislature elected him and Sam Houston to the U.S. Senate in February 1846. Rusk served with distinction in the Senate, and during the special session of March 1857 the Senate elected him president pro tem. Rusk County and the town of Rusk were named in his honor.

Navasota

Rest Haven Cemetery
Blackshear St. at N. Sixth St.
N 30 23.423, W 096 06.050

MANCE LIPSCOMB

Mance Lipscomb (1895–1976) was born near Navasota and spent almost all of his working life in Brazos County, farming a twenty-acre plot of bottomland. Lipscomb's father taught him the basics of

GRAVESITE OF TEXAS BLUESMAN MANCE LIPSCOMB. REST HAVEN CEMETERY, NAVASOTA.

fiddling and later Lipscomb taught himself the guitar. He eventually developed a distinctive finger-picking style that complemented his singing style. Mance Lipscomb was discovered in 1960, and at age sixty-five, he saw his album *Texas Songster* (his first recording) become the debut release on the Arhoolie label later that year.

Lipscomb's life and music have been well documented on film. He appeared in several 1960s and early-1970s blues documentaries, including *The Blues* (1962), *The Blues Accordin' to Lightnin' Hopkins* (1968), *Blues Like Showers of Rain* (1970), *A Well Spent Life* (1971), and *Out of the Black into the Blues* (1972).

New Braunfels

Comal Cemetery
Peace St. at Common St.
N 29 42.848, W 098 06.560

Our Lady of Perpetual Help Cemetery
Peace St. at Mather St.
N 29 42.700, W 098 06.596

Panteon-Hidalgo Cemetery
Peace St. at Dittlinger St.
N 29 42.744, W 098 06.648

These three cemeteries, all located along Peace Street and just west of the Guadalupe River, are considered here together because they are so different. Walking through them is a marvelous opportunity to compare what are dramatic contrasts between and within Texas cultures. The New Braunfels legacy of German settlement is well represented in Comal Cemetery, and the Panteon-Hidalgo and Our Lady of Perpetual Help cemeteries exemplify the city's Hispanic heritage.

Comal Cemetery is typically German—orderly and almost stern. Plots are laid out with the precision of a Teutonic engineer, and the cemetery is well kept. On the two occasions I visited this cemetery, it closed right at the appointed hour—no sooner, no later. The cemetery is replete with the surnames of German immigrants, such as Tolle, Hartmann, and many others. At rest in Comal Cemetery is one of Texas' most notable naturalists, Ferdinand J. Lindheimer (1801–1879). Educated in Germany, Lindheimer came to Texas in 1836 and served in the Texas Army under John C. Hays until 1837. By the time Lindheimer settled in New Braunfels (1844), he had spent several years collecting and studying Texas plant life. In 1852 he became the editor of the *Neu-Braunsfelser Zeitung*, a position that he held for twenty years. After leaving the newspaper, he continued to study Texas plants and is credited with classifying several hundred species.

Of all types of cemeteries, those that are predominantly the resting place of Hispanic Texans are generally my favorites. These cemeteries are all about life—full of color and passion. Pinwheels, dolls, and ornaments of every kind imaginable adorn the graves in these cemeteries. Small porcelain pictures of the deceased are often on the headstone, sometimes protected by brass covers, allowing the curious to witness the resident's corporeal visage. Hispanic cemeteries are replete with reverence, but never somber.

Across the street from Comal Cemetery are Panteon-Hidalgo and Our Lady of Perpetual Help (OLPH) cemeteries. These graveyards, particularly Panteon-Hidalgo, are polar opposites of Comal Cemetery. OLPH is a "scrape" cemetery; there is not a blade of grass to be found. The bare ground is literally covered with small shards of glass, bits of pottery, and old plastic flowers. It had a large dumpster in the middle of its principal lane on the day I visited. Statues and headstones of every conceivable design, size, color, shape, and texture mark the graves here. One in particular, located near the back of the cemetery, appears to have the likeness of Elvis Presley, draped in a priest's attire, holding aloft an angel. But for all the joy here, two graves near the very back of the cemetery mark the final resting place of young men from New Braunfels who died during the Vietnam War.

Panteon-Hidalgo is adjacent to and directly north of OLPH. This cemetery is markedly different from its sister to the south. Panteon-Hidalgo is much less colorful and, with high grass among the graves, a bit difficult to navigate. Most of the graves in the eastern section of the cemetery are those of children and young teenagers. Many of the graves have low concrete curbs around them, and the cemetery is not arranged in any particular order.

Newcastle

Fort Belknap Cemetery
East off Highway 251
N 33 09.039, W 098 44.375

Through the early years of Texas statehood, the U.S. Army established a series of forts to protect the Texas frontier. During the years

1848–1849 the frontier forts of Duncan, Inge, Lincoln, Martin Scott, Croghan, Gates, Graham, and Worth had been established and quickly become obsolete. The frontier was moving west faster than the Army could build posts. As a result, the federal government decided to adopt a plan recommended by Capt. Randolph Marcy, a plan that called for a new series of forts to the west of the existing cordon. General William G. Belknap was ordered to establish a line of forts based on Marcy's suggestions, and he established Fort Belknap on the north bank of the Brazos River.

The fort became a focal point of the Texas frontier. Soldiers from the fort ranged throughout the area in search of Indians and served as the hub for local population growth. The fort was also the crossroads for a series of overland trails, including that of the Butterfield Overland Stage. The fort was abandoned in 1867, when Fort Griffin was established.

The Fort Belknap area is rich in the lore of the west. On October 13, 1864, the Elm Creek Raid occurred just northwest of the fort, and legendary cowboy and Indian scout Brit Johnson served there in the 1850s (he was killed by Kiowa Indians in 1871). The Fort Belknap Cemetery is just north of the old fort and east of the highway. It lies at the end of a dirt road, and the exit off Highway 251 is well marked. It is reasonably well maintained and apparently is still in use. A low chain-link fence surrounds the cemetery, and the gate into the cemetery is not locked.

ROBERT S. NEIGHBORS

Robert Neighbors (1815–1859) came to Texas from Virginia in 1836 and served in the Texas Army as its quartermaster. In 1842, while serving in John C. Hays' volunteers, Neighbors was captured by Gen. Adrian Woll and imprisoned in Mexico. Released in 1844, he returned to Texas and began service as an Indian agent.

Neighbors was instrumental in establishing relations with several Indian tribes and in 1853 was appointed to the post of supervising agent for Texas. Over the course of his service, Neighbors became increasingly sympathetic to the cause of the various Texas tribes. When opposition arose to having Indian reservations in Texas, Neighbors secured the transfer of tribal members to reservations in Oklahoma. On his return to Texas in 1859, while stopping at the village of Fort Belknap, he was murdered by a man angered by Neighbors' defense of the Indian tribes. Neighbors' grave is covered by a crumbling false crypt and is prominently indicated by a Texas historical marker.

INDIAN AGENCY MAJ. ROBERT NEIGHBORS WAS MURDERED AS A RESULT OF HIS SYMPATHY WITH THE PLIGHT OF NATIVE AMERICANS IN TEXAS. FORT BELKNAP CEMETERY, NEWCASTLE.

Woolfolk Family Cemetery
Highway 380, 3 miles west of Newcastle
N 33 10.478, W 098 46.145

JOSEPH A. WOOLFOLK

On May 18, 1871, Gen. William Tecumseh Sherman and eighteen other federal cavalrymen set out from Fort Belknap, crossing Salt Creek Prairie en route to Fort Richardson, the northernmost outpost on the Texas frontier. Although the prairie had been an area of almost constant Indian raids, Sherman and his soldiers saw none on this day. However, Indians peering over Cox Mountain saw them. A band of more than a hundred Kiowas and Kiowa-Apaches hid in the rocky terrain and let the soldiers pass. A chief named Owl Prophet led the Kiowas, and in a vision he had seen the passing of two caravans across the plains and a warning that the first was not to be attacked. Only the second was to be raided. The vision of Owl Prophet clearly saved the life of General Sherman.

The second wagon train to cross the plains that day was not so fortunate. Ten wagons owned by government contractors were attacked by the Indians, led by Kiowa chief Satanta, at about 3:00 the same afternoon. Most of the teamsters were killed, but one—Thomas

Brazeal—survived to reach Fort Richardson and relay the story of the raid. The next morning, Maj. Gen. Ranald S. Mackenzie found the carnage, and the attackers were quickly identified. When confronted with the charge, Satanta (now at Fort Sill, Oklahoma) admitted that he had led the raid. General Sherman ordered that Satanta and two additional chiefs (Satank and Big Tree) be arrested and taken back to Texas for trial. One of the two attorneys selected to defend the three was Joseph Woolfolk.

A native of Kentucky and a graduate of the University of Louisville law school, Woolfolk (1836–1919) came to Texas in 1858 to practice law. Hired by the Texas Emigration and Land Company to survey land grants, he was licensed to practice law in Texas and served as county attorney and county clerk in Young County. During the Civil War, Woolfolk joined a home guard Texas Ranger unit, transferred to the regular Confederate army, and, while serving in West Virginia, was captured by Union troops in July 1863. Woolfolk spent the rest of the war in a prison camp in Ohio but returned to Kentucky and married after his release in 1865.

Moving back to Texas in 1867, he settled in Weatherford, and in 1871 he was appointed to defend the Kiowa chiefs. Although Woolfolk was commended for his defense of the two men, they were convicted. He later settled again in Young County, where he served in several positions prior to his death.

The Woolfolk Family Cemetery is a small cemetery, about 0.25 miles south of Highway 380. The cemetery is itself fenced and lies in a large field along a fencerow. It is visible from the highway but is best located by its proximity to the Texas historical marker along the south shoulder of the highway. Standing at the marker and looking just southwest, the cemetery is easily visible. I crossed the fence and walked to the nearest house to ask for permission to see the cemetery. The occupant responded, "What cemetery?" History is lost on some folks.

Norse

Our Savior's Cemetery
FM 182, north of intersection with FM 219 (Bosque County)
N 31 45.247, W 097 40.335

The small community of Norse was at the center of the Norwegian immigration to Texas in the 1840s. The exact means by which these immigrants chose Bosque County is unknown, but those who visited the area apparently found the rolling Texas plains reminiscent of the topography in eastern Norway. As settlers began to move into the area, the families began to focus their social life on a settlement they called Norse, which included a rock school. Our Savior's Lutheran Church was dedicated in 1878, and a post office opened in 1880. As towns sprang up around Norse, the tiny community began to decline, but the local Norwegian community still worships at Our Savior's Lutheran Church, and the old cemetery serves as a reminder of its presence and contribution to the culture of Texas.

CLENG PEERSON

Cleng Peerson (Kleng Pedersen) (1782–1865) was perhaps the most influential person in the immigration of Norwegians to the United States. He came to America to escape the hardships of his native Norway and lived in New York City in the early 1820s, where he helped other Norwegian immigrants. Between 1825 and 1847, Peerson helped establish communities for Norwegian Quakers and their compatriots in New York, Indiana, Illinois, Wisconsin, Minnesota, Iowa, and Missouri. Peerson moved to Texas and lived near Dallas until 1854. When he moved to Bosque County, he began urging other Norwegians to follow, and the Norwegian communities in the county began to take form. Peerson lived out his remaining days in Norse.

Oakland (Lavaca County)

Andrew Chapel Cemetery
At the terminus of County Road 138
N 29 32.299, W 096 47.963

JOSEPH LAWRENCE

Joseph Lawrence (1800–1897) was born in North Carolina and moved to Texas in 1835. At the Battle of San Jacinto, his company was part of the Texas Cavalry. The day after the battle, Lawrence killed an escaping Mexican soldier who was carrying William B. Travis' saddle and blanket. Lawrence stayed in the army until he received his discharge on June 28, and then he returned to Washington-on-the-Brazos. When he died on October 9, 1897, he was ninety-eight and the oldest surviving veteran of the Texas Revolution.

Odessa

Sunset Memorial Park
Business I-20E and Newell Rd.
N 31 52.913, W 102 17.801

ALFRED M. WILSON

Alfred M. Wilson (1948–1969) was a 1967 graduate of Odessa High School in Odessa and entered military service in Abilene, Texas. Private First Class Wilson was assigned to the Ninth Marines, Third Marine Division, in Quang Tri Province, Vietnam, on March 3, 1969. He was a rifleman, and while on a reconnaissance mission, Wilson and his comrades were attacked by enemy forces. An enemy soldier stepped from behind a tree and threw a grenade toward them. Wilson shouted to the Marine accompanying him and threw himself on the grenade. He absorbed the force of the explosion with his own body, and in so doing saved the life of his companion. For his sacrifice, Alfred Wilson was awarded the Congressional Medal of Honor.

MARVIN R. YOUNG

Marvin R. Young (1947–1968) was born in Alpine, Texas, and enlisted in the U.S. Army at Odessa in September 1966. On August 21, 1968, Staff Sergeant Young was leading a squad of Company C, First Battalion, Fifth Infantry, Twenty-fifth Infantry Division, on reconnaissance patrol near Ben Cui, Vietnam. A large force of the North Vietnamese army attacked the squad. When the platoon leader was killed, Young quickly assumed command, moving from position to position, encouraging his men, and directing return fire.

After receiving orders to withdraw, Young remained behind in order to provide covering fire. During the ensuing struggle, he was wounded three times but refused assistance, in order to remain behind to cover the withdrawal of his comrades. There the advancing enemy force killed him. For his valiant service, Marvin Young was awarded the Congressional Medal of Honor.

Old Noxville

Noxville Cemetery
County Road 473
N 30 22.208, W 099 23.426

Meandering beneath high limestone bluffs, the clear water of the Little Devil's River served as a focal point for settlement in Kimble County in the early 1870s. Among those who farmed and prospered along the stream was Illinois native Noah Nox. Nox set up business along the banks of the river, and his store served as the first Noxville post office. Nearby, townspeople quarried the local limestone, cut it onto neat blocks, and built the first rock schoolhouse in Kimble County. Like so many small Texas towns, Noxville gradually faded into history. The post office closed in the 1940s, and local children began to attend classes in Harper at about the same time. By the 1990s, Noxville had all but disappeared. Today the Noxville Cemetery is about all that remains of the community.

Getting to the cemetery is a bit tricky, as both County Road 473 and the Noxville Cemetery road (which exits east off CR 473) each include a low-water crossing of the Little Devil's. The road to the cemetery crosses land still owned and ranched by descendants of James Parker, one of the original settlers of Noxville. The old Noxville schoolhouse stands just west of the river, as sturdy and resolute as the stonemasons who built it.

As I stopped to gaze through the white-framed windows, it was easy to imagine pigtailed girls and barefoot boys sitting at wooden desks, diligently studying their lessons. Just beyond the school, the road dips into the riverbed, crosses the river, and arises alongside rhomboid limestone blocks that have split and fallen from the face of nearby cliffs. The stream was alive with sunfish and suckers on the day I visited, and American lotus along the shoreline provided sanctuary and shade for largemouth bass as they darted out to scatter surface minnows. The cemetery is on a rise overlooking the Little Devil's River, and the road terminates along its western edge. It is small and perfectly kept and has a covered pavilion in the southwest corner.

CREED TAYLOR

Just north of the entrance to Noxville Cemetery lies the grave of a very determined citizen-soldier, Creed Taylor (1820–1906). Taylor was brought to Texas by his family in 1824 and quickly became proficient with both gun and knife as a Texas frontiersman.

Taylor was a man of action. He joined the Texas Rangers as a teenager, and his service to the Texas Revolution began when (at age fifteen) he participated in the Battle of Gonzales. Creed Taylor participated in every major battle of the struggle for independence, including the Battle of Concepción, the Grass Fight, and the Siege of Bexar. After removing his family from harm's way during the Runaway Scrape, Taylor rejoined Sam Houston and fought in the decisive Battle of San Jacinto.

Returning home, Taylor married and began a family, but his itch to remain in "the fightin' area" led to skirmishes with Comanche Indians at the Battle of Plum Creek (1840) and again at Bandera Pass (1841). When Mexican forces reoccupied San Antonio in 1842, Creed Taylor again answered the call to arms and fought in the Battle of Salado Creek. When the U.S.-Mexican War broke out, Creed Taylor was off again, this time to fight with Capt. Samuel Walker's company of Mounted Texas Rangers. Taylor participated in many of the major battles of that campaign, including Palo Alto, Resaca de la Palma, Monterrey, and Buena Vista. Never a man to pass up a good fight, Taylor would serve with John S. "Rip" Ford in the Confederacy.

Eventually, Taylor settled in Kimble County near the James River. After the death of his first wife, Nancy Goodbread, he married Lavinia Spencer (thirty-five years his junior) and started a second family at age sixty-six. Old age finally succeeded in doing what no molded-lead bullet or flint-tipped arrow had ever accomplished. Creed Taylor died at age eighty-six and is buried in the Noxville Cemetery alongside Lavinia and a son. A simple marble headstone marks a true Texas legend.

Palestine

East Hill Cemetery
At the terminus of E. Market St.
N 31 45.856, W 095 37.125

THOMAS MITCHELL CAMPBELL

Thomas Mitchell Campbell (1856–1923) was born at Rusk and attended school there until he began the study of law; he was admitted to the bar in 1878. In 1897 Campbell became active in Democratic Party politics and was elected governor of Texas in 1906. He

GRAVESITE OF WILLIAM KIMBROUGH, VETERAN OF THE TEXAS REVOLUTION AND THE BATTLE OF SAN JACINTO. EAST HILL CEMETERY, PALESTINE.

served two terms in office, 1907–1911. Campbell initiated a number of reforms involving railroad regulation, antitrust laws, lobbying restrictions, equitable taxation, and pure food and drug laws. Upon leaving the governorship, Campbell returned to private law practice in Palestine but remained active in Democratic politics. In 1916 he ran unsuccessfully for the U.S. Senate.

ALEXANDER WHITE GREGG

Alexander White Gregg (1854–1919) was born in Centerville. His father was killed in the Civil War, and after his mother remarried, he lived for a time in Mississippi. He graduated from Kings College, Bristol, Tennessee, in 1874 and then studied law at the University of Virginia. He was admitted to the bar in 1878 and began to practice at Palestine, Texas. He served in the Texas Senate from 1886 to 1888. He was elected as a Democrat to the Fifty-eighth U.S. Congress and served eight terms, March 4, 1903, to March 3, 1919.

WILLIAM KIMBROUGH

William Kimbrough (Kimbro, Kimbo) (ca. 1810–1856) came to Texas from Tennessee in 1831. Kimbrough led a company of volunteer infantry in Col. Sidney Sherman's Second Regiment, Texas Volunteers. Kimbrough participated in the Battle of San Jacinto and, after the battle, was captain of the militia company. After the Texas Revolution, he served as sheriff of San Augustine County from 1836 through 1838, was elected sheriff on February 1, 1841, and held the office until 1843.

JOHN HENNINGER REAGAN

John H. Reagan (1818–1905) began his political career when Texas entered the Union. He was elected the first county judge of Henderson County and then to the Second Legislature of Texas (1847). John H. Reagan quickly rose to prominence and in 1857 was elected U.S. Congressman from the Eastern District of Texas. On January 15, 1861, Reagan resigned his congressional seat, for he realized that Texas would eventually secede from the Union. Soon after, Reagan was appointed postmaster general of the Confederacy.

In April 1865, President Jefferson Davis and his cabinet fled Richmond, but on May 9, near Abbeville, Georgia, Jefferson Davis, former Texas governor Francis R. Lubbock, and Reagan were captured. On May 25, 1865, Reagan and Vice President Alexander H. Stephens of Georgia were imprisoned at Fort Warren in Boston Harbor. For the next twenty-two weeks, Reagan was held in solitary confinement. After his release from Fort Warren, he returned to Texas early in December 1865.

Though Reagan spent several years in relative obscurity, in 1874 he received the Democratic nomination for the First Congressional District, was elected, and served from 1875–1887. He was elected to the U.S. Senate in January 1887, but before the end of his term, he returned to Texas to head the newly formed Railroad Commission of Texas. Reagan made an unsuccessful bid for the 1894 Democratic nomination for governor and then remained chairman of the Railroad Commission until his retirement in January 1903.

CHRISTOPHER COLUMBUS ROGERS

Christopher Columbus Rogers (1846–1888) was born in Anderson County, the son of county sheriff William Rogers. Christopher Rogers spent the Civil War as a guard at a Confederate prison and, after the war, worked as a printer at a Palestine newspaper. Rogers clearly had a violent nature, which was exemplified by his murder of Dan Cary, a Republican marshal of Palestine. After killing Cary, Rogers operated a saloon in Tyler for a time, where he killed a fellow saloonkeeper in a gunfight. In 1874 he was elected city marshal of Palestine, an office he held till his death.

During his tenure, Rogers is reputed to have taken the lives of nine more men. In 1887 he was involved in a gunfight with a friend, Tom O'Donnell, who was resisting arrest. In the melee, O'Donnell was killed, and Rogers was suspended, pending investigation of the killing. Rogers, while sitting unarmed in a saloon in 1888, was stabbed to death as a result of an argument over the O'Donnell incident.

Palo Pinto

Palo Pinto Cemetery
FM 4 at Elm St.
N 32 45.987, W 098 18.272

GEORGE WEBB SLAUGHTER

George W. Slaughter (1811–1895) was part of Texas' great ranching and trail-driving tradition. After arriving in Texas in 1830, Slaughter served as a message courier under Sam Houston and delivered at least one message to William B. Travis at the Alamo.

Although he was an ordained Baptist minister, Slaughter made his fortune in ranching. In 1857 he set up a ranch five miles north of the site of present Palo Pinto, preaching and practicing medicine in addition to ranching. Slaughter and his son, Christopher Columbus Slaughter, began trailing cattle in 1867 and continued until 1875. In a single drive in 1870, the Slaughters trailed more than three thousand head of cattle to Kansas. Slaughter made his home in Emporia, Kansas, until 1876, when he dissolved his partnership with his son and returned to Texas to ranch in partnership with another son, Peter Slaughter.

Paris

Evergreen Cemetery
Evergreen St. at Highway 19
N 33 38.574, W 095 33.299

SAMUEL BELL MAXEY

Samuel B. Maxey (1825–1895) was born at Tompkinsville, Kentucky. He attended the U.S. Military Academy at West Point and roomed for a period with Thomas J. (Stonewall) Jackson. He graduated in 1846 and fought in the U.S.-Mexican War battles of Cerro Gordo, Contreras, Churubusco, and Molino del Rey. In 1849 Maxey resigned from the Army and began practicing law in Albany, Kentucky, with his father. In 1857 Maxey moved to Texas and settled near Paris.

With the coming of the Civil War, Maxey assumed command of the Ninth Texas Infantry regiment and joined the forces of Gen. Albert Sidney Johnston. He was promoted to brigadier general in March 1862 and, on December 27, 1863, was appointed commander of Indian Territory, where he served until February 21, 1865. On May 22, 1865, Maxey asked to be relieved of his command after his division began to experience substantial desertion of its members.

Maxey was elected to the U.S. Senate on January 28, 1874, and served two terms. He was an ardent promoter for Texas. During the U.S.-Mexican War, he had served with Ulysses S. Grant, and his friendships and moderate politics proved to be invaluable in his drive to bring federal money and development to Texas.

Peaster

Peaster Cemetery
100 yards south off McClendon Rd., 0.7 mile east of FM 920
N 32 52.598, W 097 51.532

The Peaster Cemetery is just northeast of the community of the same name, and H. H. Peaster, who founded the town, is buried in this immaculately kept cemetery. There is a "pioneer area" in the southwest corner of the cemetery, and the kindness of the local citizens is well displayed in the neat rows of graves marked by simple granite stones inscribed with the one-word epitaph, "Unknown." Still active, the cemetery contains the graves of early area settlers and their descendants; veterans of the Civil War, World War I, and World War II; and Peaster's most famous citizen, John Alexander Fox (1883–1961), who created the "Buster Brown" character for the Brown Shoe Company's advertising campaign.

Fox's epitaph says all that needs to be said about this remarkable man:

A MEMBER OF THE MASONIC LODGE, AN ODDFELLOW, A
SCOUT-MASTER AND WELL RESPECTED FIGURE IN FORT
WORTH FOR A QUARTER OF A CENTURY; JACK FOX WAS
KNOWN AND LOVED BY AMERICANS UNDER A DIFFERENT

NAME. REPRESENTING THE BROWN SHOE COMPANY OF SAINT LOUIS, MR. FOX TRAVELED AMERICA AS BUSTER BROWN, ACCOMPANIED BY HIS DOG TIGE. DELIGHTING TENS OF THOUSANDS OF CHILDREN, MR. FOX, ALTHOUGH ONLY FOUR FEET TALL, WILL FOREVER STAND TALL BY THOSE WHOSE LIVES HE TOUCHED.

I wore several pairs of grandparentally purchased Buster Brown shoes throughout my childhood. Although they were sturdily constructed, I did not find them particularly stylish. I much preferred my U.S. Keds: they required no brown shoe polish.

Pecos

Pecos Park
120 E. First St.
N 31 25.665, W 103 29.679

ROBERT CLAY ALLISON

Clay Allison (1840–1887) was one of the Old West's most dangerous gunmen. When the Civil War erupted, he joined the Confederate forces but was discharged in 1862 as a result of his behavioral instability. Undeterred, he reenlisted and finished the war as a scout for Gen. Nathan Bedford Forrest.

After the war, Allison moved to the Brazos River country in Texas. At a Red River crossing near Denison he severely beat a ferryman named Zachary Colbert in a fistfight. This incident reportedly started a feud between Allison and the Colbert family that led to the Allisons' killing of the ferryman's outlaw nephew, "Chunk" Colbert, in New Mexico on January 7, 1874.

Allison soon signed on as a cowhand with Oliver Loving and Charles Goodnight and was probably among the eighteen cowboys on the 1866 drive that blazed the Goodnight-Loving Trail. Allison was a heavy drinker, a fact that led him straight to trouble and a series of murderous events. On October 30, 1875, he led a mob that seized and lynched a man suspected of murdering a Methodist circuit rider. Two days later Allison killed a friend of the man he had lynched only two days earlier. In December 1876, Allison and his brother John were involved in a dance hall gunfight at Las Animas, Colorado, in which a deputy sheriff was killed. Allison was charged with manslaughter, but the charges were later dismissed on grounds of self-defense. Allison was arrested as an accessory to the murder of three soldiers the following spring, but evidence was inconclusive and he was soon acquitted. In 1878 he sold his New Mexico ranch and headed to Hays City, Kansas.

In September 1878 Allison and his men are purported to have terrorized Dodge City, where Wyatt Earp is said to have convinced Allison that his presence in the town was no longer welcome. By 1880 Robert and John Allison had settled on Gageby Creek, near its junction with the Washita River, in Hemphill County. Though Allison's wild life seemed to be calmed by his marriage and family, he continued his unusual behavior. In the summer of 1886 a dentist from Cheyenne, Wyoming, was employed to remove one of Allison's teeth. Unfortunately for the dentist, he extracted the wrong tooth and seeking Biblical retribution, Allison settled the score by pulling out one of the dentist's teeth.

In December 1886 he bought a ranch near Pecos and became involved in area politics. On July 3, 1887, while hauling supplies to his ranch from Pecos, he was thrown from his heavily loaded wagon and fatally injured when run over by its rear wheel. Heck of an end for a gunman.

Port Neches

Oak Bluff Memorial Park
Block St. at Woodcrest Lee St.
N 30 00.111, W 093 57.700

WOODWARD MAURICE (TEX) RITTER

Singing cowboy Tex Ritter (1905–1974) was born in Murvaul, Texas, and grew up on a ranch in Beaumont. After graduating from high school, he majored in law at the University of Texas. During college, however, he became interested in acting and moved to New York in 1928 to join a theatrical troupe. After a few years of struggle, he briefly returned to school, only to leave again to pursue stardom.

Ritter returned to New York in 1931 to act in the Broadway production *Green Grow the Lilacs*. Building upon his stage success, he began hosting radio programs and started a recording career. He caught the attention of Hollywood producer Edward Finney and was cast in the 1936 Western *Song of the Gringo*. Before his film career ended, he had starred in eighty-five movies.

As his film career began to fade, his music career began to shine. In

1942 he became the first country artist signed to Capitol Records, and in 1944 his hit "I'm Wastin' My Tears on You" began a string of successful records over two decades. In 1963 Ritter began a two-year tenure as the president of the Country Music Association. In 1964, Tex Ritter became the fifth member of the Country Music Hall of Fame.

Proffitt

Proffitt Cemetery
U.S. Highway 380
N 33 10.990, W 098 51.975

Members of the Robert Smith Proffitt family came to this area west of Newcastle about 1862 and established homes. A son, John Proffitt (1846–1925), amassed large land holdings and built a gin and other businesses. The developing community was named Proffitt, after the founding family. On July 17, 1867, three local young men—Rice Carlton (age nineteen), Reuben Johnson (twenty), and Patrick Proffitt (nineteen)—were killed in an Indian raid near this site. They were buried in a common grave on John Proffitt's land about one mile south of town, the first burial in the community graveyard now known as the Proffitt Cemetery.

The gravesite of the three young men, marked by a Texas historical marker, lies under a large tree and is surrounded by a low brick fence. The cemetery contains both marked and unmarked graves of area pioneers. There are many gravesites of very young children in the cemetery that speak of the difficult conditions of the Texas frontier. Records indicate that the largest number of burials occurred in the years between 1910 and 1920 and includes many victims of the World War I–era influenza epidemic.

Quanah

Quanah Memorial Park
FM 2640, north of Quanah
N 34 18.506, W 099 43.849

WILLIAM JESSE McDONALD

William Jesse McDonald (1852–1918) was born in Kemper County, Mississippi. After the death of his father in the Civil War, he moved to a farm near Henderson, Texas, in 1866. In 1891 McDonald was selected to replace S. A. McMurry as captain of Company B, Frontier Battalion, Texas Rangers. He served as a Ranger captain until 1907. Capt. McDonald and his Rangers played a major part in the Brownsville Raid of 1906, for which McDonald gained the reputation as "a man who would charge hell with a bucket of water."

In 1905 McDonald served as bodyguard to President Theodore Roosevelt, and later President Woodrow Wilson appointed him U.S. marshal for the Northern District of Texas. On his tombstone is one of Texas' most famous mottoes: "No man in the wrong can stand up against a fellow that's in the right and keeps on a-comin'." McDonald is a member of the Texas Ranger Hall of Fame.

Richmond

Morton Cemetery
300 N. Second St.
N 29 35.157, W 095 45.827

The site of the Morton Cemetery was part of a Mexican land grant received by William Morton and was first used as a cemetery in 1825, when Morton buried Robert Gelaspie (or Gillespie), a fellow Mason on the grounds. Gelaspie's brick tomb is still in immaculate condition and is believed to be the first Masonic landmark erected in Texas. After Morton died in 1833, his widow sold the land to Robert Eden Handy and William Lusk, promoters of the town site of Richmond. In 1854 Michael DeChaumes acquired the burial ground, which became known as DeChaumes Cemetery. The site came to be called the Morton Cemetery after the 1890s, when it was acquired by the Morton Lodge No. 72 of the Ancient Free and Accepted Masons. In the early 1940s the cemetery became the property of the Richmond Cemetery Association, which was later renamed the Morton Cemetery Association.

ROBERT JAMES CALDER

Robert J. Calder (1810–1885) was born in Baltimore, Maryland, and moved to Texas from Kentucky in 1832. He joined the Texas Army in 1836 and was elected captain of K Company, First Regiment of Texas Volunteers, which he commanded at the Battle of San Jacinto.

After the Texas Revolution, Calder received 640 acres of land for his service, was appointed marshal of Texas in 1836, and was sheriff of Brazoria County from 1837 to 1843. He continued his life of public service as mayor of Brazoria (1838), chief justice of Brazoria County (1844, 1846), and mayor of Richmond in 1859. In 1881 he officially unveiled the monument to the memory of those who perished at San Jacinto.

MIRABEAU BUONAPARTE LAMAR

Mirabeau Buonaparte Lamar (1798–1859) came to Texas from Georgia in 1835 after a career in business, politics, and journalism. At the news of the fall of the Alamo and the Goliad Massacre, Lamar joined the revolutionary army.

When the Mexican and Texan forces skirmished at San Jacinto on April 20, 1836, Private Lamar's quick action saved the life of Thomas Rusk, who was surrounded by enemy soldiers. As the Battle of San Jacinto was about to unfold, Lamar was commissioned as a colonel and assigned to command the cavalry. Soon after the battle, he became secretary of war in David G. Burnet's cabinet and demanded that Gen. Antonio López de Santa Anna be executed as a murderer.

In September 1836, in the first election, Lamar was elected vice president of the Republic of Texas and in 1837 was elected president. His administration was a mixed bag of success and poor policy. He was opposed to annexation and substituted a harsh Indian policy in place of Houston's policy of leniency and conciliation. Lamar was instrumental in locating the state capital at Austin. Perhaps his most lasting contribution was his education policy, which resulted in legislation that set aside land for public education. Lamar's advocacy of the program earned for him the nickname "Father of Texas Education." A dictum in one of his messages to Congress, "Cultivated mind is the guardian genius of democracy," became the motto of the University of Texas. Lamar County and the town of Lamar in Aransas County were named in his honor.

JANE HERBERT WILKINSON LONG

Jane Herbert Wilkinson Long (1798–1880) was called the "Mother of Texas" because of the birth of her child on Bolivar Peninsula on December 21, 1821. Throughout her life she claimed to be the first English-speaking woman to bear a child in Texas, although she probably did not hold that distinction in actuality. Jane Long ended up stranded—and pregnant—on the Bolivar Peninsula when an ill-fated

filibuster undertaken by her husband, James Long, resulted in his accidental death in Mexico City. All the other families left Bolivar, but Jane stubbornly waited for her husband to return.

In her later years, Jane Long ran boardinghouses at Brazoria and Richmond, then ran successful farming and ranching operations. According to her, such prominent Texans as Ben Milam, Sam Houston, and Mirabeau B. Lamar courted her, but she refused them all.

Rocksprings

Rocksprings Cemetery
Highway 377, 2 miles north of Rocksprings
N 30 01.033, W 100 12.104

In 1892, J. R. Sweeten (who dug the first water well in the area) donated two acres of land to be used as a community cemetery. Two children, Willie J. Blackwell and Ben Smith, appear to have been the first people interred here (1891). Many of those buried in the Rocksprings Cemetery in the early years were travelers passing through the area. Much like Goliad, Rocksprings was struck by a killer tornado on April 12, 1927, which took the lives of at least three members of the Adams family and of the Rev. and Mrs. Hudson Spiers. Over the years, additional land acquisitions have increased the size of the cemetery. Iron fencing that once surrounded some gravesites was donated to scrap metal drives during World War II.

CLINTON LAFAYETTE SMITH

Lipans and Comanche Indians captured Clint Smith (1860–1932) and his brother, Jeff (1862–1940), on February 26, 1871. For the next five years, the boys were held as captives. They were eventually returned, and the accounts of their captivity became some of the most celebrated tales of the Old West. After their return, they both led long lives as cowboys and trail drivers. Jeff Smith lies at rest in the Coker Cemetery in San Antonio.

Round Rock

Round Rock Cemetery
Sam Bass Rd. at Meadows Dr.
N 30 31.015, W 097 41.778

SAM BASS

Sam Bass (1851–1878) was born near Mitchell, Indiana, and orphaned at age thirteen. He ran away from his uncle's home in 1869 and arrived in Denton, Texas, in 1870. For the next five years, Bass drifted between jobs until he decided to try his hand at trailing cattle in 1876. Bass' troubles began when he and Joel Collins trailed a herd to market and spent the earnings instead of paying the owners for the cattle. Then in 1877 Bass and Collins took their criminal careers a step further when they decided to graduate to the practice of stage-coach and train robbery. In September 1877 they held up a Union Pacific train near Big Springs, Nebraska, where their take included $60,000 in $20 gold pieces from the express car and $1,300 plus four gold watches from the passengers. The bandits split up, and Collins and two other gang members were soon killed by law enforcement authorities. But Bass, disguised as a farmer, made it back to Texas, where he formed a new outlaw band.

Soon, Sam Bass and his gang became the target of the Texas Rangers, who were tipped by one of Bass' gang members that Bass intended to rob the Round Rock bank. With that information in hand, Maj. John B. Jones—commander of the Frontier Battalion of Texas Rangers—set up an ambush.

On July 19, 1878, Bass, Seaborn Barnes, and two other gang members scouted the area before the actual robbery. They bought some tobacco at Henry Koppel's store, where Williamson County deputy sheriff A. W. Grimes noticed their movements. When Grimes approached the three, he was shot and killed. Within seconds, the Rangers opened fire on Bass and his gang. As the bandits returned fire, another deputy was wounded, and a bullet struck Bass.

Barnes, Bass, and a third bandit named Frank Jackson quickly mounted their horses, firing at Major Jones and Ranger Dick Ware. Ware shot Barnes dead as he mounted his horse, and as Sam Bass galloped away, he was shot again in the back. Jackson escaped, but Bass died from his wounds the next day. In 1879 Bass' sister came to mark his grave with a tombstone in the Round Rock Cemetery. Buried nearby are Seaborn Barnes and Deputy Sheriff Grimes.

Round Top

Florida Chapel Cemetery
Florida Chapel Rd., 0.2 mile east of intersection with Highway 237
N 30 02.598, W 096 42.633

Florida Chapel Cemetery is a country cemetery on a hill overlooking the Fayette County landscape. This small cemetery is similar to other small cemeteries in which German and Czech surnames abound. As is typical of such cemeteries, Florida Chapel appears to have experienced absolutely no vandalism, despite the minimal security afforded by a single chain surrounding the grounds. Here one can find many beautiful, old wrought iron fences, all situated such that about four inches of space is left between the bottom rail and the surrounding ground. Easier to mow and trim around them, I suspect.

FRIEDERIKE C. E. M. RECKNAGEL

Friederike Recknagel (1860–1956) was a gifted and important amateur photographer. Her studies of local people, buildings, and her family are Texas treasures. Her avenue to photography is unknown, but during most of the years surrounding the beginning of the twentieth century, Mrs. Recknagel carefully recorded the simplest, and yet most profound, events of her life. Her photographs are considered an important link to nineteenth-century Texas.

Salado

Salado Cemetery
Baines St. at Santa Maria Rd.
N 30 56.176, W 097 31.907

In 1859 Elijah Sterling Clack Robertson (1820–1879) offered to donate land for development of a college and town near the Salado Springs. The area had long been a gathering spot for Indians in the years before Spanish exploration. The small town of Salado grew into an important business and educational center with the founding of Salado College. Among the attendees at Salado College was Miriam Ferguson, who would later become Texas' first female governor. The town's importance as an agricultural center was solidified when, in 1873, the first Texas Grange was organized there.

Salado's history is well represented in its cemetery, which is just north of FM 2268 on Baines Street. The cemetery itself was founded on 2.5 acres of land donated by Robertson in 1856, and pioneer Hermon Aiken (1809–1860) is purported to have been the first person to be buried in this cemetery. The entrance to the cemetery has several large oaks, under which are a series of plain but pleasant concrete tables and chairs. The Salado Cemetery has an unusual number of false crypts, and in some cases entire families, most notably the Barton family, have false crypts overlying their gravesites. Low iron fences, reminiscent of the German cemeteries in Fayette, Comal, and Gillespie counties, surround many of the family plots. The cemetery is well maintained, appears to be active, and is the final post of numerous veterans of the Civil War.

Of particular interest in this cemetery is the plot of the Reynolds family. In the course of just under two months, three teenage members of the Reynolds family perished. Lelia Reynolds (age nineteen), on November 16, 1875; B. J. Reynolds (age twenty-two), on December 12, 1875; and Mary E. Reynolds (age twenty-one), on January 2, 1876. One can only imagine the cause of the Reynoldses' loss, be it disease or something else. But the loss of three older children in such a short span is reminiscent of the clustered dates on gravestones in Old Indianola or Brenham's Prairie Lea Cemetery after those communities were swept by disease. Clearly, life on the Texas prairie was difficult for all children, even those who had reached adulthood.

Ancestors of two of Texas' most flamboyant and famous politically significant figures are at rest in the Salado Cemetery. Buried here is the family of James E. Ferguson (1824–1876), who was a circuit-riding Methodist minister and father of Texas governor James E. Ferguson (1871–1944). Near the Ferguson gravesite is that of George Washington Baines, Sr. (1809–1892), a pioneer settler and great-grandfather of President Lyndon Baines Johnson.

San Angelo

Fairmount Cemetery

1116 W. Ave. N
N 31 26.574, W 100 26.965

HOUSTON HARTE

Houston Harte (1893–1972) graduated from the University of Missouri's School of Journalism in 1915 and in 1920 purchased the San

Angelo *Evening Standard.* In 1927 he formed a partnership with Bernard Hanks that eventually became Harte-Hanks Communications. By 1972 Harte-Hanks owned nineteen newspapers, with a circulation of more than six hundred thousand.

JACK MATHIS

Jack W. Mathis (1921–1943) enlisted in the U.S. Army on June 12, 1940, and transferred to the Army Air Corps to serve with his brother, Mark. Second Lieutenant Jack Mathis was assigned duty as a bombardier on a B-17 bomber crew in the 303d Bombardment Wing. On March 18, 1943, Mathis took off from England for his fourteenth mission, a bombing run over Vegesack, Germany. As his aircraft approached its target, the plane was hit by antiaircraft fire that mortally wounded Mathis. Although severely wounded, he struggled back to his bombsight, released the bombs directly onto the target, and then fell at his bombsight. He was awarded the Medal of Honor for conspicuous gallantry and intrepidity beyond the call of duty.

Mark Mathis replaced his brother in the crew of the B-17 in which Jack was killed. Mark was killed in action when his severely damaged airplane ditched in the North Sea in May 1943.

OSCAR RUFFINI

Oscar Ruffini (1858–1957) was one of Texas' finest architects. In 1883 he moved to Austin to work for his brother, Frederick, who was already an established architect. Working as a draftsman, Oscar Ruffini designed plans for the Texas Capitol and for the main building of the University of Texas.

By 1884 Oscar Ruffini had gained enough experience to set himself up as an architect in San Angelo, the newly established county seat of Tom Green County. His first major commission was the Tom Green County Courthouse, the building that established his reputation as a designer of courthouses. During his career, Oscar Ruffini designed beautiful courthouses in Sutton, Blanco, and Concho counties, as well as many other structures in San Angelo and west Texas.

San Antonio

Coker Cemetery
Coker United Methodist Church, 231 E. North Loop Rd.
N 29 33.277, W 098 29.361

JOHN COKER

John Coker came to Texas in 1834 and served at the Battle of San Jacinto. He was one of the party that accompanied Erastus "Deaf" Smith in the destruction of Vince's Bridge, the only avenue of escape for General Santa Anna's army at the Battle of San Jacinto. In recognition of Coker's service, he was awarded 1,920 acres, where he and his brother Joseph founded the Coker Community.

JEFFERSON DAVIS SMITH

See entry for Clinton Lafayette Smith under Rocksprings Cemetery, Rocksprings.

SAN ANTONIO CITY CEMETERIES

The San Antonio City Cemeteries are a complex of graveyards that lie in the heart of east San Antonio. This expansive cemetery system (according to the historical marker on the site, twenty-nine cemeteries were originally platted by city aldermen) is the final resting site of many of San Antonio's and south Texas' most influential citizens. Unfortunately, these cemeteries, with the exception of the Veterans Administration National Cemetery, have been demonstrably vandalized, and many of the beautiful obelisks and headstones have been pushed to the ground or broken.

Dignowity Cemetery
Monumental St. at Potomac St.
N 29 25.371, W 098 28.016

JOHN RUFUS BLOCKER AND ABNER PICKENS BLOCKER

John Blocker (1851–1927) and Abner Blocker (1856–1943) were two of three brothers (Bill Blocker, 1850–1921, is the third) who were among Texas' most successful trail drivers. The Blocker family came to Texas in 1852 and settled near Austin. John started in the cattle business in Blanco County with his brother Bill, and Abner Blocker joined them there. Over the next two decades, the brothers trailed cattle to markets throughout the west. Their brand was an inverted numeral seven, and the Blockers developed a style of roping that became known as the Blocker Loop. Excellent accounts of the many trail-driving adventures of the Blocker brothers can be found in *The Trail Drivers of Texas*, by J. Marvin Hunter.

Masonic Cemetery
E. Commerce St. at Monumental St.
N 29 25.177, W 098 28.153

CLARA DRISCOLL

Clara Driscoll (1881–1945) was born into a wealthy south Texas family. She left Texas to study abroad and, upon her return, found the Alamo both in disrepair and in danger of destruction. Teaming with the Daughters of the Republic of Texas, she paid most of the costs related to the Daughters' procurement of the Alamo, an act for which she became known as the "Savior of the Alamo." Mrs. Driscoll later pursued a writing career and authored a novel and a collection of short stories.

After moving to New York with her husband, she later returned to Austin, where he established the *Austin American* newspaper. She directed construction of "Laguna Gloria" and eventually donated the mansion to the Texas Fine Arts Association to be used as an art museum. After the end of her marriage, Clara became active in civic activities and politics. She built the Hotel Robert Driscoll in Corpus Christi as a memorial to her brother and served sixteen years as the Democratic Party's national chairwoman. A truly remarkable woman, Clara Driscoll left a legacy of great generosity and a genuine love for Texas art and history.

GEORGE WASHINGTON WEST

George West (1851–1926) was one of the first Texas cattlemen to drive Longhorns to the Kansas railhead. In 1870 he is reputed to have bossed the longest recorded trail drive, which began in Lavaca County and terminated within one hundred miles of the Canadian border. The town of George West, Texas, is named in his honor.

San Antonio City Cemetery #1
E. Commerce St. at Monumental St.
N 29 25.154, W 098 28.006

JACK HARRIS, BEN THOMPSON, AND JOHN KING FISHER

Few times in Texas history have the lives and fate of three such men crossed in events with equal drama and disastrous results. Jack Harris (1834–1882) was born in Connecticut and went to sea at age twelve. He came to San Antonio around 1860, where he served as a police officer and enlisted in the Confederate army at the outbreak of the Civil War. After the war, he returned to police work in San Antonio.

In 1872 he rented a building in San Antonio and opened an establishment he named the Jack Harris Vaudeville Theater and Saloon. Within ten years he had become one of San Antonio's most prominent citizens, and his saloon, theater, and gambling rooms had become the most popular—if not dangerous—watering hole in the city.

Ben Thompson (1842–1884) was born in England but arrived in Austin as a child. Much like John Wesley Hardin, Thompson took to the art of killing his fellow man at an early age and killed his first two victims somewhere around the advanced age of seventeen. While serving in the Confederacy, he killed a fellow soldier and a teamster. In June 1868 he was sentenced to prison in the Texas State Penitentiary at Huntsville, where he served two years for killing his brother-in-law. Upon his release, Thompson left Texas and went to Abilene, Kansas.

There, in 1871, he opened the Bull's Head Saloon with his partner, Philip H. Coe (1839–1871). Coe was born in Gonzales and served with distinction during the Civil War. During the war and its aftermath, Coe made gambling his profession, quite possibly at the foot of his mentor, Ben Thompson. In 1869 it appears as if Coe was in Brenham, but by the spring of 1871 he was again in company of Thompson in Abilene, Kansas.

By any measure Abilene of the early 1870s was a tough town, and its city marshal—James B. (Wild Bill) Hickok—was up to the challenge of taming its rowdy visitors. Although there may have been many reasons that Hickok and Philip Coe did not care for each other, it is likely that the basis of their dislike was a woman they both cherished. Apparently she chose the gambler over the lawman and was going to leave town with Coe—or so she thought. During the evening of October 5, 1871, Hickok shot Coe, who had apparently been firing his pistol into the evening air on a street in Abilene. Tragically, in the confusion of the shots taken at Coe, Hickok also shot and killed his

deputy. Coe received a mortal abdominal wound, suffered in agony for four days, and died on October 9, 1871. His remains were transported back to Texas and buried in the Prairie Lea Cemetery in Brenham. Philip Coe may have the distinction of being the last person killed by Hickok.

Tired of both the outlaws and Hickok, the citizens of Abilene decided in 1872 no longer to allow Texas cattle drivers access to the rail yards in the city. After the shooting of Coe, Ben Thompson left town for Ellsworth, Kansas, where he met Wyatt Earp in one of the Old West's classic "in the street" confrontations. Looking down the barrel of Earp's gun, Thompson backed down and soon left Ellsworth for the Texas Panhandle. There Thompson would meet and, in the ensuing years, form a lifelong friendship with Bat Masterson.

Thompson eventually returned to Austin and opened his own business, the Iron Front Saloon, at Sixth and Congress. As always seemed to be the case, trouble arrived with him. On Christmas Eve in 1876 he was in a rival establishment when a fight erupted. When

Thompson tried to intervene, Mark Wilson (owner of the establishment) fired a shotgun blast at Thompson, who immediately returned three shots, killing Wilson.

By 1880, at age thirty-seven, Thompson had established a formidable reputation for fearlessness and proficiency with a six-gun. "It is doubtful," wrote Bat Masterson of Thompson, "if in his time there was another man living who equaled him with a pistol in a life and death situation."

But Thompson's love of gambling, whiskey, and gunplay was an addiction that would prove his undoing. His downward spiral began in 1880, when he traveled to the Jack Harris Vaudeville Theater in San Antonio. There during a night of drinking and gambling, he lost heavily. Angered and drunk, he vowed he would return. Joe Foster, Harris' partner in the Vaudeville Theater, made it known that Thompson was no longer welcome in their establishment.

Despite the trouble that seemed to follow Thompson, the citizens of Austin elected him city marshal in 1881. But on July 11, 1882, Thompson made the first of a series of errors in judgment; he returned to Jack Harris' San Antonio saloon. In a brief gunfight that followed, Jack Harris was struck in the chest and died a few hours later. His death was mourned throughout the city of San Antonio, and Jack Harris was laid to rest just inside the Commerce Street entrance to the San Antonio City Cemetery #1. Though Thompson was indicted for the murder—and resigned as marshal—he was acquitted after a successful claim of self-defense. He returned to Austin as a hero. But Thompson's days were already numbered, as were those of a cattle-rustler-turned-lawman from Uvalde.

John King Fisher (1854–1884) was once the undisputed czar of a five-thousand-square-mile territory in southwest Texas known as the Nueces Strip, an area of Texas where cattle rustling was a flourishing industry. Fisher's path of lawlessness began when, as a teenager, he was convicted of burglary in Goliad and spent four months in the state prison at Huntsville. But prison life apparently did not diminish his love of the wild life. Within a few years, Fisher had established himself as king of the Nueces Strip, where as many as a hundred outlaws had taken refuge in his dominion. Tall, handsome, and impeccably dressed, Fisher and his followers rustled cattle and terrorized resisting settlers, but he kept intruders out of his part of Texas. On the road to his ranch he had placed a sign that read, "This is King Fisher's Road. Take the other."

As local stockmen quickly learned, these outlaws were not the least bit afraid to take whatever they wanted in broad daylight. The lawlessness of the Nueces Strip soon attracted forces under the command of Texas Ranger Captain Leander McNelly (1844–1877). Although McNelly arrested Fisher several times for cattle rustling and horse thievery, the flamboyant outlaw was never convicted. Still, the tribulations that come with the life of an outlaw seemed to have convinced Fisher that a presence within the law would be more peaceful than one outside its bounds. In 1881 he was appointed deputy sheriff of Uvalde County and was made acting sheriff in 1883. He made plans to run for office in 1884.

In March 1884, Fisher had come to Austin on Uvalde County business when he ran into Ben Thompson. The two of them decided to catch the train back to San Antonio to see a play before Fisher returned to Uvalde. After the performance, they unwisely strolled into the Jack Harris Vaudeville Theater, where Thompson ran into Jack Harris' partners, Joe Foster and Billy Simms.

Thompson and Fisher had been drinking heavily in the saloon. Inside, Simms, Foster, and three confederates were waiting. When the subject of the murder of Jack Harris came up, Fisher wanted to leave. But Thompson pushed on, eventually slapping Foster and placing a pistol in the saloon owner's mouth. Almost immediately, shooting broke the tension and silence of the room. As the smoke cleared, both Thompson and Fisher lay dead on the floor. Fisher had never drawn his gun, and Thompson had managed but a single shot. Yet the bodies of the outlaw lawmen had nine and thirteen wounds, respectively. Ironically, a coroner's jury in San Antonio ruled the killings self-defense.

The bullet-riddled body of Ben Thompson was returned to Austin for burial at Oakwood Cemetery. John King Fisher's body was returned to his home. He now lies in the Pioneer Park, Uvalde.

Confederate Cemetery (San Antonio City Cemetery #4)
E. Commerce St. at New Braunfels Ave.
N 29 25.173, W 097 27.823

George W. Baylor

George Baylor (1832–1916) served gallantly in the Civil War battles at Mansfield and Pleasant Hill, but his career was forever blighted for his killing of fellow officer John Austin Wharton (1828–1865) in the Fannin Hotel in Houston during a quarrel over military matters. On April 6, 1865, Baylor, apparently angered after having been slapped by Wharton, drew his pistol and shot the unarmed officer. Wharton, who had served valiantly at the battles of Shiloh and Chickamauga, is buried in the Texas State Cemetery. Baylor is said to have regretted the death of Wharton for the remainder of his own life.

After the war, Baylor entered the service of the Texas Rangers and spent much of 1879 and 1880 in pursuit of Apache chief Victorio. He was elected to the Texas House in 1885 and later served as clerk of the district and circuit courts.

Hamilton P. Bee

Hamilton P. Bee (1822–1897) was born in South Carolina and came to Texas as a youth. During the U.S.-Mexican War, he served briefly as a private with Benjamin McCulloch, as a second lieutenant with Mirabeau B. Lamar's company of Texas Cavalry and with Col. Peter Hansborough Bell's regiment of Texas Volunteers. After that war, Bee was elected to the Texas Legislature, where he served as Speaker of the House from 1855–1857.

As the Civil War erupted, Bee was elected brigadier general of militia in 1861 and appointed brigadier general in the Confederate army to rank from March 4, 1862. He first served in the Rio Grande District but in 1864 led his brigade in the Red River campaign, where he led the cavalry charge at Pleasant Hill, Louisiana.

John Salmon Ford

John S. (Rip) Ford (1815–1897) came to Texas in 1836 and served in the Texas Army under John Coffee (Jack) Hays (1817–1883). Salmon was elected to the Texas Congress in 1844 and introduced the resolution that accepted the terms for Texas' annexation to the United States. After a stint editing an Austin newspaper, Ford served in the U.S.-Mexican War, in which he earned the nickname "Rip" for his habit of sending notices of death that began with the words, "Rest In Peace." Hence, Rip.

In the late 1840s, Ford was selected by Robert S. Neighbors to participate in an exploration of southwest Texas for the purpose of establishing a route to El Paso, and in 1849 Ford was appointed captain in a Texas Ranger unit stationed in the Nueces Strip. Ford was later elected to the Texas Senate (1852), fought in Indian battles in the Panhandle (1859), served as a member of the Secession Convention (1861), and led Confederate troops in the last battle of the Civil War, at Palmito Ranch. "Rip" Ford was reelected to the Texas Senate in

GRAVESITE OF TEXAS LEGEND JOHN S. "RIP" FORD, CONFEDERATE CEMETERY, SAN ANTONIO.

1876 and was appointed as superintendent of the Deaf and Dumb School (1879). He was a charter member of the Texas Historical Association.

Odd Fellows Cemetery
Paso Hondo St. at Monumental St.
N 29 25.269, W 098 28.155

The Odd Fellows Cemetery is directly across Paso Hondo Street from the Masonic Cemetery, one block north of East Commerce Street. I found the Odd Fellows Cemetery to be the most interesting of all the cemeteries in the complex. It has many unusual statues (including a very interesting statue of a north-facing angel), stone markers, and metal markers. The cemetery also houses an absolutely huge mausoleum marked only by the family name "Scholz." There are no posted hours for the cemetery, and the gates are apparently never closed. This cemetery has experienced substantial vandalism, but the city of San Antonio has assumed its maintenance and it is reasonably well kept.

In the southeast corner of this cemetery are the gravestones of two great Texas patriots, Samuel H. Walker and Robert A. Gillespie. Both Walker and Gillespie were among the Texans killed in the U.S.-

Mexican War. On the twentieth anniversary of the Battle of San Jacinto, April 21, 1856, a large crowd gathered at San Antonio to witness the reinterment of these two Texas Rangers. Under the auspices of the Independent Order of Odd Fellows (IOOF), Walker and Gillespie were laid side by side in the Odd Fellows Cemetery. The orator that day was James C. Wilson, one of the three men with whom Walker escaped from imprisonment in Mexico.

ROBERT A. GILLESPIE

Robert Gillespie (1815–1846) participated in the Battle of Salado Creek and was a member of the Somervell expedition. He was wounded in action in Mexico on September 22, 1846, and died the next day. Gillespie County was later named in his honor.

SAMUEL WALKER

Samuel Walker (1817–1847) was a member of the Somervell expedition, but he remained with the invading Texans and was a member of the ill-fated Mier expedition. He avoided execution by drawing a white bean during the Black Bean Episode. Walker later escaped from imprisonment with two others; together they reached Tampico and caught a vessel to New Orleans.

By 1844 Walker was back in the service of the Texas Rangers. After several skirmishes with Indians, one in which he was severely wounded, Walker left the service of Texas in March 1846. At the outbreak of the U.S.-Mexican War, Walker was authorized by Gen. Zachary Taylor to raise a company of Texas Mounted Rangers to act as scouts for Taylor's army. Walker served with bravery and distinction until he was killed on October 1847. The bodies of both Walker and Gillespie were reinterred at the Odd Fellows Cemetery, where their graves are marked by a decaying limestone obelisk. Although Walker's remains have been reported to have been moved to Waco, it appears that did not take place.

San Antonio City Cemetery #5
Paso Hondo St. at Palmetto St.
N 29 25.263, W 098 27.955

NATHANIEL C. LEWIS

Nathaniel C. Lewis (1806–1872) was born in Falmouth, Massachusetts, and went to sea at age fourteen in a whaling vessel. He came to San Antonio in 1830, entered the mercantile business, and became a prominent businessman. Lewis apparently supplied the defenders of the Alamo from his store and may have been the last man to leave the mission prior to the March 6, 1836, battle. He later served in the House of Representatives of the Fourth Congress of the Republic of Texas and several terms as an alderman in San Antonio.

Saint Mary's Cemetery
Palmetto St. and Wyoming St.
N 29 24.976, W 098 27.934

ADINA EMILIA DE ZAVALA

Adina Emilia de Zavala (1861–1955) was born in Harris County. The family lived at Galveston, where Adina attended Ursuline Academy, before moving to a ranch near San Antonio about 1873. Adina graduated from Sam Houston Normal Institute at Huntsville in 1879 and taught school in Terrell from 1884 to 1886 and later in San Antonio.

Perhaps de Zavala's greatest contribution to Texas was the preservation of a portion of the Alamo, which her San Antonio historical group prevented from being razed in the early twentieth century. In 1886 a wholesale grocery company purchased the Alamo mission convent and the "long barracks." As early as 1892, before her historical group affiliated with the Daughters of the Republic of Texas (DRT), she negotiated a verbal agreement that would give her group the first chance at buying the landmark property.

Clara Driscoll (buried in the Masonic Cemetery—San Antonio) joined the society and the DRT in 1903, and the next year she purchased the property. The Texas Legislature authorized state purchase of the property from Driscoll in January 1905 and gave custody of the Alamo to the DRT.

De Zavala was active in historical preservation for the rest of her life. In 1912 she organized the Texas Historical and Landmarks Association, and in 1923 Governor Pat Neff appointed her to the Texas Historical Board. De Zavala was a member of the United Daughters of the Confederacy, the Texas Folklore Society, the Philosophical Society of Texas, and the Texas Woman's Press Association, and she authored several publications on Texas history.

GEORGE K. KITCHEN

Sergeant George K. Kitchen (1844–1922) was in Texas with Company H, Sixth U.S. Cavalry, on the upper Washita River on September 9, 1874. While attempting to reach Gen. Nelson A. Miles' forces on the Washita River, the company was attacked by a large force of Indians. For his gallantry in action during the five-day battle, Kitchen was awarded the Congressional Medal of Honor.

SAM LUCCHESE

Sam Lucchese (1868–1929) was born in Sicily in 1868 and immigrated to the United States in 1883. Upon his arrival in San Antonio, he and his brothers opened the Lucchese Boot and Shoe Factory. In 1919 the factory had a daily production of thirty-five pairs of custom boots, along with various other types of shoes. As his business prospered, Lucchese invested in real estate, and his theaters became a mainstay in Spanish-language entertainment.

Veterans Administration National Cemetery
517 Paso Hondo St.
N 29 25.262, W 098 28.006

The Veterans Administration (VA) National Cemetery is one of two (along with Fort Sam Houston National Cemetery) national cemeteries located in San Antonio. The VA National Cemetery is small, relative to the other cemeteries in the complex, and is immaculately kept. This cemetery is unique in its number of Medal of Honor awardees from the Indian Wars, including William De Armond, Frederick Deetline, Henry Falcott, John Given, John Harrington, John Hooker, Henry McMasters, James Nash, Solon Neal, George Smith, and Lewis Warrington.

DAVID B. BARKLEY

David B. Barkley (1899–1918) was born in Laredo and entered the U.S. Army as a private when the United States entered World War I. He was assigned to Company A, 356th Infantry, Eighty-ninth Division. While serving in France, Barkley was assigned a reconnaissance mission that required swimming the Meuse River and infiltrating German lines. Barkley and another soldier completed the initial crossing, but on the return, Barkley drowned. His death on November 9, 1918, took place only two days before the armistice. For his heroic service, this young Texan was awarded the Congressional Medal of Honor. He lay in state in the Alamo, only the second person to be so honored. Camp Barkley was named in his honor.

WILLIAM H. BARNES

William Barnes (1845–1866) served in the Thirty-eighth U.S. Colored Troops during the Civil War. On September 29, 1864, he was cited for gallantry at Chapin's Farm, Virginia. Although wounded, he led a charge into the Confederate defenses and for that action was awarded the Congressional Medal of Honor.

JOHN L. BULLIS

John Bullis (1841–1911) was a career soldier. As a member of the Union army, he participated in several important battles, including Gettysburg, where he was captured. After a prisoner exchange, he served with the 118th U.S. Infantry, Colored, and rose to the rank of captain.

After the war, Bullis reenlisted in the regular army and returned to Texas. In 1869 he was transferred to the Twenty-fourth Infantry, a unit composed of white officers and African American enlisted men. While stationed at Fort Clark in 1873, he was given command of a special troop, the famous "Black Seminole" scouts. The scouts were assigned to Col. Ranald S. Mackenzie's expedition in 1873, where Bullis and his twenty scouts distinguished themselves in battle.

In later years, John Bullis served as an Indian agent and as paymaster at Fort Sam Houston. During the Spanish-American War and Philippine Insurrection, he saw duty in both Cuba and the Philippines. He gained considerable wealth through wise investments, and after his death in 1911, a military training base near San Antonio was named in his honor.

JESSE LEIGH HALL

Jesse Leigh Hall (1849–1911) was born in Lexington, North Carolina. Hall moved to Texas in 1869 and changed the spelling of his middle name to "Lee." He started his career as a schoolteacher but soon signed on as city marshal in Sherman, then deputy sheriff of Denison, and later, sergeant at arms of the Texas Senate. In August 1876 he received a commission as second lieutenant of Leander H. McNelly's Special Force of Texas Rangers, operating in the Nueces Strip. In October 1876, Hall became acting commander of the company and soon was in Cuero to control the Sutton-Taylor feud. In January 1877, Hall was promoted to first lieutenant and company commander.

Hall left the Rangers in 1880 and proceeded to fail at several business ventures. After serving as agent to the Anadarko Indians, he was indicted in 1888 for embezzlement and for making false claims, but the suits were dismissed for lack of evidence. With the coming of the Spanish-American War, Hall raised two companies for service in the First U.S. Volunteer Infantry Regiment. When the regiment was released from service, Hall reentered the army as a first lieutenant and saw action as a leader of the Macabebe Scouts in the Philippine Islands. He received a promotion to captain for conspicuous gallant service at Aringay and Batangas before he was discharged on October 6, 1900.

George E. Kelly

Lieutenant George E. Kelly (1879–1911) was killed in a plane crash at Fort Sam Houston on May 10, 1911. He was the first American military aviator to lose his life while piloting a military aircraft. In 1947, Kelly Air Force Base in San Antonio was named in his honor.

Harry McLeary Wurzbach

Harry McLeary Wurzbach (1874–1931) was born in San Antonio and attended law school at Washington and Lee University in Lexington, Virginia. After admission to the bar in 1896, he settled in to practice law in San Antonio. During the Spanish-American War, he volunteered as a private in the Texas Volunteer Infantry. On November 2, 1920, Wurzbach was elected to the Sixty-seventh U.S. Congress from the Fourteenth Texas District, the first native Texan to be a Republican representative. He was also the first Republican from Texas to be elected for more than two terms, serving in the Sixty-eighth through Seventy-second Congresses.

Fort Sam Houston National Cemetery
1520 Harry Wurzbach Rd.
N 29 28.735, W 098 25.987

Roy P. Benavidez

Roy Benavidez (1935–1998) was awarded the Congressional Medal of Honor in 1981 for actions in Vietnam on May 2, 1968, west of Loc Ninh. As an Army Green Beret, Benavidez volunteered to participate in a rescue mission to aid 12 Green Beret comrades who were surrounded by more than 350 of the enemy. Within seconds of jumping from the rescue helicopter, Benavidez was wounded four times. While trying to lift a fallen comrade to his shoulders, he was struck again. In hand-to-hand combat he was struck on the back of his head by an enemy rifle butt, bayoneted in his right arm, and suffered a broken jaw when struck in the face a second time before killing his assailant with a knife. Benavidez was responsible for bringing back 17 men, including his wounded Green Beret comrade, downed helicopter crewmen, and three North Vietnamese soldiers he loaded by mistake, plus classified material.

CECIL BOLTON

Cecil Bolton (1908–1965) received the Congressional Medal of Honor for his valiant efforts during a pitched battle that followed the crossing of the Mark River in Holland, November 2, 1944. Wounded, he led a bazooka team against an enemy machine gun. He charged the nest, killing the two gunners, and then attacked a second machine gun and an 88-mm artillery piece.

WILLIAM J. BORDELON

William J. Bordelon (1920–1943) was awarded the Congressional Medal of Honor for service during the invasion of Tarawa. Bordelon single-handedly destroyed four Japanese machine gun positions, ignoring several serious arm and facial wounds of his own, and then gave his life while rescuing two Marine buddies from certain death. His body was exhumed from Honolulu, Hawaii, in November 1995, and he was the fifth person to lie in state at the Alamo shrine prior to final burial.

JOHN B. CHARLTON

John B. Charlton (1848–1922) was known as the "Old Sergeant" for his years as a soldier and an Indian fighter. Charlton first served in the U.S. Army during the Civil War and reenlisted in 1870 to serve in Col. Ranald S. Mackenzie's Fourth U.S. Cavalry. Charlton was the escort for William T. Sherman on a frontier inspection tour that narrowly escaped the Kiowas in 1871. Charlton killed Kiowa chief Satank during an escape attempt. Charlton spent the next three years fighting Indians and participated in the Battle of Palo Duro Canyon on September 27, 1874. He left the military in 1876 and began a freight operation between Cheyenne and Deadwood, South Dakota.

BARNEY M. GILES

Barney McKinney Giles (1892–1984) was a deputy commander of the U.S. Army Air Corps during World War II. He became brigadier general in charge of the Fourth Bomber Command in February 1942 and took over the Fourth Air Force in September of that year, with the temporary rank of major general. In July 1943, Gen. Henry "Hap" Arnold appointed Giles chief of the Air Staff and later promoted him to be deputy commanding general of the Air Force. After the surrender of Japan, Giles attended the signing of the treaty on the battleship *Missouri*.

WILLIAM G. HARRELL

William G. Harrell (1922–1964) was refused entry into the U.S. Air Force because he was color blind, but he was accepted in the Marines. On March 3, 1945, Sergeant Harrell went ashore with the other members of the First Marine Battalion, Twenty-eighth Marines, Fifth Marine Division, at Iwo Jima. While holding a defensive position, Harrell opened fire on Japanese soldiers who had attacked in the darkness, but as he fought, a grenade explosion destroyed his left hand and fractured his thigh. As he lay wounded, Harrell was attacked by a Japanese soldier and was wounded by his assailant's saber. Although Harrell managed to kill his attacker, a second grenade was placed near his head by two additional enemy soldiers. Harrell killed one of his foes and pushed the grenade back at his remaining attacker. As the grenade detonated, the enemy was killed, but Harrell's right hand was also destroyed. For his heroic sacrifice, William Harrell was awarded the Congressional Medal of Honor.

MILTON A. LEE

Milton A. Lee (1949–1968) enlisted in the U.S. Army in San Antonio and arrived in Vietnam in January 1968. Assigned to Company B, Second Battalion, 502nd Infantry, First Brigade, 101st Airborne Division, Private First Class Lee was serving as a radio operator when on April 26, 1968, near Phu Bai, South Vietnam, his unit came under intense fire from North Vietnamese regulars. His platoon was decimated, and as casualties began to mount, Lee administered first aid in the midst of the assault. During a subsequent assault on the enemy position, Lee spotted an enemy ambush and charged the position, killing the enemy soldiers. As he charged a second position, he was mortally wounded but continued to deliver covering fire for his comrades. For his heroic service and gallant saving of lives, Milton Lee was awarded the Congressional Medal of Honor.

JAMES E. ROBINSON, JR.

James E. Robinson (1918–1945) entered military service at Waco, Texas, and was assigned to the 861st Field Artillery Battalion, Sixty-third Infantry Division, U.S. Army. On April 6, 1945, Robinson was a field artillery observer attached to Company A, 253rd Infantry, near Untergriesheim, Germany. After heavy fighting and the loss of most of his unit's leadership, Robinson led his remaining riflemen in a charge against an enemy objective. During the engagement, he killed ten enemy soldiers and his unit secured the area. During an advance on the town of Kressbach, Robinson was mortally wounded but refused medical aid and continued to direct artillery fire. For his gallant service, James Robinson was awarded the Congressional Medal of Honor.

CLETO L. RODRÍGUEZ

Cleto L. Rodríguez (1923–1990) entered the U.S. Army in early 1944 and served as a technical sergeant with Company B, 148th Infantry. During the battle for Manila, Rodríguez and his partner, John M. Reece, were part of a unit that attacked the strongly defended Paco Railroad Station. The two men killed eighty-two enemy soldiers and disorganized the enemies' defense, thus facilitating the defeat of the Japanese at their strong point. Two days later, Rodríguez single-handedly killed six enemy soldiers and destroyed a 20-mm gun. Rodríguez was the fifth person of Hispanic descent to win the Medal of Honor and the first Mexican American soldier to win the nation's highest combat medal for service in the South Pacific.

MARVIN STALLINGS

I know nothing more about Corp. Marvin Stallings (1922–1944) other than that he was a member of Third Battalion, Company I of the 506th Parachute Infantry Regiment, a unit of the 101st Airborne Division. He was one of eighteen paratroopers onboard the *Donna Mae*, a troop transport plane piloted by 1st Lt. Ray Pullen. In the late hours of June 5, 1944, Marvin Stallings and roughly thirteen thousand paratroopers of the 82nd and 101st Airborne Divisions began climbing onto 821 C-47 troop planes for the massive airborne assault carried out in the early hours of D-day.

One can imagine Stallings and his comrades sitting in the hold of the plane, waiting for the green "jump light," and wondering what

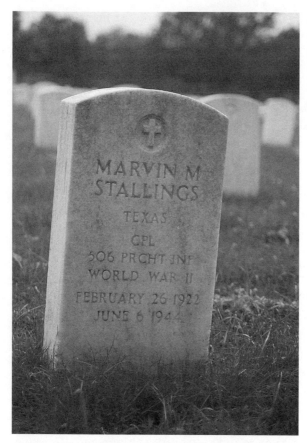

CORPORAL MARVIN
STALLINGS WAS
KILLED IN ACTION ON
D DAY, JUNE 6, 1944.
FORT SAM HOUSTON
NATIONAL CEME-
TERY, SAN ANTONIO.

would await them when they hit the ground. Perhaps Stallings thought of his parents or a girlfriend back home (the *Donna Mae* was named for Ray Pullen's fiancée). Perhaps he prayed or bummed a stick of gum from another trooper.

As the *Donna Mae* neared the drop zone, antiaircraft fire began to light the night sky. At about two minutes from the drop zone, one of the pilots in formation reported a bright flash of light when the *Donna Mae* was hit. Lieutenant Pullen struggled to keep the plane in the air and managed to fly the mortally wounded C-47 for twenty miles before it crashed near the small village of Magneville, France. Marvin Stallings, his seventeen paratrooper comrades, and the four aircrewmen perished.

Corporal Marvin Stallings was brought home for interment at Fort Sam Houston in 1948. A small memorial stands even today at Magneville in honor of the twenty-two brave Americans who died that night in the Normandy Invasion.

SETH WELD

Corporal Seth Weld (1879–1958) was awarded the Congressional Medal of Honor for service at La Paz, Leyte, Philippine Islands, on December 5, 1906. Corporal Weld, although wounded, went to the assistance of a wounded officer and a fellow soldier who were surrounded by about forty Philippine insurgents, and using his disabled rifle as a club, he beat back the assailants and rescued his companions.

EDWARD T. XIMENES

Edward T. Ximenes (1915–1992) was born in Floresville, Texas, where he was a schoolmate of future governor John B. Connally. An excellent student, Ximenes attended the University of Texas, where he received his bachelor's degree in 1937, and in 1941 he was awarded a medical degree from the University of Texas Medical Branch at Galveston. After service in World War II, Ximenes moved to San Antonio, where he practiced internal medicine. In 1967, Governor John B. Connally appointed Ximenes to the University of Texas Board of Regents, and Ximenes thus became the first Hispanic appointed to that position.

San Fernando Cemetery #1
1100 N. Colorado St.
N 29 24.933, W 098 30.756

THOMAS JEFFERSON DEVINE

Thomas J. Devine (1820–1890) settled in La Grange after having studied law in the East. He served as city attorney for San Antonio until 1851, when he was elected district judge. In 1861 Devine served as a member of the Texas Secession Convention and helped in the surrender of federal troops and property in Texas.

After the Civil War, Devine went to Mexico to avoid taking an oath of allegiance to the federal government. He later, along with Jefferson Davis, was one of only three men charged with treason during the war, a charge for which he was never tried. Devine continued to practice law and was held in high esteem for his knowledge and ethics. The town of Devine is named in his honor.

JOSÉ ANTONIO NAVARRO

José Antonio Navarro (1795–1871) was a Texas patriot and one of three Hispanic signers of the Texas Declaration of Independence.

ALEJO PÉREZ SURVIVED THE FALL OF THE ALAMO AND LIVED A LONG LIFE AS A SAN ANTONIO CITIZEN. SAN FERNANDO CEMETERY #1, SAN ANTONIO.

Navarro served in the Texas Republic House of Representatives, 1838–1839; as the sole Hispanic delegate to the Texas state constitutional convention, 1845; as a member of the Texas Republic Senate, 1845; and as Texas state senator, 1846–1849. Navarro County is named in his honor.

ALEJO PÉREZ, JR.

Alejo Pérez, Jr. (1835–1918), was the son of Juana de Navarro Alsbury and her first husband, Alejo Pérez, Sr. He was brought into the Alamo by his mother and was seventeen days shy of his first birthday at the time of the Alamo battle. Alejo, Jr., survived the battle and grew up in San Antonio, later serving on its police force. At his death on October 19, 1918, he was probably the last surviving occupant of the Alamo.

ANDREA CASTAÑÓN VILLANUEVA

Andrea Castañón Villanueva (1785–1899) may have been a survivor of the Battle of the Alamo. She claimed to have been in the fortress during the battle in 1836 and to have nursed James Bowie. Although there is some question as to her presence, most historians believe she was actually in the Alamo during the battle. Records indicate that she is indeed buried in this cemetery, but I have never been able to locate a headstone marking her grave.

Sunset Memorial Park
1701 Austin Highway
N 29 29.750, W 098 25.835

POMPEO LUIGI COPPINI

Pompeo Coppini (1870–1957) was perhaps Texas' most noted sculptor. Born in Italy, he moved to Texas in November 1901. Coppini created the statue of Jefferson Davis and other figures for the Confederate Soldier Monument that stands on the Capitol grounds in Austin. Coppini also was commissioned to create the Littlefield Fountain Memorial at the University of Texas at Austin. In addition, he created the seven bronze statues along the south mall of the university grounds, all of which (except the sculpture of George Washington) were associated with the Littlefield commission.

AN ELABORATE SCULPTURE ADORNS THE GRAVESITE OF SCULPTOR POMPEO COPPINI IN SUNSET MEMORIAL PARK, SAN ANTONIO.

Many of Coppini's finest works are found in Texas cemeteries. These include the monument at his own gravesite; the statues of Stephen F. Austin and Johanna Troutman (Texas State Cemetery); the gravesite monument of Sam Houston (Oakwood Cemetery, Huntsville); and the Woodmen of the World Memorial to those who lost their lives in the Galveston Hurricane of 1900 (Lakeview Cemetery, Galveston).

WALDINE AMANDA TAUCH

Waldine Tauch (1892–1986) was born in Schulenberg, Texas, and moved to Brady as a teenager. While she was in Brady, Pompeo Coppini took Tauch as his pupil, and the two artists would share a life-long association. In 1923 Tauch moved to New York, where she assisted Coppini in his crafting of the Littlefield Fountain for the University of Texas at Austin.

Waldine Tauch became a superb sculptor in her own right. Her best works include the statue of Douglas MacArthur at Howard Payne University, Brownwood; *Higher Education Reflects Responsibility to the World*, a bronze statue at Trinity University, San Antonio; *Texas Ranger of Today*, an eight-foot bronze statue at the Union Terminal in Dallas; and *Pippa Passes*, a bronze statue at Baylor University, Waco.

Mission Burial Park
1700 S.E. Military Dr.
N 29 21.111, W 098 28.240

ANTOINETTE POWER HOUSTON BRINGHURST

Antoinette (Nettie) Bringhurst (1852–1932) was one of eight children of Sam and Margaret Houston. She was state historian of the Daughters of the Republic of Texas from 1906 to 1908 and, as a result of her published poetry, was elected poet laureate for life in 1908.

OSCAR JULIUS FOX

Oscar J. Fox (1879–1961) was born in Burnet County, Texas, and after studying music abroad, he returned to San Antonio and a career in music. In 1923 he published the first of more than fifty songs; for most of the western songs he published, he took existing lyrics by John A. Lomax and set them to music. Among his most famous compositions were "Whoopee Ti Yi Yo, Git Along, Little Dogies" and "The Cowboy's Lament."

ADOLPH AND ELIZABETH TOEPPERWEIN

Adolph (Ad) Toepperwein (1869–1962) and his wife, Elizabeth (1882–1945), were two of America's finest sharpshooters. Adolph became interested in shooting after watching another sharpshooter, and by 1892 he was touring the country as he displayed his phenomenal marksmanship. In 1903 he married Elizabeth Servaty, who had never fired a gun in her life. But within a matter of only two years, they were traveling the country as a pair, exhibiting their remarkable shooting skills.

In 1906 Adolph shot 19,999 of 20,000 hand-tossed wooden blocks during a three-day shooting exhibition. Elizabeth was the first woman in the United States to qualify as a national marksman with a military rifle. She was also the first woman to successfully break 100 consecutive targets in trapshooting (which she repeated more than 200 times). In 1969 she was inducted into the Trapshooting Hall of Fame, Vandalia, Ohio.

GEORGE EDWARD (RUBE) WADDELL

Considered by many as one of the greatest left-handed pitchers of all time, Rube Waddell (1876–1914) exceeded twenty wins in each of his four years with the Kansas City Athletics and led the American League in strikeouts for six consecutive years. He was elected to the Baseball Hall of Fame in 1946.

ROSS YOUNGS

With a physique that resembled a fire hydrant in its strength and stature, Ross Youngs (1897–1927) was one of the outstanding right fielders in baseball history. He hit over .300 in seven straight seasons, and his lifetime batting average of .322 led manager John McGraw to call him "the greatest outfielder I ever saw." The Committee on Baseball Veterans elected him to the Baseball Hall of Fame in 1972.

Ruiz-Herrera Cemetery

From San Antonio, take I-35 south; exit Somersett Rd. and proceed under Loop 410 to Fisher-Howard intersection. Turn left on Quesenberry Rd., and proceed to the cemetery at the road's terminus. This cemetery is difficult to locate.
N 29 16.349, W 098 36.637

The Ruiz-Herrera Cemetery is one of San Antonio's oldest cemeteries that is still used by its founding family. Started in the 1840s, this small cemetery was terribly overgrown on the day I visited. If you decide to visit this cemetery, I would recommend going during the winter. The chiggers and grass burrs were plentiful in this cemetery.

BLAS M. HERRERA

Blas Herrera (1802–1878), who has been referred to as the "Paul Revere" of the Texas Revolution, was born on February 2 in San Antonio de Béxar. In late 1835, during the Siege of Bexar, Herrera served under the command of Captain Juan Seguín, participating in the assault of the city on December 5–9, 1835. Seguín dispatched Herrera to Laredo in early 1836 to watch for Mexican troop activities and to report back to the Alamo any news of a Mexican advance toward San Antonio.

In mid-February, Herrera rode all night to reach the city with information that Mexican general Santa Anna was at the head of a large force that appeared to be approaching the city. Herrera then escorted José Antonio Navarro and José Francisco Ruiz to Washington-on-the-Brazos, where they signed the Texas Declaration of Independence (March 2, 1836). Herrera may have served Gen. Sam Houston by providing intelligence before and during the Battle of San Jacinto.

FRANCISCO ANTONIO RUIZ

Francisco Antonio Ruiz (ca. 1804–1876) was mayor (alcalde) of San Antonio during the Battle of the Alamo and was held under house arrest until the Alamo fell. Upon Ruiz fell the harsh duty of identifying the Alamo dead and disposing of their bodies. He also provided an eyewitness account of the fall of the Alamo. So opposed to annexation was Ruiz that when Texas became part of the Union, he went to live among the Indians. Better a recluse than a Unionist, I guess.

San José Burial Park
8235 Mission Rd.
N 29 20.715, W 098 28.456

JOHN E. KILMER

John E. Kilmer (1930–1952) was a U.S. Navy hospital corpsman attached to duty with a Marine rifle company in the 1st Marine Division. On August 13, 1952, his company was defending an important position during an assault by large concentrations of hostile troops. As the attack progressed, Kilmer repeatedly braved intense enemy mortar, artillery, and sniper fire to move from one position to another, administering aid to the wounded and expediting their evacuation.

Painfully wounded when struck by mortar fragments, he inched his way to the side of a stricken Marine through a barrage of enemy shells around him. Undaunted by the shell fire, he administered first aid to his comrade and, as another salvo of enemy fire encased the immediate area, unhesitatingly shielded the wounded man with his body. He gallantly gave his life for another and was awarded the Congressional Medal of Honor.

San Saba

San Saba City Cemetery
Highway 16, north of Highway 190 intersection
N 31 11.730, W 098 42.425

SION R. BOSTICK

Sion Bostick (1819–1902) came to Texas about 1828 after Stephen F. Austin granted his father, Caleb Bostick, land in what would become Matagorda County. Sion Bostick was a soldier by nature; apparently he never saw a military operation he did not like. He took part in both the Battle of Gonzales and the Siege of Bexar (1835). Rejoining the Texas Army in March 1836, he participated in the Battle of San Jacinto. On April 22, 1836, Bostick, along with Joel Robinson and James A. Sylvester (both are interred in the Texas State Cemetery), captured General Santa Anna, returning him to General Sam Houston. In 1840 Bostick participated in the Battle of Plum Creek, where Texas militiamen fought a decisive engagement with Comanche Indians who were returning from a raid on Victoria.

A Texas Historical Commission marker at the very front of the cemetery directs visitors to Bostick's grave "275 yards to the west." I broke out my trusty compass, determined due west, and set out to find his gravestone. Almost an hour later, I still had not found it. It is much easier to find by walking or driving down the road that forms the south boundary of the cemetery while looking for the marker, which is just off the north edge of the road. Look for the name "Bostick" at the base of the upright stone.

Santa Anna

Santa Anna Cemetery
FM 1176, east of Crockett St.
N 31 44.229, W 099 18.781

The Santa Anna Cemetery lies just southeast of the City of Santa Anna on FM 1176. It is open and windswept, with many mature cedar trees and little else in the way of shade. Most of the family plots in the cemetery are curbed with concrete and are orderly if not attractive. At rest in the Santa Anna Cemetery is my grandmother, Martha Goodson Carlock (1898–1995). She was never famous, but she taught me to read and write before I started elementary school and she instilled in all her grandchildren the hunger for education that she carried with her for more than ninety-five years.

JOHN RILEY BANISTER AND EMMA D. BANISTER

At rest in the Santa Anna Cemetery are John Riley Banister (1854–1918) and his wife, Emma D. Banister (1871–1956). John Banister came to Texas from Missouri in 1867 and began to "cowboy" in Coleman and Mason counties. In 1876 he joined the Texas Rangers and served in the Frontier Battalion, escorting John Wesley Hardin to Comanche for trial in the murder of Brown County deputy sheriff Charles Webb. Banister also aided in the capture of the legendary bank robber Sam Bass. Banister left Ranger service in 1888, worked running a livery stable, as a railroad detective, and as an inspector for the Texas Cattle Raisers Association.

After his first wife died in 1894, leaving him with four children, John Banister married his second wife, Emma Daugherty. John and Emma would have five children of their own. In 1914 John Banister became sheriff of Coleman County but was struck down by a stroke in 1918. Emma, who had served as John's office deputy, assumed the job of sheriff and, in doing so, became the first female sheriff in the United States. After completing her husband's term, she returned to her farm in Santa Anna.

Seguin

Juan Seguín Memorial Site

Nelda St. at S. Saunders St.
N 29 33.699, W 097 58.297

JUAN NEPOMUCENO SEGUÍN

Juan Seguín (1806–1890) was born in San Antonio on October 27, 1806. Seguín began his long career of public service as an alderman in 1828 and as alcalde in 1833. His military career began in 1835, when he assumed command of a militia company in opposition to the Centralist government in Mexico. In October 1835, Stephen F. Austin commissioned him to the rank of captain. Seguin participated in the Siege of Bexar but left the Alamo as a courier before the fatal battle.

Juan Seguín participated in the Battle of San Jacinto and was military commander of San Antonio through most of 1837. He was elected to the Texas Senate that year and, as the only Hispanic Texan in the Senate of the Republic, served in the Second, Third, and Fourth Congresses. He left the Senate in 1840 and was elected mayor of San Antonio.

As was often the case, however, Seguín's heritage (much like that of the De León family in Victoria) caused problems in the new Republic of Texas. Seguín found himself in the middle of growing hostilities between Anglos and Mexican Texans, and he was suspected of having aided the Mexican invasion of San Antonio in March 1842. Fearing for the safety of his family, Seguín was forced to flee Texas for Mexico, where he spent six years. He returned to Texas after the U.S.-Mexican War and settled in Wilson County, although he eventually retired to Nuevo Laredo. He died there in 1890, and his remains were returned to Texas in 1974 for burial in Seguin, which had been named in his honor.

Riverside Cemetery

South River St. at E. Klein St.
N 29 33.668, W 097 57.732

This cemetery traces its origin to the Smith family graveyard established by early settlers Ezekiel Smith (1781–1854) and Susanna Smith (1774–1848). In 1837 Ezekiel Smith was granted land in Guadalupe County, and the Smiths' son French Smith (1809–1880) was one of the first shareholders of the city of Seguin. Ezekiel Smith and two of his sons were members of the Somervell expedition, and although his sons chose to return home, sixty-year-old Ezekiel decided to stay on and continue in the ill-fated Mier expedition. In 1880, French Smith deeded the family cemetery to the city of Seguin, and a public cemetery north of the Smith Cemetery was founded, later called Riverside. George B. Hollamon deeded additional land to the city for the cemetery in 1888, and in 1896 W. E. Goodrich deeded a third parcel.

JAMES CLINTON NEILL

J. C. Neill (1790–1845) was born in North Carolina and moved his family to Texas in 1831. In September 1835 he entered the Texas militia as a captain of artillery and was a participant in the Battle of Gonzales. John Holland Jenkins recorded that Neill actually "fired the first gun for Texas at the beginning of the revolution"—the famous Gonzales "Come and Take It" cannon. In December 1835, Neill's artillery skill proved to be a key factor in the successful assault on San Antonio de Béxar. In late December 1835, Neill was left to hold the town of San Antonio with fewer than a hundred men, and he began the task of fortifying a mission fort called the Alamo. On January 17, James Bowie arrived with orders to remove the artillery and blow up the fort, but after viewing Neill's buttressing of the structure, he decided instead to defend the Alamo.

Then James C. Neill walked out of history when he left the Alamo to care for his family in Bastrop, all of whom had been stricken with a serious illness. He left William B. Travis in temporary command, assuring the garrison that he would return within twenty days. He was riding back to rejoin his command when the Alamo fell to Mexican forces.

On March 13, 1836, Neill joined Sam Houston's army on the Brazos River, and on April 20 he commanded the Twin Sisters during the skirmish that preceded the Battle of San Jacinto, in which he was seriously wounded when a fragment of grapeshot caught him in the hip. He was therefore unable to participate in the Battle of San Jacinto. It is ironic that the man who fired the first shot of the Texas Revolution and whose resourceful strengthening of the Alamo led to its eventual destruction would find himself in such circumstances as to miss the two most important battles of the entire Texas Revolution. After independence, Neill continued to serve Texas, and in 1844 he was appointed as an Indian agent. Although Neill is purported to be buried in this cemetery, I could not locate his marker after several slow walks through the cemetery on two different occasions.

CLAIBORNE WEST

Claiborne West (1800–1866) came to Texas about 1831. At the Convention of 1836 he signed the Texas Declaration of Independence. He was elected to represent Jefferson County in the House of the First Congress of the Republic of Texas in 1836–1837.

San Geronimo Cemetery
E. Walnut, east of intersection with Highway 123
N 29 34.394, W 097 56.210

HENRY EUSTACE MCCULLOCH

Henry Eustace McCulloch (1816–1895) was born in Rutherford County, Tennessee, and was the younger brother of Benjamin McCulloch. Ben and Henry McCulloch moved to Gonzales in the late 1830s to survey and locate lands. Henry McCulloch joined the Texas Rangers and was wounded during the Battle of Plum Creek in 1840. In 1842 McCulloch participated in the Battle of Salado Creek. In 1843 he was elected sheriff of Gonzales and began a business that he moved to Seguin the following year.

During the U.S.-Mexican War and afterward, he served as a captain of a volunteer company guarding the Indian frontier. In the early 1850s McCulloch served in both the Texas House and the Senate from Guadalupe County, and in the late 1850s he was appointed U.S. marshal for the Eastern District of Texas. He served as a Confederate brigadier general during the Civil War and commanded the Northern Sub-District of Texas from 1863 to the end of the war.

ANDREW JACKSON SOWELL

Andrew Jackson Sowell (1815–1883) took part in the battles of Gonzales and Concepción and the Grass Fight during the Siege of Bexar. Sowell was a member of the Alamo garrison, but shortly before the final battle, he and Byrd Lockhart left to forage for supplies. Delayed in Gonzales, Sowell was unable to return to the Alamo before it fell. After Texas gained its independence, Sowell served for many years with the Texas Rangers and fought in the U.S.-Mexican War and with the Confederate army during the Civil War. He was a noted scout and friend of Christopher "Kit" Carson.

MAXIMILIAN HUGO STARCKE

Maximilian (Max) Starcke (1884–1972) was born at York's Creek (now Zorn), Texas. After graduation from the Agricultural and Mechanical College of Texas (now Texas A&M University) and a San Antonio business college, he began a successful business career in Seguin. Starcke served as an alderman in Seguin from 1909 to 1912 and as mayor from 1928 to 1938. As mayor, he built the city's first water filtration plant and a hydroelectric power plant on the Guadalupe River.

In 1938 Starcke was hired as first operations manager of the Lower Colorado River Authority and in 1940 was promoted to general manager of the LCRA, a position he held for fifteen years. Under his leadership the LCRA built two more dams and hydroelectric power plants on the Colorado River and extended its services to thirty-three cities and eleven rural electrification cooperatives in a forty-one-thousand-square-mile area. In retirement, Starcke continued his lifelong civic work and was a powerful force in the business and political environment of central Texas.

Sherman

West Hill Cemetery
Highway 56 at South Woods
N 33 37.923, W 096 37.178

OLIVE ANN OATMAN FAIRCHILD

Olive Ann Fairchild (1839–1903) was born in Illinois. In 1850 her family joined a wagon train headed for California, but the Oatmans and their seven children were eventually left to travel alone. On February 18, 1851, they were attacked by Indians on the Gila River in Arizona. Olive and her sister Mary were captured, their brother Lorenzo left for dead, and the rest of the family massacred. The girls were held as slaves for a year, then sold to a Mojave chief near Needles, California. During captivity, Mary died of starvation and abuse. In the winter of 1855–1956, the army located Olive and began negotiations to free her. On February 28, 1856, Olive was ransomed at Fort Yuma, Arizona, and reunited with her brother Lorenzo.

In 1857 the story of Olive Oatman and her family, entitled *Life among the Indians*, by R. B. Stratton, was published. The volume sold out three printings in a year, and the book royalties paid for the college education of Lorenzo and Olive. In 1858 the Oatmans moved to New York, and Olive went on the lecture circuit to promote Stratton's book. She married cattleman John Brant Fairchild (1830–1907) in 1865 and moved to Sherman in 1872.

Stonewall

LBJ Ranch

1.5 miles east of Stonewall
N 30 14.460, W 098 37.456

LYNDON BAINES JOHNSON

Lyndon Johnson (1908–1973) was born near Stonewall, Texas, and became perhaps the most significant political figure in Texas history. Johnson's U.S. congressional service began in 1937, and he spent eleven years in Congress. After losing a close senatorial race in 1941, he entered the U.S. Navy during World War II. In 1948 he defeated Coke Stevenson for a seat in the U.S. Senate. Johnson became Senate majority leader and was selected as the vice presidential nominee on the 1960 Democratic ticket.

Johnson assumed the U.S. presidency when John F. Kennedy was assassinated, and he was elected to a full term in 1964. During his presidential years, Johnson was the architect of the "Great Society" and the driving force in passage of the Civil Rights Act of 1964 and the Voting Rights Act of 1965. Johnson chose not to run for a second full term as president, retiring to his ranch to write his memoirs and tend his cattle. No Texan has left a greater mark on the history of the United States.

Tehuacana

Tehuacana Cemetery

County Road 226 (Limestone County)
N 31 44.990, W 096 32.833

ROBERT MARSHALL LOVE

Robert M. Love (1847–1903) was born in Franklin, Texas, and grew up in Tehuacana. At seventeen he volunteered for service in the Confederate army and served from 1862 through the end of the war. He entered politics as deputy sheriff of Limestone County (1872) and later served as the county sheriff (1884–1890), the U.S. marshal for the Northern District of Texas (1894–1896), and the state comptroller (1901–1903).

In 1873 Love and his brother John took the rather outrageous action of arming themselves to guard the north and south entrances of the Texas Capitol to protect the members of the legislature who had been prohibited to convene by incumbent governor Edmund J. Davis. Richard Coke had been elected governor, but Davis contested the election. The Fourteenth Legislature was therefore able to administer the oath of office to Coke.

In 1903, while serving as state comptroller, Love was shot at his desk in the Capitol at Austin by W. G. Hill, a former employee of the department. His last words were, "I have no idea why he shot me. May the Lord bless him and forgive him. I cannot say more."

Texarkana

Hillcrest Cemetery
Highway 67, approximately 3.5 miles west of Texarkana
N 33 24.920, W 094 06.32

JOHN WILLIAM WRIGHT PATMAN

Wright Patman (1893–1976) was born near Hughes Springs in Cass County, Texas. Patman began his political career as assistant county attorney for Cass County and in 1920 was elected to the Texas House of Representatives. After two terms in the legislature, he served four years as district attorney of the Fifth Judicial District.

In 1928 he won election as a Democrat to the U.S. House, representing the First Texas Congressional District. Patman was a "New Deal" Congressman and favored sweeping social and economic reforms. During his twenty-four terms in Congress, he became one of its most influential members. During his final four years of service, he was the senior member of Congress.

JOHN MORRIS SHEPPARD

Morris Sheppard (1875–1941) was born near Wheatville, Morris County, Texas. After earning his law degree, he ran for Congress in 1902 as a Democrat and was elected to the seat once held by his father. He served five terms in the Congress and in 1913 was elected to the U.S. Senate. He was a strong supporter of women's suffrage and prohibition. Sheppard introduced the prohibition amendment to the U.S. Constitution, which was ratified in 1919. In 1934 Sheppard became the most senior member of Congress and served there until his death.

Tyler

Oakwood Cemetery
W. Oakwood St. at N. Palace St.
N 32 21.239, W 095 18.558

HORACE CHILTON

Horace Chilton (1853–1932) was born near Tyler, Texas. Chilton studied law, was admitted to the bar in 1872, and began his practice in Tyler. He served as assistant attorney general of Texas from 1881 to 1883, and when he was appointed by Governor James Hogg to fill the congressional seat vacated by John H. Reagan in 1891, Chilton became the first native Texan to sit in the U.S. Congress. In 1895 Chilton was elected to follow Richard B. Coke in the Senate and served there until March 3, 1901.

RICHARD BENNETT HUBBARD, JR.

Richard (Dick) Hubbard, Jr. (1832–1901), was born in Walton County, Georgia, and came to Texas with his parents after having graduated from Harvard Law School in 1853. In 1857 he was U.S.

GRAVESITE OF SENATOR HORACE CHILTON, OAKWOOD CEMETERY, TYLER.

district attorney for the western district of Texas, but he resigned in 1859 to run for the Texas Legislature. He won the election and served in the Eighth Legislature. During the Civil War, he commanded the Twenty-second Texas Infantry Regiment and served in the Trans-Mississippi Department in Arkansas and Louisiana.

Hubbard was elected lieutenant governor in 1873 and 1876 and succeeded to the office of governor on December 1, 1876, when Richard Coke resigned to become a U.S. Senator. His administration was lackluster, largely as a result of the politics of reconstruction in Texas. He lacked the political support necessary for election to a second term and left the office in 1879. He was minister to Japan (1885–1889) and later wrote a book based upon his diplomatic experience entitled *The United States in the Far East*, which was published in 1899.

Utopia

Jones Cemetery

On unnamed road that intersects Highway 187 just north of Utopia, in Bandera County
N 29 37.752, W 099 32.472

BENJAMIN FRANKLIN HIGHSMITH

Benjamin F. Highsmith (1817–1905) was born in St. Charles District, Missouri Territory. Highsmith came to Texas with his family by wagon train in 1823, and they settled near the present site of La Grange.

At age fifteen, Benjamin Highsmith fought in the Battle of Velasco (1832). He was involved in all the major actions of the Texas Revolution, including the skirmish for the Gonzales "Come and Take It" cannon, the Battle of Concepción, the Grass Fight, and the Siege of Bexar. He remained in Bexar after the siege until February 18, 1836, when he carried the appeal for aid sent by Alamo commander William B. Travis to Col. James W. Fannin, Jr., at Goliad. When he returned to San Antonio, he found that the Alamo and its garrison had been surrounded by the Mexican army.

Highsmith next served as a courier for Gen. Sam Houston and, along with David B. Kent, carried the message to Fannin from Houston that ordered Fannin to abandon Goliad. Highsmith fought in the Battle of San Jacinto as a member of Capt. William Ware's company. After the revolution, Highsmith had a long career with the Texas

CYNTHIA BOLIN WAS THE VICTIM OF AN 1866 INDIAN ATTACK NEAR PRESENT-DAY UTOPIA. WARESVILLE CEMETERY, UTOPIA.

Rangers, and during the U.S.-Mexican War, he fought in the battles of Monterrey, Palo Alto, and Buena Vista.

Waresville Cemetery
Waresville Cemetery Rd. at Highway 187 (Uvalde County)
N 29 35.763, W 099 31.555

Utopia was founded by R. H. Kincheloe when he decided to move from his home on Little Creek after an 1866 Indian raid left his wife, Sarah, seriously injured and took the life of her friend Cynthia Bolin. The original town was named Montana, but postmaster George Barker changed the name to Utopia.

Sarah, who is said to have been struck seventeen times, survived the attack and died in 1938. Both she and her husband lie at rest in this cemetery. The gravesite of the unfortunate Cynthia Bolin, who was killed in the Indian attack, is near that of Sarah Kincheloe and has a fitting epitaph:

FAREWELL DEAR FRIENDS
I CAN NO LONGER STAY,
THE VILE HANDS OF INDIANS
HAVE TAKEN ME AWAY

WILLIAM WARE

William Ware (1801–1853) was a prominent figure in the Texas Revolution. He raised and commanded a company of volunteers at the Siege of Bexar (where he was slightly wounded), and as captain of the Second Company of Col. Sidney Sherman's Second Regiment, Texas Volunteers, Ware fought in the Battle of San Jacinto. He founded the small community of Waresville, just south of present-day Utopia.

Uvalde

Pioneer Park
W. Leona St. at N. Park St.
N 29 12.894, W 099 47.583

JOHN KING FISHER

King Fisher (1854–1884) had his first serious encounter with the law at the age of fifteen, when he was accused of stealing a horse after he borrowed it without telling the owner. He was later sent to prison for housebreaking in Goliad, and after serving four months for the crime, he moved to Dimmit County and established a ranch. Fisher quickly became the recognized ruler of the Nueces Strip, a region between the Nueces River and the Rio Grande, where cattle rustling was the major industry. His ranch became a haven for outlaws, and one of the roads to his spread was marked by a sign that read, "This is King Fisher's road. Take the other."

Fisher was a dashing figure, handsome and impeccably dressed. He was arrested several times by two of Texas' most famous Rangers, Leander McNelly and his successor Lee Hall, who had been sent to the Nueces Strip to bring some semblance of law and order.

Though charged with murder and horse and cattle theft, Fisher was never convicted. Still, after several arrests and a marriage, he decided to undertake a more lawful approach to life. In 1881 he was appointed deputy sheriff of Uvalde County and became acting sheriff in 1883. Fisher proved to be an effective and popular sheriff and had planned to run for the office in 1884. However, on the night of March 11, 1884, in the Vaudeville Variety Theater in San Antonio, Fisher and his companion, gunman Ben Thompson, were involved in one of the most famous shootouts in Texas history. Fisher was caught in the middle of a quarrel between Thompson and the theater's owners. When the smoke cleared, both Fisher and Thompson lay dead on the floor.

CATTLE-RUSTLER-
TURNED-LAWMAN
JOHN KING
FISHER WAS
KILLED IN A SAN
ANTONIO
AMBUSH.
PIONEER PARK,
UVALDE.

Uvalde Cemetery
Highway 90 at FM 481
N 29 11.987, W 099 48.680

JOHN NANCE GARNER

John Nance (Cactus Jack) Garner (1868–1967) was born in a log cabin near Detroit, Texas. He was admitted to the Texas bar in 1890 and settled in Uvalde to practice law. Garner was elected in 1898 to the state legislature, where he served until 1902. In 1903 he was elected to Congress and went on to represent his district for fifteen terms. He became Speaker of the House in 1931 and made a run at the presidency in 1932, but he lost the nomination to Franklin Roosevelt. Garner was offered the vice presidential nomination and assumed the office with Roosevelt's election.

Garner's political acumen was invaluable in the implementation of the New Deal. Colorful, persuasive, and well respected, he served as Roosevelt's pipeline to Congress. His influence with the Texas delegation was invaluable (from 1933 to 1938, eight Texans held regular committee chairmanships, and two chaired special committees), and his close friend Sam Rayburn became House majority leader in 1937.

Eventually, the philosophy and realities of the New Deal split the relationship of Garner and Roosevelt. Garner eventually began to oppose Roosevelt, and his support for the president's programs dwindled to nonexistence. In the latter days of his tenure, he and Roosevelt apparently rarely spoke. Garner made a bid at a nomination for the presidency in 1938, but Roosevelt proved to be unbeatable. Garner then returned to private life in Uvalde.

Van Alstyne

Van Alstyne Cemetery
Baihard Rd. at Sherman Rd.
N 33 25.173, W 096 34.315

COLLIN McKINNEY

Collin McKinney (1766–1861) was one of five delegates from Red River to the Convention of 1836 at Washington-on-the-Brazos. He was also one of five appointed to the committee to draft the Texas Declaration of Independence, and as the oldest member of the convention, at seventy years of age, he was given the pen after the signing. He was also a member of the committee that produced the Constitution of the Republic of Texas, and later he was elected a delegate from Red River County to the First, Second, and Fourth Congresses of the republic.

In 1840 he joined other family members who earlier had moved to the part of Fannin County that became Grayson and Collin counties. Collin County and McKinney, the county seat, were named in his honor.

Victoria

Evergreen Cemetery
Red River St. at N. Vine St.
N 28 48.677, W 097 00.604

EDWARD CONRAD

Edward Conrad (1811–1836) was one of four representatives from Refugio Municipality at the Convention of 1836 at Washington-on-the-Brazos, and there he signed the Texas Declaration of Independence. He also served as a member of the committee to draft the Texas Constitution.

THE DE LEÓN FAMILY

Martín De León (1765–1833) was the only Mexican impresario to found a colony in Texas. He was born into an aristocratic family who had settled in Mexico after emigrating from Spain. After service in the Mexican army, he decided to settle in Texas, and in 1807 he petitioned the Spanish governor at San Antonio to establish a colony. His request and a subsequent one were denied, and De León began ranching in Texas. By 1816 he had more than five thousand head of cattle, and when he drove a large herd to New Orleans, he became interested in establishing a colony on the lower Guadalupe River.

In 1824 De León successfully petitioned the provincial delegation at San Fernando de Béxar to settle forty-one Mexican families on the lower Guadalupe and then founded the town of Nuestra Señora Guadalupe de Jesús Victoria. His colony prospered, as did he. His ranch grew to more than twenty-two thousand acres, and in 1807 he registered the first brand in Texas, an "E" and "J" connected, signifying "Espíritu de Jesús." Though Martín De León was struck down in a cholera epidemic in 1833, his family had already become a powerful force in the area.

Silvestre De León (1802–1842), the second son of Martín and Patricia De León, was a merchant in the colony and served as third alcalde of the colony. His older brother, Fernando De León (1798–1853), was a leader in the colony as well. Silvestre and Fernando De León were central figures in gathering support from the colony for the Texas Revolution. In November 1835 the brothers drove a large herd of livestock to New Orleans, exchanging it for $35,000 worth of munitions and provisions intended for the colony and the Texas Army. Silvestre participated in the Siege of Bexar in December 1835, and upon the occupation of Guadalupe Victoria, the Mexican army arrested the brothers as traitors. Both were released after the victory at San Jacinto but then fell victim to the prejudice directed against all Texans of Mexican descent. Forced to leave Texas, the De León brothers had to abandon their property and possessions as they fled to Louisiana.

Though the brothers eventually resettled in Victoria, their lives were forever changed. Silvestre was murdered in 1842 while returning from selling horses, mules, and cattle in Louisiana. Fernando returned in 1844 to reclaim his property and was involved in lawsuits until his death—after recovering only a portion of his ranch and livestock holdings.

MARGARET THERESA ROBERTSON WRIGHT

Margaret (Marguerite) Theresa Robertson Wright (1789–1878) came to Texas about 1825 after the death of her husband in Louisiana. In 1826 or 1827 she settled in De León's colony at Guadalupe Victoria and applied for a league of land on the west bank of the Guadalupe River, five miles from town. In 1828, before title to the land was granted, she married John David Wright, who settled with her on the league. After her husband left to escape prosecution for an outstanding debt, Margaret remained and operated a prosperous cattle ranch.

Margaret Wright's place in history was secured with events surrounding the Goliad Massacre. Several of the fleeing survivors found refuge on her ranch. Under the guise of visiting the Guadalupe to draw water, she located other hidden survivors and arranged a system for providing them support. The soldiers left notes for her in a hollow tree, and she hid food and medicine for them in her water pail. She also managed to obtain a firearm from the Mexican soldiers camped on her land. She continued aiding them until the wounded men could rejoin the army. Sam Houston, in a speech given more than two decades later, praised Margaret Wright's heroism and called her the "Mother of Texas."

In 1842 J. D. Wright returned to find that in his absence Margaret had purchased an additional half league of land and had deeded 640 acres of it to her son. A series of bitter court actions resulted as Wright filed suit to recover the land, arguing that control of their joint property was entirely his and could not be conveyed without his consent. He lost. Half of the joint property—5,535 acres of land and 570 head of cattle— were awarded to Margaret in what may have been the first divorce granted in Texas. I think she did the right thing.

Waco

Greenwood Cemetery
S. Price St. at Oak Ave.
N 31 34.320, W 097 06.722

JULIUS LORENZO COBB BLEDSOE

Julius (Jules) Bledsoe (1897–1943) was born in Waco, Texas, and was a gifted singer. After earning an undergraduate degree from Bishop

College in Marshall (1918), he studied medicine at Columbia University in New York City (1920–1924). While attending Columbia, he studied voice and made his professional singing debut on April 20, 1924, at Aeolian Hall in New York. His best-known role was his portrayal of "Joe" in the Jerome Kern's production of *Showboat* (1927). Bledsoe's rendition of "Ol' Man River" is an American classic.

JEFFIE OBREA ALLEN CONNER

Jeffie O. A. Conner (1895–1972) was born near Waco and educated at Prairie View State Normal and Industrial College. She taught in county schools from 1914 until she began her service as a cooperative extension agent for the rural African American population of McLennan County in 1923. Jeffie Conner spent the next decade working to improve farm practices, home sanitation, and nutrition of the African American residents of the county. She continued her own education and earned a B.S. in home economics from Prairie View in 1934 and an M.S. in 1944 after completing a thesis entitled "A Study of 460 Negro Farm Families in Three Texas Counties." In 1946 she did additional coursework at Cornell University.

She resigned in 1948 to become supervisor of McLennan County schools, a position she held until 1957. Governor John Connally appointed her to the Governor's Committee on Public School Education in 1967, and she served on the Waco Human Relations Commission from 1969 to 1972. Jeffie Conner's awards included an honorary doctor of humanities degree from Paul Quinn College, a citation from Prairie View A&M University for outstanding service in the humanities, and a Woman of the Year award from Zeta Beta Phi Sorority.

ROBERT LLOYD SMITH

Robert Lloyd Smith (1861–1942) was born a freeman at Charleston, South Carolina. After receiving his B.A. degree from Atlanta University, he came to Texas around 1880. Smith was a powerful advocate of education and self-help for African Americans, and in 1890 he founded the Farmers' Home Improvement Society in Colorado County. The organization encouraged farmers toward economic independence through home and farm ownership, cooperative buying, cash purchases instead of credit buying, and raising much of their own food. Under his leadership, the organization spread throughout much of the South.

Smith was elected as a Republican to the Twenty-fourth and Twenty-fifth Texas Legislatures in 1894 and 1896 from Colorado

County. His legislative agenda strongly supported education, race relations, and the advancement of Prairie View Normal School. He was appointed deputy U.S. marshal for the Eastern District of Texas by President Theodore Roosevelt and served from 1902 to 1909. He later began a garment manufacturing business and in 1907 was elected the first president of the Texas branch of the National Negro Business League.

Oakwood Cemetery
2124 S. 5th St.
N 31 32.247, W 097 06.610

Before Oakwood Cemetery was established in 1878, the tract of land where it now stands held a fairgrounds and a racetrack. The 157-acre burial ground was successor to First Street Cemetery, the oldest large cemetery in Waco, which was frequently inundated by the nearby Brazos River. Many bodies from early graveyards were moved here beginning about 1878 because of better grounds maintenance. Since 1898 the Oakwood Cemetery Association (a private group) has managed the operations of the cemetery, although the land remains the property of the city.

Oakwood Cemetery is the home of one of the most unusual tombstones imaginable. It is actually an abstract sculpture rather than a headstone, and it graces the gravesite of Charles George Smith (1891–1967). His epitaph probably says a great deal about the man: "Strange cosmic curve integrated arc of space. Unrolling rhythm swinging out from time into eternity." Clearly, Charles G. Smith was not your average thinker.

WILLIAM COWPER BRANN

William Cowper Brann (1855–1898) was born in Coles County, Illinois. His mother died when he was two years old, and he was raised in the home of a nearby farmer. At age thirteen, Brann packed his belongings, struck out on his own, and never returned. Though educated only through the third grade, he became a gifted and brilliant writer. He worked at a series of odd jobs until he finally became a reporter. Brann eventually wrote for the *St. Louis Globe Democrat* (1883–1886) and then for the *Galveston Evening*. In Austin he wrote for the *Austin Statesman*, and there began his self-proclaimed "journal of personal protest," the *Iconoclast*, which soon failed. In 1894 Brann landed in

ECLECTIC GRAVESITE OF CHARLES SMITH, OAKWOOD CEMETERY, WACO.

Waco as an editorialist for the *Waco Daily News,* and the next year he revived publication of the *Iconoclast.* This time it was successful and eventually attained a circulation of one hundred thousand.

It must have seemed as if no one was immune from Brann's vitriolic attacks, and Brann seemed to enjoy taking direct aim at the Baptists and Baylor University. On October 2, 1897, Brann was kidnapped by student-society members and taken to the Baylor campus, where he was asked to retract his statements about the university. On October 6, having failed to leave town, he was soundly beaten by a Baptist judge and two other men. Brann seemed particularly to enjoy attacking Baylor president Rufus Burleson (also buried in Oakwood Cemetery, Waco). On April 1, 1898—in broad daylight and in the middle of a Waco street—an angry Baylor University supporter named Tom E. Davis shot Brann in the back. But before he died, Brann managed to draw his own pistol and kill Davis.

Brann's headstone in Oakwood Cemetery is adorned with his full profile. Soon after the stone was erected, an angry gunman apparently

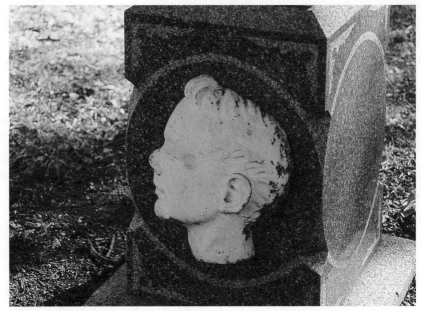

FIREBRAND WILLIAM COWPER BRANN FANNED SUCH FLAMES OF DISLIKE THAT HIS LIKENESS, CARVED INTO HIS GRAVE MARKER, WAS SHOT IN THE TEMPLE. OAK-WOOD CEMETERY, WACO.

shot Brann's likeness (in the temple) with a pistol, and the bullet impression remains to this day. I guess some guys just cannot be dead enough for some people.

RICHARD COKE

Richard Coke (1829–1897) was born near Williamsburg, Virginia; graduated from William and Mary College in 1843; and in July 1848 earned a law degree. In 1850 he moved to Waco to practice law, and in 1861 he served as a delegate to the Secession Convention in Austin (he voted for secession, by the way). After service in the Civil War, he was appointed judge of the Nineteenth Judicial District in September 1865. Coke won the Democratic nomination for governor in 1873, defeating Governor Edmund J. Davis, and was reelected for a second term in 1875. The next year he resigned the office of governor upon his election to the U.S. Senate. Coke was reelected to the Senate in 1883 and again in 1889 but declined to run in 1894. Coke's life-size statue was the work of prominent sculptor Frank Teich and faces the grave of his lifelong "friend through eternity," Dr. David Wallace.

George Bernard Erath

George B. Erath (1813–1891) was born in Vienna, Austria, and immigrated to America after graduation from college. He first settled in Cincinnati but moved to Texas in 1833 and served as a surveyor in Robertson's colony. In 1835 he joined the Texas Rangers to help control Indian depredations and in 1836 enlisted in Company C of Col. Edward Burleson's First Regiment, Texan Volunteers, for service in the Texas Revolution. As a member of that unit, he fought in the Battle of San Jacinto. In 1842 he participated in the Somervell and Mier expeditions but escaped capture.

Erath served in the Texas House of Representatives of the Eighth and Ninth Congresses of the Republic (1843–1845). After annexation he served in the First Texas Legislature. In 1846 he laid out the towns of Waco and Stephenville and later served in the Senate of the Seventh, Eighth, and Ninth Legislatures. Erath returned to the Senate for the final time in the Fourteenth Legislature. Erath County is named in his honor.

Neil McLennan

Neil McLennan (1777–1867) was a pioneer settler in Robertson's colony and in 1839 joined George Erath in a scouting and surveying trip near the present site of Waco. McLennan exchanged his land grant for claims on the Bosque River and moved his family there in 1845. McLennan County is named in his honor.

Pat Morris Neff

Pat Neff (1871–1952) was born in Coryell County, Texas. He earned an undergraduate degree at Baylor University in 1894 and a law degree in 1897 from the University of Texas. He settled in Waco, where he began his law practice and a political career by election to the Texas House of Representatives (1899–1905). After a six-year stint as county attorney, Neff decided to run for governor in 1920. A tireless campaigner, Neff forced a runoff election against former U.S. Senator Joseph Weldon Bailey and was elected.

As governor, Neff championed reforms in education, prisons, public health, law enforcement, and taxation proposals to establish a state park system. Though most of his policies were not implemented, he did succeed in establishing Texas Technological College and Texas State Teachers College and the Texas State Park system. After reelection in 1922 and completion of his second term, Neff was appointed to the U.S. Board of Mediation by President Calvin Coolidge. Governor Daniel J. Moody named him to the Railroad Commission in 1929, a position he held until 1932, when he assumed the presidency of Baylor University.

WILLIAM ROBERT POAGE

W. R. (Bob) Poage (1899–1987) was born in Waco and grew up on a ranch in Throckmorton and Shackelford counties. Educated at Baylor University, he graduated from law school there in 1924. Poage remained at Baylor, teaching in the law school until 1928. During his last semester in law school, Poage decided to run for the state legislature; he was elected and served from 1925 to 1929. Subsequently he was elected to the Texas Senate (1931–1937). He then made his first run for the U.S. Congress in 1934 but lost. Two years later, however, he was elected to represent the Eleventh District.

Poage was a firm supporter of agriculture and improvement of rural life in America. As a member of the Agriculture Committee, he helped write early rural electrification law and establish the Rural Electrification Administration. He sponsored the 1949 Rural Telephone Act to extend rural telephone service and the important Poage-Aiken Act of 1965, which established water and wastewater systems in rural areas nationwide. Poage represented his district until he retired in 1978.

FELIX HUSTON ROBERTSON

Felix H. Robertson (1839–1928), the son of Confederate general Jerome Bonaparte Robertson, was the only Texas-born general officer to serve the Confederacy. He was born at Washington-on-the-Brazos, attended Baylor University, and was appointed to West Point in 1857. He resigned from the military academy to serve in the Confederate army and rose rapidly through the officer ranks.

Robertson, an artillery officer, participated in the assault on Fort Sumter that began the Civil War. He fought in the Battles of Shiloh, Murfreesboro, and Chickamauga and in the Atlanta campaign. He was promoted to brigadier general in July 1864, but his military career ended soon afterward, when he was severely wounded in November 1864. After the war, Robertson settled in Waco, and at the time of his death in April 20, 1928, he was the last surviving general of the Confederacy.

JEROME BONAPARTE ROBERTSON

Jerome Bonaparte (Polly) Robertson (1815–1890) came to Texas from Kentucky to participate in the Texas Revolution but arrived after the conflict had concluded. He settled at Washington-on-the-Brazos in 1837 to practice medicine. He served in the Texas House of Representatives (1847) and the Texas Senate (1849) and was a delegate to the Secession Convention (1861).

At the outbreak of the Civil War, he raised a company that became part of the Fifth Texas Infantry, Hood's Texas Brigade. As did his son, he rose rapidly through the officer ranks to that of brigadier general (1862). Robertson participated in many of the most important and tragic battles of the Civil War, leading the Texas Brigade into battle at Fredericksburg, Gettysburg, and Chickamauga. After the surrender, Robertson returned to Texas, where he practiced medicine and served as superintendent of the state bureau of immigration and as passenger and emigration agent for the Houston and Texas Central Railroad.

LAWRENCE SULLIVAN ROSS

Lawrence S. (Sul) Ross (1838–1898) was born at Bentonsport, Iowa (Territory), and came to Texas in 1839 with his family. They settled in Waco in 1849 after a period in Milam County and in Austin. Ross enrolled at Baylor University in Independence, Texas, and then at the Wesleyan University in Florence, Alabama, where he obtained his A.B. degree in 1859.

Ross was the quintessential Texas man of action and a great leader of men. In 1858, while home on vacation from college, he volunteered for service with the U.S. Army as leader of a band of Indian auxiliaries from the Brazos Indian Reservation (in Young County). He was seriously wounded in a battle at the Wichita Village but was able to return to college and graduated the next year.

Back in Texas, Ross joined the Texas Rangers in its defense of the Texas frontier. In 1860 his unit engaged the Comanche Indians in the battle at the Pease River in which Cynthia Ann Parker was recovered after years of captivity. Sul Ross enlisted in 1861 in the Confederate army and served with the Sixth Texas Cavalry. He participated in several important engagements, including those at Pea Ridge, Corinth, and Vicksburg. He was promoted to brigadier general in 1864 and commanded the Texas Cavalry Brigade until the end of the war.

After the war, Ross farmed for several years and then in 1873 was elected sheriff of McLennan County. He was elected to the Texas Senate (1880) from the Twenty-second District and to the office of governor in 1886 and 1888. He assumed the presidency of the Agricultural and Mechanical College of Texas (now Texas A&M University) in 1891 and proved to be both a visionary and an effective leader of the institution.

EMILY DOROTHY SCARBOROUGH

Dorothy Scarborough (1878–1935) was born into a family of writers at Mount Carmel (near Tyler). After receiving her B.A (1896) and M.A. (1899) from Baylor University, she studied literature at the University of Chicago and was awarded a doctorate in literature from Columbia University (1917).

Emily Scarborough was one of Texas' most gifted novelists and an important folklorist. She was an early member of the Texas Folklore Society, which was founded in 1910, and served as president of the society in 1914–1915. She published two volumes of folklore, *On the Trail of Negro Folksongs* (1925) and *A Song Catcher in the Southern Mountains* (1937, posthumous). Her writings often depicted the harsh life of tenant farmers, and her novel *The Wind* (1925) is considered a Texas classic.

DAVID RICHARD WALLACE

David Richard Wallace (1825–1911) came to Texas in 1855 after earning a medical degree (1853) from the New York City Medical College. He settled in Independence (then the site of Baylor University), where he practiced medicine and taught Latin and Greek at Baylor. In 1861 he moved to Waco when the university moved there, and there he continued his medical practice and teaching responsibilities.

During the Civil War, Wallace served as a surgeon, and with the end of the war, he returned to Waco to practice medicine until his appointment as superintendent of the State Lunatic Asylum (later renamed Austin State Hospital) from 1874 to 1879. In 1883 he was appointed to help establish the North Texas Lunatic Asylum (later renamed Terrell State Hospital) and began a specialty practice in mental health that would firmly establish him as a pioneer in the psychiatric field in Texas. Wallace's monument was created by prominent Texas sculptor Frank Teich and faces the monument of his lifelong friend Richard Coke.

Stanfield-Walker Cemetery
Stanfield Dr. at N. Lacy Dr.
N 31 37.592, W 097 06.357

The Stanfield-Walker Cemetery, a small family cemetery, was begun in 1853 upon the death of Missouri V. Cobbs, infant daughter of county judge John Allen Cobbs and his wife, Eleanor. The cemetery contains one section with twenty-one graves of the Cobbs and related families, and another section with several unmarked graves of former slaves. Also interred here are two veterans of the Texas War for Independence, William Collett Walker (1818–1896), husband of the Cobb's daughter, Rebecca; and his father, James F. Walker, Jr. (1793–1873), who served at the Battle of San Jacinto.

SARAH WALKER

Sarah Walker (1811–1878) was the widow of Jacob Walker, who was reputedly the last man to die in the Alamo. She received a land grant in Sabine County, a league and a labor east of the Brazos River. Sarah Walker exemplifies the pioneer spirit, having once ridden three hundred miles by horseback to warn Gen. Sam Houston of an impending Indian attack.

Weatherford

Greenwood Cemetery
Front St. at E. Water St.
N 32 45.780, W 097 47.479

CHESTER BOWEN

Chester Bowen (1842–1905) is one of a handful of Union soldiers laid to rest in Texas who were awarded the Congressional Medal of Honor during the Civil War. While serving as a corporal in Company I, Nineteenth New York Cavalry (First New York Dragoons), Bowen was awarded the medal for his actions in capturing a Confederate flag at Winchester, Virginia, on September 19, 1864.

BOSE IKARD

Though born into slavery in Mississippi, Bose Ikard (1843–1929) was one of the great African American cowboys of the trail-driving era and perhaps the best nightrider who ever herded cattle. The Civil War

THE EPITAPH ON THE GRAVESTONE OF BOSE IKARD SPEAKS TO HIS LONG FRIEND-
SHIP WITH TEXAS LEGEND CHARLES GOODNIGHT. GREENWOOD CEMETERY,
WEATHERFORD.

left Bose Ikard a freeman, and in 1866 he began trailing cattle to market. During his first cattle drive, he formed a lifetime friendship with
Charles Goodnight.

After the 1867 cattle drive, which resulted in the death of Oliver
Loving, Ikard is thought to have been one of the cowboys who
accompanied Loving's body back to Texas for its final interment.
When his cowboy days were finished, Bose Ikard returned to Parker
County to farm. In the late 1860s he married Angeline Ikard, and they
reared five children to adulthood. Bose Ikard died of influenza in
1929 in Austin, and as with his friend Oliver Loving, his remains were
brought back to Weatherford for burial. Charles Goodnight, his lifelong friend, had a simple granite marker placed at Ikard's gravesite.
Its epitaph is one of the most noble in all of Texas:

SERVED WITH ME FOUR YEARS ON THE GOODNIGHT-LOVING
TRAIL, NEVER SHIRKED A DUTY OR DISOBEYED AN ORDER,
RODE WITH ME IN MANY STAMPEDES, PARTICIPATED IN
THREE ENGAGEMENTS WITH THE COMANCHES, SPLENDID
BEHAVIOR.

C. GOODNIGHT

SAMUEL WILLIS TUCKER LANHAM

S. W. T. Lanham (1846–1908) came to Texas after the Civil War. Settling in Weatherford, he taught school while studying law. In 1871 he was appointed as district attorney for the Thirteenth District of Texas and in that year prosecuted Kiowa Indian chiefs Satanta and Big Tree for their part in the Warren Wagon Train Raid. He began his political career in 1880 and was elected to the U.S. House of Representatives in 1882. In 1902 he was elected as twenty-second governor of Texas.

OLIVER LOVING

Oliver Loving (1812–1867) came to Texas in 1843 from his home in Kentucky. By 1855 he had settled in Palo Pinto County near Keechi Creek, where he began a cattle operation. In 1866 Loving and Charles Goodnight combined a herd to be taken to Fort Sumner, New Mexico, to provide beef for several thousand Indians on the reservation there. The route became known as the Goodnight-Loving Trail. Their route, which followed the path of the Butterfield Overland Mail, led to Fort Sumner and then on to Denver.

In the spring of 1867, Loving and Goodnight prepared for a new drive from Texas. After traveling about a hundred miles, Loving decided to go ahead of the herd on horseback to reach markets in New Mexico and Colorado prior to the time contracts were to be let in July. Loving pushed ahead with one companion, Bill Wilson, whom Goodnight described as "the clearest headed man in the outfit."

Although instructed to travel only at night, Loving apparently did not like "night riding" and persuaded Wilson to change tactics. On the third day, Comanche Indians intercepted Loving and Wilson. The two trail drivers immediately broke for the cover of the Pecos River. However, the Indians followed and surrounded them in the river bottom. There Loving was wounded and sustained a broken arm.

Sure that he would die from his wounds, Loving begged Wilson to leave him and find Goodnight. Loving had no intention of being taken alive, but if he did survive, he would move downstream from their present position. Wilson managed to escape and retraced his route back to the cattle herd, where he waited in a cave for Goodnight and the others' eventual appearance. Bill Wilson was in miserable condition when Goodnight found him but was able to relay the information concerning Loving's injuries and location. Goodnight and fourteen cowboys immediately set out to find their comrade. After riding

PIONEER TRAIL DRIVER OLIVER LOVING DIED AFTER BEING WOUNDED IN AN INDIAN ATTACK, AND HIS BODY WAS RETURNED TO TEXAS FOR BURIAL BY HIS FRIEND CHARLES GOODNIGHT. GREENWOOD CEMETERY, WEATHERFORD.

for a day, they found the spot where Loving was supposed to have been, but he was not there.

Oliver Loving did not die immediately from his wounds. He managed to elude the Indians and found the road to Fort Sumner, New Mexico, hoping that a friendly traveler would find him. Despite his serious wounds, Loving survived five days before passersby found him and took him to Fort Sumner.

About two weeks later, Goodnight heard that Loving was at the fort. Goodnight found his friend near death, and Loving asked Goodnight to take him back to Texas for burial. As he died, Oliver Loving was assured that his last wish would be granted. After temporary burial at Fort Sumner, Goodnight took his friend back to his home in Texas, where he was laid to rest.

MARY MARTIN

Mary Martin (1913–1990) was born in Weatherford and began music and voice lessons as a young child. She operated a dance school in Weatherford for a period but, after a divorce, moved to California to try show business. By 1939 she had become a film star and soon became a successful Broadway actress. Perhaps her most famous role was that of Peter Pan, for which she won a Tony Award. Her lifetime achievements brought Martin a coveted award from the John F. Kennedy Center for the Performing Arts in Washington, D.C., in 1989.

West Columbia

Columbia (Presbyterian) Cemetery
E. Jackson St. at S. 16th St.
N 29 08.486, W 095 38.831

JOHN SMITH DAVENPORT BYROM

John Byrom (1798–1837) came to Texas in 1830 and settled in what is now Brazoria County. He participated in the Battle of Velasco (1832), and in 1835 he represented Brazoria at the Consultation. Byrom was one of the four representatives from the municipality to the Convention of 1836 at Washington-on-the-Brazos and signed the Texas Declaration of Independence.

West Point

Woods Prairie Cemetery

1.5 miles west of West Point on Highway 71
N 29 57.027, W 097 01.407

Zadock Woods, one of Stephen F. Austin's Old Three Hundred, was born in Brookfield Township, Massachusetts. In 1797 he married Minerva Cottle, who bore six children. The Woods family moved to Missouri about 1801 and established a "fort" in Woodville near Troy, Missouri. During the War of 1812, Lt. Zachary Taylor garrisoned Woods Fort, and Woods himself served with Andrew Jackson at New Orleans.

Financially ruined as a result of a business venture with Moses Austin, Woods decided to join Austin's Texas Colony in 1824. Settling first in Matagorda County, he later moved his family north on the Colorado River to Fayette County. There his home near West Point, called Woods Fort (or Woods Prairie), became a traveler's safe haven from Indian raids.

In 1842 Woods and two of his sons, Norman and Henry, joined a force of men from Fayette County recruited by Capt. Nicholas M. Dawson to fight with Mathew Caldwell's command against Mexican forces at Salado Creek. On September 18, 1842, Zadock Woods was killed in a skirmish that became known as the Dawson Massacre. His son Henry managed a daring escape, but Norman, severely wounded in the battle, was captured and imprisoned in Perote Prison, Mexico. Zadock Woods was buried in a mass grave by Salado Creek, but his body was reinterred six years later at Monument Hill–Kreische Brewery State Historic Site in La Grange.

Woods Prairie Cemetery is a small cemetery located about a mile up a gravel road north of Highway 71 in Fayette County. The exit off the highway to the cemetery is clearly marked, and the road is easily passable from Highway 71 to the cemetery location on the left side of the road. This cemetery is poorly kept and was largely overgrown with waist-high Johnson grass on the day I visited. The majority of marked graves in the cemetery lie on the southern half and northwest quadrant of the cemetery. The northeast side of the cemetery is largely clear of markers; however, the presence of bits of sandstone and rocks without inscription suggests that there are several unmarked graves in Woods Prairie. Marked stones in the cemetery are predominantly those of the Young, Reeves, and Moore families.

The western part of the cemetery appears to be the site of the earliest burials, including that of Minerva Cottle Woods (1776–1839), the wife of Zadock Woods. Close by are the graves of the first members of the Young family to be buried here, Sam Young (1786–1867) and his wife, Jane (1794–1851).

Nearby stands the monument of Laurana Young (1816–1864), but the marker for her husband, James (who is noted on her marker), was not to be found. Her gravesite speaks to the hardships of pioneer families. The marker bears the names of five children, Robert, D.K., Laura, Annie, and Pleasant. All died before age fifteen.

Wichita Falls

Riverside Cemetery
Highway 277, west of intersection with I-44
N 33 54.670, W 098 30.469

JAMES BURR V ALLRED

James Allred (1899–1959) was born in Bowie, Texas. After naval service in World War I, Allred began the study of law and received an LL.B. from Cumberland University, Lebanon, Tennessee. In 1923 Governor Pat M. Neff named him to an unexpired term as district attorney for the Thirtieth Texas District. In 1930 Allred made a successful race for attorney general and was elected governor in 1934 and again in 1936.

President Roosevelt, in his second term, nominated Allred to a federal district judgeship, which Allred assumed as his term as governor ended. In 1942 Allred resigned the bench to run for the U.S. Senate but lost the race to the colorful W. Lee "Pappy" O'Daniel. In 1949 President Harry S. Truman reappointed Allred to the federal bench, where he remained until his death.

Crestview Memorial Park
Crestview Memorial Dr. at W. Rathgeber Rd.
N 33 50.503, W 098 30.414

THOMAS W. FOWLER

Thomas Fowler (1921–1944) was born in Wichita Falls and there entered the U.S. Army. On May 23, 1944, while he was serving as a second lieutenant, First Armored Division, in the vicinity of Carano, Italy, his unit engaged the enemy in a full-scale armored infantry attack. Acting as a scout three hundred yards in front of the infantry, Fowler led the two platoons forward until he had gained his objective, where he spotted several dug-in enemy infantrymen. Having taken them by surprise, Fowler dragged them out of their foxholes and sent them to the rear; twice, when they resisted, he threw hand grenades into their dugouts.

Realizing that a dangerous gap existed between his company and the unit on his right, Lieutenant Fowler decided to continue his advance until the gap was filled. He reconnoitered to his front, brought the infantry into position where they dug in, and, under heavy mortar and small arms fire, brought his tanks forward.

Within minutes, the enemy began an armored counterattack. Several Mark VI tanks fired their cannons directly on Fowler's position, setting one of his tanks afire. With no regard for his own safety, Fowler ran directly into the enemy tank fire to reach the burning vehicle. Under withering fire from the enemy tanks and left alone by withdrawing friendly forces, he remained in his forward position, attempting to save the lives of the wounded tank crew. Only when the enemy tanks had almost overrun him did he withdraw a short distance, where he personally rendered first aid to nine wounded infantrymen in the midst of the relentless incoming fire.

Thomas Fowler's courage and his ability to evaluate the situation and to take his full responsibility as an officer in the U.S. Army exemplify the high traditions of the military service. For his courage and leadership, he was awarded the Congressional Medal of Honor. Although Thomas Fowler survived the engagement, he was killed in combat approximately ten days later.

Wortham

Wortham Cemetery
Highway 14, north of Wortham
N 31 47.840, W 096 27.776

BLIND LEMON JEFFERSON

Blind Lemon Jefferson (1897–1929) was born in Coutchman, Texas. Blind from birth, he was known all his life as Blind Lemon Jefferson. As a young man, Jefferson took up the guitar and became a street musician, playing in Wortham and nearby East Texas towns. Drawn to the city of Dallas sometime before 1917, he became a resident

BLUES LEGEND BLIND LEMON JEFFERSON ASKED ONLY FOR A CLEAN GRAVE. WORTHAM CEMETERY, WORTHAM.

there, playing in the area centered on Deep Ellum, Dallas' equivalent of Memphis' Beale Street. It was here that he met up with Leadbelly, who many years later paid tribute to Lemon's greatness by recording several pieces inspired by Jefferson's playing (notably, "Blind Lemon's Blues").

Jefferson was discovered by a talent scout for Paramount Records while in Dallas and was taken to Chicago. Jefferson completed upwards of a hundred recordings in the early 1920s, several of which were estimated to have sold one hundred thousand copies. He recorded spirituals under the pseudonym "Deacon L. J. Bates." Jefferson is generally considered one of the earliest representatives of the "classic blues" genre and was one of the most popular folk blues singers of the 1920s. He influenced many other artists and is said to have been a major influence in the career of the young Sam "Lightnin'" Hopkins. Jefferson was inducted into the Blues Foundation's Blues Hall of Fame in 1980.

Yoakum

Oak Grove Cemetery
FM 318 at Old Church Rd.
N 29 17.038, W 097 08.033

JAMES A. JAMISON

James Jamison (1841–1906) was a member of the Quantrill Raiders, along with Jesse James and the Younger brothers. After the Civil War, he left the Quantrill gang and moved to Texas, where he became a noted peace officer. He served as city marshal in several cities, including Halletsville, Schulenburg, and Gonzales. Jamison had always expected to "die with his boots on" and did so, of pneumonia, while sitting in a chair.

Yorktown

Woods Cemetery
Woods Cemetery Rd., north of Highway 72
N 29 01.250, W 097 27.320

The community of Shiloh began in the mid-1840s when several families settled in the vicinity of nearby Shiloh Creek. The Shiloh Methodist Church was organized in 1851, and the church school started classes in 1856. Among the first settlers in this small community were members of the Woods family, and the small cemetery on Woods Cemetery Road is all that now remains of Shiloh. Woods Cemetery lies at the end of a dirt road that snakes through the countryside north of Highway 72. The cemetery is replete with "No Trespassing" signs, but the gate across a railroad-tie cattle guard was open. The cemetery is neat and well kept, with a huge covered pavilion.

The first burial in the cemetery was that of Montraville Woods (1817–1857), who is buried here with his brothers, Henry Gonzalvo Woods (1816–1869) and Norman B. Woods (1805–1843). Henry and Norman Woods participated in one of Texas' most tragic military engagements, the Dawson Massacre. On September 18, 1842, a group of fifty-three Texans under the command of Capt. Nicholas Dawson found themselves locked in a hopeless battle with Mexican cavalry and artillery at Salado Creek (near San Antonio). They had undertaken a forced march from Fayette County to aid fellow Texans commanded by Mathew Caldwell. Caught on the open prairie by

HENRY WOODS, KILLED DURING THE SUTTON-TAYLOR FEUD, WAS A MEMBER OF
ONE OF TEXAS' GREAT PIONEER FAMILIES. WOODS CEMETERY, YORKTOWN.

Mexican soldiers, Dawson's force retreated to a nearby mesquite thicket to fight it out with the numerically superior force. But the outnumbered and outgunned Texans were soon defeated. The field lay strewn with the dead, including Dawson and seventy-nine-year-old Zadock Woods, who had brought two sons, Norman and Henry, from their home in Fayette County (see Woods Prairie Cemetery). Woods' older son, Norman, lay on the field of battle, seriously wounded. But Henry was one of only two men able to miraculously escape capture.

Taken captive and imprisoned at Perote Prison in Mexico, Norman wrote letters expressing his hope of returning to his wife, Jane, and their children. But he would not see his family again—Norman Woods died in prison. In a letter to Henry, he asked his brother to take care of his family, and in October 1844, Henry married Norman's widow, Jane. Together they raised Norman's five children and four of Henry's. In 1856 the Woods family left Fayette County and settled near Shiloh, where Henry became a successful rancher. Eventually, Henry recovered the body of his brother and brought it back to Texas for burial in the family cemetery. Jane died in 1866 and was buried in a beautiful stone crypt in Woods Cemetery, adjacent to the grave of Montraville. Henry was later killed in an ambush after being drawn into the famous Sutton-Taylor feud and is buried next to Jane.

Woods Cemetery is testament to a great Texas family. They were here at the beginning: Zadock and Minerva Cottle Woods were part of Stephen F. Austin's first colony. Their prairie fort in Fayette County protected settlers and travelers from Comanche Indians. They answered every call in the defense of Texas: Henry fought in the Texas Revolution and enlisted for service in the Civil War, and Zadock and Norman gave their lives in service to the Republic. From the day the Woods family set foot on Texas soil, they established a legacy of courage, determination, commitment, and all that can be called noble.

BIBLIOGRAPHY

ༀ

Primary Sources

Abalafia-Rosenzweig, Mark. *Monument Hill State Historical Park: The Dawson and Mier Expeditions and Their Place in History.* Austin: Texas Parks and Wildlife Department, 1986.

Allen, Tom. *Those Buried Texans.* Dallas: Hendrick-Long Publishing Co., 1980.

Biffle, Kent. *A Month of Sundays.* Denton: University of North Texas Press, 1993.

Bixel, Patricia B., and Elizabeth H. Turner. *Galveston and the 1900 Storm.* Austin: University of Texas Press, 2000.

Bomar, George W. *Texas Weather.* Austin: University of Texas Press, 1995.

Brown, Norman D., ed. *Journey to Pleasant Hill: The Civil War Letters of Captain Elijah P. Petty, Walker's Texas Division.* San Antonio: University of Texas Institute of Texan Cultures, 1982.

Conger, Roger N. *A Pictorial History of Waco.* Waco, Tex.: Texian Press, 1964.

Conger, Roger N., Rupert N. Richardson, Kenneth Neighbors, Joe B. Frantz, Ben Proctor, Dorman H. Winfrey, Roger N. Conger, James M. Day, Harold B. Simpson, and W. C. Nunn. *Frontier Forts of Texas.* Waco, Tex.: Texian Press, 1966.

Constable, George, ed. *The Gunfighters.* New York: Time-Life Books, 1974.

Daughters of the Republic of Texas. *The Marked Gravesites of the Citizens of the Republic of Texas.* Austin, 1982.

Debo, Angie. *A History of Indians of the United States.* Norman: University of Oklahoma Press, 1970.

Durham, George. *Taming the Nueces Strip.* Austin: University of Texas Press, 1962.

Fehrenbach, T. R. *Lone Star: A History of Texas and the Texans.*
New York: Macmillan, 1968.

Fenley, Florence. *Oldtimers: Their Own Stories.* Uvalde, Tex.:
Hornby Press, 1939.

Ford, John S. *Rip Ford's Texas.* Edited by Stephen Oates. Austin:
University of Texas Press, 1963.

Hardin, Stephen L. *Texian Iliad.* Austin: University of Texas Press,
1994.

Haynes, Sam W. *Soldiers of Misfortune.* Austin: University of Texas
Press, 1990.

Humphrey, David C. *Austin: An Illustrated History.* Northridge,
Calif.: Windsor Publications, 1985.

Hunter, J. Marvin. *The Trail Drivers of Texas.* Austin: University of
Texas Press, 1985.

James, Marquis. *The Raven.* Austin: University of Texas Press, 1994.

Jenkins, John Holland. *Recollections of Early Texas: The Memoirs
of John Holland Jenkins.* Edited by John Holland Jenkins III.
Austin: University of Texas Press, 1958.

Jones, William Moses. *Texas History Carved in Stone.* Houston:
Monument Publishing Co., 1958.

Jordan, Terry G. *Texas Graveyards.* Austin: University of Texas
Press, 1982.

Kemp, Thomas J. *Virtual Roots.* Wilmington, Del.: Scholarly
Resources, 1997.

Larson, Erik. *Isaac's Storm.* New York: Vintage Books, 2000.

Little, Carol Morris. *A Comprehensive Guide to Outdoor Sculpture
in Texas.* Austin: University of Texas Press, 1996.

Massey, Sara R., ed. *Black Cowboys of Texas.* College Station: Texas
A&M University Press, 2000.

Matovina, Timothy M. *The Alamo Remembered: Tejano Accounts
and Perspectives.* Austin: University of Texas Press, 1995.

Mayhall, Mildred P. *The Kiowas.* Norman: University of Oklahoma
Press, 1962.

McKee, Gary E. *The Fayette County Men of the Dawson and Mier
Expeditions.* La Grange, Tex.: Echo Publishing Co., 1998.

Newcomb, W. W., Jr. *The Indians of Texas.* Austin: University of
Texas Press, 1961.

Oates, Steven B. *Confederate Cavalry West of the River.* Austin: University of Texas Press, 1995.

Poage, W. R. *McLennan County—Before 1980*. Waco, Tex.: Texian Press, 1981.

Selcer, Richard F. *Hell's Half Acre: The Life and Legend of a Redlight District*. Fort Worth: Texas Christian University Press, 1991.

Smithwick, Noah. *The Evolution of a State or Recollections of Old Texas Days*. Austin: University of Texas Press, 1983.

Stephens, Hugh. H. *The Texas City Disaster, 1947*. Austin: University of Texas Press, 1997.

Struve, Walter. *Germans and Texans*. Austin: University of Texas Press, 1996.

Texas State Historical Association. *The New Handbook of Texas*. Austin: 1996.

Wallace, Ernest, and E. Adamson Hoebel. *The Comanches*. Norman: University of Oklahoma Press, 1952.

Webb, Walter P. *The Texas Rangers*. Austin: University of Texas Press, 1935.

Williams, Mack. *In Old Fort Worth*. Fort Worth, Tex.: 1977.

Winfrey, Dorman H., James M. Day, Ben Proctor, Harold B. Simpson, Roger N. Conger, Billy Mac Jones, and Joe B. Frantz. *Rangers of Texas*. Waco, Tex.: Texian Press, 1969.

WEBSITES

Congressional Medal of Honor Society Website: http://www.cmohs.org

Find a Grave: http://www.findagrave.com

506th Airborne Infantry Regiment Association: http://currahee.hispeed.com

NavSource Online: http://www.navsource.org/archives/04/04032.htm

Rock and Roll Hall of Fame and Museum: http://www.rockhall.com

Texas Historical Commission, Texas Historical Sites Atlas: http://atlas.thc.state.tx.us

Texas Ranger Hall of Fame and Museum: http://www.texasranger.org

Texas State Cemetery: http://www.cemetery.state.tx.us/Index.htm

U.S. Geological Survey, Geographic Names Information System: http://mapping.usgs.gov/www/gnis

The Wild West: http://www.thewildwest.org

Newspaper Articles

Austin American-Statesman. "Island's Cemetery Lady Finds the Dead Do Tell Tales." April 30, 1998.
Dallas Morning News. "Final Destinations." April 26, 1998.
Dallas Morning News. "Final Destinations." June 21, 1998.

INDEX

࿊

Boldface page numbers indicate gravesite photos.